GW01451686

PIRKEI AVOS
with a Twist of Humor

Other Books by the Author

Torah with a Twist of Humor

And You Thought There Were Only Four! 400 Questions to Make Your Seder Enlightening, Educational and Enjoyable

From Fasting to Feasting: A Unique Journey through the Jewish Holidays

Torah News U Can Use: I Didn't Know That!

Can I Play Chess on Shabbas?

PIRKEI AVOS

with a Twist of Humor

JOE BOBKER

gefen ‎גפן
publishing house ‎בית הוצאה לאור
JERUSALEM ◆ NEW YORK

Copyright © Joe Bobker
Jerusalem 2008 / 5768

All rights reserved. No part of this publication may be translated, reproduced,
stored in a retrieval system or transmitted, in any form or by any means,
electronic, mechanical, photocopying, recording or otherwise, without
express written permission from the publishers.

Typesetting: Raphaël Freeman, Jerusalem Typesetting
Cover Design: S. Kim Glassman

ISBN 978-965-229-419-7

Edition 1   3   5   7   9   8   6   4   2

Gefen Publishing House Ltd.   Gefen Books
6 Hatzvi Street, Jerusalem 94386, Israel   600 Broadway, Lynbrook, NY 11563, USA
972-2-538-0247 • orders@gefenpublishing.com   1-800-477-5257 • orders@gefenpublishing.com

www.israelbooks.com

Printed in Israel   *Send for our free catalogue*

Contents

"A smile is a small curve that
sets many things straight!"

— Yiddish proverb

Foreword

> "With God's help, I starved to death three
> times a day, not counting supper!"
>
> — *Tevye*

$\mathbf{A}$re we allowed to laugh during Torah study?

Of course!

Does God laugh?

Of course!

In the forty-two references to laughter in the Torah,[1] God laughs not in frivolity nor to be amused, but in derision at enemies and the wicked, and reluctantly at the Jews' calamity.[2]

The Mishna encourages a happy face and disposition, whilst Koheles[3] puts humor in its place: "There's a time to weep, and a time to laugh; a time to mourn, and a time to dance!"

If you want to get closer to God you can't do it through apathy, sadness, jest or levity – but only through joy; thus, a person in a happy mood can learn more Torah in an hour than a depressed person can learn in several hours.[4]

God's presence doesn't dwell in a place where there is no joy, and the centrality of Sinai is the mitzva of being *sameach* (happy); thus, being in a good mood is a part of the *Yiddishe zeitgeist*.

So laugh and learn away with *Pirkei Avos*, which declares that the world endures on three pillars: justice, truth, peace – and a fourth – humor!

Humor?

Yes, Jewish tradition actually *legislates* that the Jew smile!

⤳

God was about to appoint King Chizkiyahu, one of the most righteous and moral of all Jews, as the Messiah, but He did not. Why? Because the king failed to raise his own son (King Menashe) to "fear God."

Our Sages, baffled by this family tragedy, concluded that Menashe's descent into evil was caused by his father's failure to smile and sing, thus creating an environment that deprived the boy of Torah warmth and inspiration.

This caused Bar Kapara to make a stunning declaration: the Messiah, the redeemer of mankind, will be recognized by his willingness to sing.

≈

Postscript: After Chizkiyahu died, all Jewish learning ceased, showing that Judaism has no future in the absence of a song in your heart and a smile on your face!

Acknowledgments

I would like to thank my mentor and teacher, HaRav Osher Abramson, *zt"l*, a Holocaust survivor, and my wife Miriam, who gives new meaning to the words patience and understanding, and without whose support and serenity this book, like all the others, would still be on my shelf instead of yours!

Caution

This book is only intended as an introduction to Jewish law and lore, and should not be used as a halachic guide, nor as halachic rulings, no matter how definitively they are worded, nor as a replacement for studying Judaism and Torah in the conventional way (by *chavrusa*). Its sole purpose is to give the reader a peek into the world of *Yiddishkeit* in order to inspire more study. If you have specific questions, consult a qualified rabbi.

The information contained in the endnotes may not always be entirely accurate but will lead you in the general direction for further study.

"When I get to heaven, they'll ask me, why didn't you learn more Torah? And I'll tell them that I'm slow-witted.

Then they'll ask me, why didn't you do more kindness for others? And I'll tell them that I'm physically weak.

Then they'll ask me, why didn't you give more *tzedaka*? And I'll tell them that I didn't have enough money.

But then they'll ask me: If you were so stupid, weak and poor, why were you so arrogant?

And for that I won't have an answer!"

— *Rabbi Raphael of Bershad*

Introduction

Pssst! Pass It On!

A student of Rebbe Mordechai of Nadvorna once asked permission
to leave the yeshiva. When asked why, the boy replied that it
was *erev Rosh Hashana* and that, since he was the *chazan*, he needed
time to look through the *machzor* and put his prayers in order.

"The prayer book is the same as last year," replied Rebbe Mordechai.
"Far better to look into your deeds and put yourself in order!"

The Jewish year has its highs and lows: the mere mention of Pesach causes excitement; the thought of an approaching Elul generates tension.

Our rabbis understood that there needed to be a "bridge" between these peaks and lows of the calendar cycle, something to help keep emotions on an even, "peaceful" keel.

Welcome to *Pirkei Avos*, a rabbinic inauguration of a weekly study session whose moral dicta's appeal is so popular and so compelling that it is second only to the appeal and charm of the Haggada.

As early as the eighth century, starting on the first Shabbas after Pesach, up to and including the Shabbas before Rosh Hashana,[5] the Babylonian students in Rav Amram's yeshiva would read one chapter of *Pirkei Avos* every Shabbas after *Mincha* (the entire *Pirkei Avos* was included in the early days of the *siddur*, which is why most Jews knew this Mishna by heart, more so than any other Mishna!).

Why on Shabbas?

The *Machzor Vitry* explains why: Shabbas afternoons in the spring and summer months of the northern hemisphere were long and more relaxed, and thus more conducive to learning "wisdom" Torah. (So what do Jews like those in Sydney, Australia, in the southern hemisphere, where I grew up, do? Since our days were shorter, we had to make a special effort to fit in the weekly *perek*).

Why after *Mincha*?

I

To honor the memory, explains Egyptian-born Sa'adia Gaon, *rosh yeshiva* of Pumbedita and Sura, of Moses, who died on Shabbas, at *Mincha* time.

✦

Originally, *Pirkei Avos* had only five chapters, but a sixth chapter was added later.[6] Why? For pragmatic purposes! There are six Sabbaths between Pesach and Shavuos.

This "add-on" final chapter, called *Perek Kinyan Torah*, literally "The Chapter of the Acquisition of the Torah" (or *Perek d'Rabbi Meir*, because it opens with a quote from Rabbi Meir), is not technically a part of *Pirkei Avos*, and consists of a collection of writings (*baraisos* – literally, "omitted doctrines") that were added about a thousand years ago.

How is this sixth chapter different?

The first five chapters revolve around individual values and morality; in contrast, the "add-on" chapter, as a form of spiritual preparation for Shavuos, focuses on the majesty of Torah.

Taken together, the themes merge into a simple adage: think globally (in Torah terms), act locally (in ethical terms).

But why was there a need to link it to Shavuos in the first place?

David ben Joseph Abudarham, the fourteenth-century Spanish-born medieval writer (*Arba Turim, Sefer Abudarham*)[7] saw it in terms of a lover who eagerly awaits the coming of his or her beloved: reading *Pirkei Avos* up to Shavuos was akin to arriving at the *chuppa*, the "marriage and merger" of Israel and Torah, bride and groom.

Jewish mystics had a different insight: since Shavuos was the time of the *omer* harvest, the day seemed ripe for the evil inclination (*yetzer hora*) to tempt, lure and entice. But have no fear! Reading the *middos* and manners of *Pirkei Avos* would provide the shield of spiritual resistance – and return everyone to Torah!

Some Jews, wary of the *yetzer hora's* reputation of trickery, read *Pirkei Avos* until Rosh Hashana or Succos; others play it safe and read it all year round!

Why?

After the original Ten Commandments were shattered by Moses, who was shocked to find a calf of gold, a second set was handed down on Yom Kippur. These tablets were inscribed with a compassionate Divine message, "I have forgiven (*salachti*)"; thus some Jews began reading *Pirkei Avos* until Rosh Hashana as a recurring symbol to show God that their original disloyalty had been replaced by a joyful fidelity to their "second chance."

Rav Shlomo Breuer, in his *Sefer Chochma v'Mussar*, links this custom to a famous Gemora which attempts to explain why one *rav* who drank the four cups of wine on Pesach had a headache until Shavuos, and another great rabbi had a headache until Succos.

The cause of both headaches was the rabbinic concern that the Jews would be unable to handle the freedoms granted via Pesach and would stray from

Yiddishkeit. One *rav* was convinced that the acceptance of Torah on Shavuos was sufficient protection; the other felt that only the *hakoras hatov* of Succos would protect his people.

And so they compromised: one *rav*'s followers learned *Pirkei Avos* until Shavuos, the others through Succos.

⤳

So what is *Pirkei Avos*?

It is a philosophical and insightful manuscript, a teaching tool *par excellence* of the Mishna, the thirty-ninth out of sixty-three tractates (volumes of thematically related rabbinic teachings)[8] – and the *only* one exclusively devoted to ethics.

It's the best summer read, a Judaic "Bartlett's" of the collective wit and wisdom of the Jewish people, a fascinating accumulation of bite-size phrases and age-old values, chock-a-block full of folk wisdom, common sense, practical advice, proverbs, sayings, biographies and maxims, all presented in an educational style that is concise and stimulating, thought-provoking and inspiring; in short, *Pirkei Avos* has something for everybody!

There is no elitism, nor intellectualism, nor special literacy required in studying the Mishna; it appeals to the masses (a Mishna that survived the Nazi onslaught is stamped "The Society of Woodchoppers for the Study of Mishna in Berdichev").

Go ahead! Open it at random: you will be pleasantly surprised. Actually, satisfaction is guaranteed. It's as though you have interrupted a long rabbinic tête-à-tête that spans the first and second centuries.[9]

And if you look closely, you'll notice something strange.

None of the sayings has any social, political, financial, historic or economic context, despite the fact that they arose from a Jewish world in upheaval, ruin and destruction.[10]

The reason is obvious: the modest ethics they impart, inspired by a startling Midrash ("*Derech eretz* [ethical conduct] takes precedence over the Torah"), are so transcendent and uplifting that they cannot be shackled to any time or place; in short, they're timeless!

This is why the Mishna begins and ends abruptly, and why so many of its authors are anonymous.[11] It is not *they* who claim importance; what they have to say is the important message.

And what was that message?

A cogent attempt to preserve the holiness of the people of Israel, in an unholy world without the Temple, Jerusalem or sovereignty.

Incredible as it sounds, especially considering that the Mishna forms the basis for the two Talmuds, the Babylonian and the Jerusalem,[12] it contains very little theology; instead of being a "source book" *for* halacha it is simply a teaching guide *about* halacha (using *mishnayos* solely to arrive at halachic decisions will, according to Rashi, cause errors in Jewish law; this is why the rabbis of the

Talmud frowned on those scholars who *paskened* [ruled in matters of Jewish law] based on the Mishna, *even* if they got all their rulings right!).

⤝

What does *Pirkei Avos* mean?

In its original format, it was simply known as *Avos*.[13]

This title was expanded to *Pirkei Avos*, "Chapters of our Fathers," when it became a custom to read it in "chapter" form (in Hebrew, a "chapter" is called a *perek*). It's also known as *Mishnas Chassidim*, "the Mishna of the Pious" (the Lubavitcher Rebbe's commentary on *Pirkei Avos* is titled "Paths of our Fathers"). Ironically, its common title, "Sayings (or Ethics) of our Fathers," is incorrect.

But who are the "fathers (*avos*)"?[14] Anybody specific? No.

The term is a sweeping affirmation of *all* our early spiritual teachers and rabbis, reverently referred to as the "fathers to the world."

The choice of *fathers*, in plural, is no accident.

The *Tosafos Yom Tov* defines the intergenerational gamut of Sages as our fathers (Elisha calls his teacher Elijah "My father, my father!"), on the basis that a father brings and guides a child into and through *this* world, whereas his rebbe-mentor-teacher helps guide the child into the *next one* (i.e., the World to Come).[15]

The first of the eighteen blessings in the *Shemoneh Esrei* speaks of "the" fathers, not "our" fathers, conferring a universality on the fathers of all mankind (meanwhile Rashi links *avos* to "ancestors" because its opening salvo immediately informs us that this Torah was transmitted from generation to generation):

> Moses received [*kibbeil*] the Torah from Sinai and transmitted it [*umsara*] to Joshua; Joshua transmitted it to the elders, the elders to the prophets, and the prophets transmitted it to the Men of the Great Assembly [*Anshei Knesses Hagedola*].[16]

Thus, *Pirkei Avos* begins with a history lesson: an outline of how, some fifteen hundred years after Sinai, the Torah went from Moses to the (120) Men of the Great Assembly (*Anshei Knesses Hagedola*)[17] whose debut coincides with the restoration of Jewish life in Judea, an era we call the Second Commonwealth.[18]

The catalyst for this renewal was an aliya from Babylon (today's Iraq), when Zerubavel led about forty-two thousand Jews back to the Holy Land after an absence of seventy years. Their ambitious mission? To rebuild the Temple, a monumental yet successful task, thanks to two underrated Jewish heroes: Nehemiah, who first came up with the idea, and Ezra, a kohen and scribe,[19] who implemented it.

These two Jews single-handedly ensured the continuity of Judaism: "When the Torah was forgotten from Israel, Ezra came up from Babylon and established it!"

What exactly did the Great Assembly do? A lot!

This religious-judicial body of Israel's greatest and wisest scholars picked up the torch of Judaism just as the flickering lights of prophecy and prophets were dying out.

Their challenge was to reconstruct, reestablish, rejuvenate.

They sought a viable Jewish community immersed in Jewish law and Torah study to replace a hybrid Judaic society that had deteriorated after assimilating "foreign elements."

The *Anshei Knesses Hagedola* spread knowledge of Torah, established regular prayer (*siddur*), extended the public reading of Torah from Shabbas morning to Shabbas afternoon (*Mincha*) and Monday and Thursday mornings (because these were market days, when outlying Jewish farmers brought their produce to town and would have the opportunity to hear words of Torah), started schools, appointed judges, reintroduced the halacha that had "been forgotten," arranged the *Tanach* and formulated a genealogy of Jewishness to make certain that only Jews were involved in the Temple – all inspired by their own three-pronged Mishna principle: "Be deliberate in judgment, raise up many disciples, make a fence around the Torah!"

A foundation of ethical discipline (*mussar*), more so than fidelity to mitzvos, is *the* indispensable support pillar of Torah; this explains the Mishna's choice of words: Moses receives Torah *not* from "God" but from "Sinai," a broad term that embraces everything about Judaism.

A question: why does Moses "transmit" – yet no one "receives" the Torah?[20]

And why does the Torah use the term *mesira* (transmits) between Moses and Joshua, and not when Joshua passes it on to "elders and prophets," the term only reappearing from the prophets to the Great Assembly?

"Elders" is a generic term, and by the time Torah wisdom reaches the prophets, it's a different group of scholars. How do we know? The original elders are no longer alive when the first prophet (Shmuel) appears; thus an accurate chronology reads as follows: Joshua hands (not "transmits") the knowledge to the elders, and it goes from elders to elders, and finally to those elders who transmit it to the first of the prophets.[21]

The Torah obviously considers the multi-generations of elders akin to *avos* (fathers), as "one," not to be distinguished separately.

So why doesn't the Mishna say that Joshua "received" the Torah, that the elders "received" the Torah, etc.?

Because they didn't.

The Torah that Moses received was directly from God, and thus unique in presentation, whilst its transmission *ad infinitum* from then on was, by its very nature, fallible. Infinite wisdom filtered in human terms becomes finite – this is why our Sages accept the notion that each Jew "receives" (i.e., understands) Torah differently, according to his capacity and situation in life.

Furthermore, by using the term *kibbeil* for "received," the Mishna suggests that Moses *earned* the right of receipt, whilst all those who followed had to "accept" Torah through exertion, discipline and hard work.

An obvious question: why is this introduction – of the transmission of Torah from Moses onwards – placed at the beginning of *Pirkei Avos* and not at the beginning of the Mishna itself?

The authenticity of both the Written Torah and the (technical) oral laws of observance as coming from Sinai was generally accepted; but our Sages felt that a specific reminder was necessary that Sinai also included such (nontechnical) "self-help" areas as ethics and character development.

By starting *Pirkei Avos* with "Moses received the Torah from Sinai…," the infinite and intricate word of God, as absolute truth, was wrapped around the informal "folksy" messages, sayings, morals, aphorisms and advice of our Sages.

☞

Who gets credit for *Pirkei Avos*?

A charismatic and wealthy rabbi called Yehuda the Nasi (prince),[22] also known as *Rabbeinu Hakodesh*, "Our holy master" (by virtue of his legendary piety), was a seventh-generation descendant of Hillel, who migrated from Judea to the Galilean towns of Beit Sha'arayim and Sepphoris.[23]

Rabbi Yehuda[24] was extremely concerned that the sudden and devastating murder of more than a million Jews during two revolts,[25] including thousands of Torah scholars and students, would create a spiritual vacuum and cause Torah to be forgotten.

So, around 200 CE, the rabbi, together with students and colleagues (known as "the *Tanna'im*," plural of the Aramaic *Tanna*, for "one who studies or teaches")[26] broke with long-held tradition and undertook the enormous task of collecting, reviewing, interpreting, editing and patiently reducing five centuries of *Torah sheb'al Peh* (Oral Torah) to writing.

The Mishna was composed entirely in Eretz Yisroel and every Sage quoted was active in the Holy Land even if he originally came from *chutz la'aretz* (Babylonia, Rome, etc.). After Constantine the Great, a convert to Christianity, made Christianity the official religion of Rome, the center of Jewish gravity shifted from the Holy Land (where the rabbis, prevented by the authorities from studying and teaching Torah, suddenly became an endangered species) to new Torah centers in Sura, Nehardea and Pumbedita in Babylon. The Mishna owes its existence to a remarkable group of Sages who, over six generations, with the permission of the enemy (the Roman occupiers), regrouped in a defeated Judea under the leadership of its first presidents, Yochanan ben Zakkai and Rabban Gamliel II.

The result is the ultimate *how-to guide*, a unique window into Jewish law and lore.

But why did our rabbis place *Pirkei Avos*, which deals with such non-halachic issues as manners,[27] within *Seder Nezikin* (Damages), the section of the Mishna that concerns itself with such halachic legal issues as damages, torts, law and legal procedure?

The Rambam provides the answer: "Because none is so in need of ethics as the judges!" Or as Hillel might have put it: If not for them (the Jewish courts), then for whom?

The brilliance of Rabbi Yehuda was his realization that intricate Jewish law, in the absence of succinct ethics and values, was akin to a choir without a conductor; and so, the moral directives of Torah were included in order to "round out" the proper behavioral requirement of a Jew who might be so immersed in the "technicalities" of mitzvos as to miss the trees for the (messianic) forest.

Ethics are the leaves and branches on the tree of religion. *Pirkei Avos* and some *baraisos* (e.g., Avos d'Rabbi Nathan), are almost exclusively occupied with it, and ethical tips appear abundantly throughout the Talmud, within aggadic passages, and interspersed amongst discussions of Jewish law.

There is no concise or specific text of Jewish ethics. Considering themselves purely public teachers and not philosophers, our Sages preferred to sprinkle occasional moral gems throughout, rather than any methodically arranged code.

Thanks to Rabbi Yehuda & Company, character development and attitude mattered, and greeting others in a cheerful manner (in other words, good *middos*) appeared as the word of God side-by-side with such precise ritual laws as those on the slaughter of animals (*kashrus*).

The Mishna, from the Hebrew root "to repeat,"[28] is the earliest known religious writing that teaches tradition through the vehicle of controversy and opposing opinions.

This is perfectly legitimate. Why? Because "all [opposing] words are [considered] given by one God!"[29]

Pirkei Avos has now been published in forty-eight languages,[30] proof positive that Torah insights are not restricted by time, space, place or culture.

A Zen Master from Tibet, visiting Manhattan on a hot summer day, orders a drink from Hymie, a little ol' Jewish vendor.

Hymie hands over a nice cold soda can and the Zen Master gives him a $100 bill which the little ol' Jewish guy puts in his pocket. After several minutes go by, the Zen Master asks politely, "Oh, Sir, where's my change?"

"Change?" Hymie replies, "Change must come from within!"

AGE AND YOUTH

My parents didn't want to move to Florida,
but they turned sixty and that's the law!

— *Jerry Seinfeld*

Age and Youth

What's the one thing in life that people want to become but don't want to be? Old.

✒

"What's the best thing about being your age?" the reporter asks a 104-year-old woman. "No peer pressure!"

✒

You know you're getting old when your back goes out more than you do, when you decide to procrastinate but never get around to it, and when you sink your teeth into a steak – and they stay there!

The hunt for the elixir of life is the oldest search in history. But our Sages relate to aging differently. "You're never too old," is the message: at a time when living to a ripe old age was the exception and not the rule, the Torah was proud of the fact that age provided no barrier to the significant achievements of the first patriarchal couple, Abraham and Sarah (Abraham started his journey to Judaism at the age of seventy-five!).[31]

The Torah sees aging not as a burden but as a challenge.

"The gray-haired head," proclaimed Jerusalem-based ben Sira, a second-century Sage, "is a crown of glory!"

I'm not sixty, say the Yiddishists, I'm eighteen with forty-two years of experience!

King David wanted to be blessed with the ability to make the years count ("Teach us to number our days that we may gain a heart of wisdom"),[32] cognizant that longevity was no accident but a Godly reward for a life of morality and lofty ethics.

To Mark Twain, age was "an issue of mind over matter; if you don't mind, it doesn't matter!" Maurice Chevalier once told a reporter, "Old age isn't so bad when you consider the alternative."

How do you know you've reached middle age? When a doctor, not a policeman, tells you to slow down, and it takes you longer to rest than to get tired!

❧

During the Israel-Lebanon War of 2006, Max, an elderly Jew, refuses to leave his home for the air raid shelter until he can find his dentures. His wife yells at him, "Hey! What do you think they're dropping? Sandwiches?"

❧

Over the centuries different scholars have attributed their long life to certain virtues.

Rav Adda ben Ahaba credited his long life to the fact that he was "never impatient, never walked in front of a man greater than himself, never walked four cubits without meditating over Torah, never fell asleep in the Beis Midrash, and never rejoiced at the disgrace of my friends."[33]

Since wisdom was associated with age, the Torah demands that we "rise in the presence of the aged, and show respect for the elderly"[34] (defined as seventy and over).

What if the elderly person is not learned?

No matter. Aging itself is an accumulated educating process, a "seasoned wisdom," explains the author of *Torah Temimah*, an invaluable and irreplaceable link in the tradition of the generations. This is why the Hebrew word for elderly is *zaken*, for *zeh shekaneh chachma*, "a person who has acquired wisdom."

And so the holy Gerer Rebbe would regularly visit senior citizens in Jewish nursing homes, not for their greatness in learning or devoutness, but because of their age.

❧

A group of seniors are sitting around *kvetching* at a Jewish nursing home.

"Oy," says Rosy, "my arms are so weak these days that I can hardly lift this cup of coffee!"

"At least you can see," replies Mimi. "My cataracts are so bad I can't even see my drink!"

"Oy," chips in Jackie, "my hands are so crippled I couldn't even sign the bill at the restaurant last night!"

"What? Speak up! What? I can't hear you!" shouts Freddy.

"Oy," complains another, "I can't turn my head because of the arthritis in my neck."

"And my blood pressure pills," cries Suzy, "make me so dizzy I can hardly walk!"

"Oy, I forget where I am, and where I'm going," rasps Beryl, "but I guess that's the price we pay for getting old." Everybody nods in agreement.

"Well, we should still count our blessings," adds a cheerful Ida, "thank God we can all still drive!"

❧

Warts and All!

> Rabbi Shimon ben Yehuda[35] said: Beauty, strength, wealth, honor, wisdom, old age,[36] fullness of years, and children are fitting for the righteous and the world.[37]
>
> — *Mishna 6:8*

This Mishna raises an obvious question: why should the blessings of the righteous revolve around physical indulgence – looks, wealth, strength and honor – and not spiritual rewards?

Is it possible? Did Rabbi Shimon truly believe that the pious crave to be good-looking, muscular, seekers of fame and fortune?

As bizarre as it sounds, the answer is "yes," because those whose lives are involved in "deeds of righteousness" already feel good about themselves, warts and all; this is why Isaiah concludes that, unlike the wicked who are in constant pursuit of pleasures, the righteous Jew exists in a permanent state of tranquility (i.e., peace of mind).

Rabbi Shimon doesn't *guarantee* that righteous Jews receive "physical" rewards, but merely observes that it would be *na'eh* (nice, or becoming) if it happened – but don't count on it!

Thus the Mishna supports beauty (Joseph's good looks helped him achieve greatness), strength (it helps in Torah study), wealth (how else can one be charitable?), honor (as long as it doesn't come with arrogance), children (God's greatest *nachas*) and old age (experience is wisdom, which movie mogul Adolph Zukor displayed on his hundredth birthday by confessing, "If I'd known how old I was going to be, I'd have taken better care of myself!").

❧

Mrs. Greenberg notices a little ol' man rocking in a chair on his front porch.

"Hello, there! I couldn't help but notice how cheerful you look. Tell me, what's your secret for a long, happy life?"

"Well, I smoke three packs of cigarettes a day, I drink a case of whiskey a week, I eat nothing but fast food, and I never exercise."

"Wow! How old are you?"

"Twenty-three!"

❧

Stuffed Like an Ox!

> Elisha ben Avuya[38] said: One who studies Torah as a child is compared to ink written on fresh paper;[39] and one who studies Torah as an old man is compared to ink written on blotted paper.
>
> — *Mishna 4:25*

"You don't know how much you don't know," warned humorist S.J. Perelman, "until your children grow up and tell you how much you don't know!"

According to Rabbi Elisha, Torah knowledge is more easily absorbed by those of tender age, and Torah values become second nature for the young, when they are impressionable – a potency of *chinuch* not seen in later years.

This is what the Rambam would describe as "self-evident!" ("If I do not develop character and acquire ideals when I'm young, when will I?"); and so the rabbis of the Talmud are blunt: at the age of six, "stuff him [*chinuch*-wise] like an ox!"

Why the metaphor of paper and ink?

In those days "paper" was a papyrus leaf, a product that could be recycled by erasing the words with a stone; however, the new writing, on top of the old one which still remained visible, turned out unclear.

Thus the Mishna analogy: new writing (i.e., education) in old age leaves a blurred impression.

And more!

The Mishna is directed towards the recipient (child) and not the writer (teacher); thus, just as "fresh paper" (symbolic of the innocence of youth) better absorbs ink, children, more receptive and open to ideas than the adults (likened to "smudged paper"), better absorb Torah ideas ("that which one learns when he is young is not easily forgotten!").

❧

Two elderly Jewish ladies have been friends and neighbors for years, having grown up and continued to live in the same community. Once a week for a decade, they played cards. One day, one turns to the other and apologizes: "You know, we've been friends for a long time, but I just can't remember your name. I've thought and thought, but I can't recall it. I guess it's old age. Perhaps you can refresh my memory and tell me what your name is?"

Her friend glares at her for at least three minutes, and finally she says: "How soon do you need to know?"

❧

Old Wine, New Cups

> Rabbi Yose bar Yehuda[40] said: One who learns from the young is compared to one who eats unripe grapes and drinks wine from the press; and one who learns from the old is compared to one who eats ripened grapes and drinks aged wine.
>
> — *Mishna 4:26*

This Mishna states the obvious: it's better to learn Torah from an elderly scholar. Why? What's wrong with the young?[41]

Nothing, but to Rabbi Yose, "unripe grapes" are not as fully "shaped" as their more mature (i.e., "older," and thus wiser) counterparts – or as Plato put it: "The spiritual eyesight improves as the physical eyesight declines!"

Wine from "the press" refers to wine not matured, a warning that learning Torah from the young could be immature, inexact, error-prone!

This honor-the-aged dogma is derived straight from the Torah: "Before the elderly [i.e., over seventy] rise!" a directive with no restrictions, because God expects *all* the elderly, whether educated or not, to be respected.

Why?

Two reasons: firstly, the elderly are a bridge of tradition between the generations, and secondly, respect for the aged is considered educational.

"Even an ordinary elderly person," writes the *Torah Temimah*, "has acquired wisdom simply by enduring the many trials of his life!"

And so Rabbi Meir cautions, "Do not look at the flask but at what is in it!" – the precursor for today's saying "Don't judge a book by its cover!"

⮞

After concluding his *drasha*, the rabbi begins the social announcements. "Tomorrow night we'll be having our annual dinner and the admission is $6.00. However, if you're over 65, the price will be only $5.50."

From behind the women's curtain comes a cranky old voice: "Do you really think I'd give you that information for only fifty cents?!"

⮞

No Children – No Adults!

> Shimon ben Yehuda said: The crown of the aged is grandchildren, and the glory of children is their fathers.
>
> — *Mishna 6:8*

The "glory" that this Mishna refers to is the national heritage of Judaism, an attribute that the Torah turns into a positive obligation: "And you shall teach them [Jewish laws and lore] thoroughly to your sons!"

The result? Jewish schooling became a communal obligation.[42]

This Mishna talks about *dor l'dor*, generational respect: sons to fathers, grandparents to grandchildren, or in Eleazer ben Pedat's words, "No children – no adults! No adults – no sages!"

It also addresses the special bond between grandparents and grandchildren. (The reason grandparents and grandchildren get along so well is that they have a common enemy: the sandwich generation!) In Yiddish there is no word for a "grandson" or "granddaughter"; the term *einikel* is unisex, a nod to the fact that, although parents might have preferences for a *zin* (son) or a *tochter* (daughter), grandparents are content simply to have a grandchild!

Although the gender of the word "grandchildren" is ambiguous in the original Hebrew (*b'nei banim* is technically masculine but syntactically refers either to boys or to a mix of boys and girls), the word for the parent in the Mishna is unambiguously masculine: *avos* (fathers). The question is obvious: where are the mothers? Why does this Mishna reveal only the "glory" of fathers?

When he heard his mother approaching, Rabbi Joseph ben Chiya would stand "for the *Shechina* [God's Presence]!" whilst eighteenth-century scholar Elijah ben Raphael urged his *talmidim* to "honor your mother in your heart, your speech, and by action!"

In other words the glory of mothers didn't need to be mentioned specifically because it was an already established Torah principle. Or, as the Yiddishists would put it: God couldn't be everywhere, so He created mothers!

⇥

The family is off to the bungalows for the summer.

"If you meet a bear," the mother says, "don't run."

"Why not?" her little boy asks.

"Because bears like fast food!"

⇥

Two Sides of One Coin

Rabbi Akiva said: Beloved is Israel for they
are called the children of God.

— *Mishna 3:18*

The Talmud describes that on "the coin" of Abraham appeared "an elderly man and woman on one side and a young boy and girl on the other."

What sort of currency did the first Patriarch have?

The reference is to the spiritual revolution that he spearheaded, wherein the symbol of success for monotheism lay in combining the wisdom and experience of the old with the youthfulness, energy, enthusiasm, idealism and vigor of the young.

In his eulogy for Rabbi Hayyim Heller, the Rav (J.B. Soloveitchik) used this "double-sided coin" theme: "On the one hand, he [the Torah scholar] is knowledge-sated, strong of intellect, rich in experience, sober-sighted, crowned with age, great of spirit. On the other hand, he remains the young and playful child; naive curiosity, natural enthusiasm, eagerness and spiritual restlessness have not abandoned him."

This Mishna reaffirms that Jewish children are the apple of God's Eye, the personification of His first command, "*Pru u'revu* (Be fruitful and multiply)."

When God bestows blessings, it is to have children ("Beget sons and daughters, that you may be increased, and not diminished!"); thus Judaism considers Jewish children the source of happiness, and the more children, the greater the joy – until the Yiddishist throws in a dose of reality: "Small kids interfere with your sleep, big kids with your life!"

Ask the Yiddishists, they'll tell you: Insanity is hereditary, gotten from one's kids!

꠷

Arriving at Tel Aviv's Ben-Gurion Airport from a long overnight flight from Los Angeles, a weary Rivka gets off with her thirteen children in tow. As she drags her kids and multiple suitcases through customs, she is asked, "Ma'am, do you have any weapons, contraband, or illegal drugs in your possession?"

"Mister," she calmly answers, "if I'd had any of those items, I would have used them by now!"

꠷

Young at Heart

Rabbi Yishmael[43] said: Be pleasant to the young.

— Mishna 3:16

This Mishna is a counsel to parents and us old folks: be patient with kids!

Rabbi Yishmael is echoing a Midrash: let kids be kids. Sometimes it's better to indulge (short-term) youthful indiscretions rather than run the risk of rebuke and (long-term) repercussions!

Why? "The world exists because of the innocent breath of children!"

Benjamin Disraeli identified "youth" as one of the two greatest stimulants in the world (the other one was debt!), and our Sages created an entire rabbinic litany on how to raise them.

"Who spares the rod hates his son," was Proverbs' blunt prescription for punishment; "Do not play favoritism," was Eleazar ben Azariah's advice (based on the disastrous chain of events after Jacob gave his favorite son Joseph a multicolored coat); in his *Iggeres Hamussar*, Rabbi Moshe Hasid cautioned parents not to reprimand a child immediately, but to wait "until the irritation has been replaced by serenity."

The importance of children in Jewish history is revealed in this exchange between Pharaoh and Moses: "Tell me exactly who is going," the tyrant demands, in response to a request to let the Jews take a three-day leave to pray to God.

"*Our young* and our old," replies Moses, mentioning Jewish children first.

This was his order of priorities; in contrast to pagan Egyptian religions, wherein the young were of no significance, Jews place their children on a spiritual pedestal, considering it incomprehensible not to have the young (symbolizing the future) stand together with the old (a holy link with the past).

❧

Little Yossi goes to the front desk of the local library and says, "Excuse me, miss, but I borrowed a book last week, and it was the most boring I've ever read. There was no story whatsoever, and there were far too many characters!"

"Oh, you must be the one who took our phone book!"

❧

AFTERLIFE

If you want to make God laugh,
tell him your future plans.

Afterlife

There is no reference in the Torah to a life after death.

Why is the Torah silent on this issue?

Two reasons. First, the Torah is a guide to living *this* life; secondly, the Torah, handed down to a people that had just left Egypt, a country that worshipped death and obsessed over the afterlife (the holiest Egyptian book was *The Book of the Dead*) rather than life itself, tends to avoid references to the practices of Egypt.

On the contrary, with its "dust you are and to dust shall you return," the Torah makes it clear that existence ends with death.[44] And then? Jews believed the body goes to a place called *Sheol*, but nobody knows for sure where that is.[45]

The Torah says it's a pit below the earth; some of the prophets (Jonah, for one) place it at the base of a high mountain; others (see Job) put it beneath the waters; Isaiah describes it as being "enclosed by barred gates"; King David sees it as a generic place of darkness and silence and his *Tehillim* (Psalms) lyrics are blunt: death is the end of all existence ("The dead cannot praise the Lord!").[46]

The earliest reference to death is in connection with rejoining one's ancestors. After Abraham, Isaac, Jacob and Moses die, they are "gathered to their people"; in contrast, the wicked are "cut off" (this is the punishment of *kareis*) from their people.[47]

Later, Daniel and Nehemiah discuss the concept of conscious life after death ("Many of them that sleep in the dust of the earth shall awake, some to everlasting life and some to everlasting abhorrence").[48]

Our Sages however discuss a form of spiritual immortality, in that the soul continues after the physical body dies. The *rosh yeshiva* of Sura in the tenth century, Sa'adia ben Yosef al-Fayyumi, struggled with the issue: "Suppose a lion ate a man, and then the lion drowned and a fish ate him up, and then the fish was caught and a man ate him, and then the man was burned and turned into ashes. Whence would the Creator restore the first man? Would God do it from the lion or the fish or the second man or the fire or the ashes?"

What about reincarnation?

Jewish mystics believe in it as a form of future *teshuva*, known as *gilgul haneshama* (transmigration), via *gilgul, ibbur,* or *dybbuk,* in that the sinful soul reappears implanted in another body that is given a "second chance," an opportunity to atone for the sins of the previous life (or perhaps as a form of punishment, akin to Adolf Hitler coming back as a cockroach!).

But wait! Isn't reincarnation a Christian belief? Yes – and a Jewish one, too, although there is no rabbinic concensus on this. The *Zohar*,[49] Rabbi Menashe ben Israel, Abraham bar Chiya and Moshe Teitelbaum all embraced it; but Judah Halevi, Rambam, Sa'adia ben Yosef and Abraham ibn Daud rejected it as a dogma of illogic.[50]

What about *techiyas hameisim* (resurrection)? When Ezekiel described his Valley of Dry Bones vision, he prophesied the restoration of national life, not individuals.[51]

This is a fundamental belief. It separated the rabbinic Pharisees from the Sadducees, who rejected it because it wasn't explicitly mentioned in the Torah (there are three accounts in the Torah, each involving Elisha and Elijah, that are resurrection-oriented, but none is conclusive).[52]

The Talmud argues that belief in resurrection is a prerequisite to the reward of entering *Olam Haba*, the World to Come (Rabbi Chiya ben Joseph writes, "The dead will come up through the ground and rise up in Jerusalem"),[53] whilst Jewish law prohibits necromancy (communicating with the dead to predict the future, on the basis that the dead have no power, despite King Saul's use of a witch to summon the dead prophet Samuel for guidance on how to defeat the Philistine army).[54]

Nevertheless, the Rambam made *techiyas hameisim* one of his thirteen "Articles of Faith," and the daily prayer (*Shemoneh Esrei*) contains several references to resurrection.

When Job's story was told after the destruction of the First Temple, wherein uncomfortable questions were raised about God's system of justice, the notion of a life for the righteous after death was clarified as the only viable explanation for why bad things happen to good people.

During the Maccabean era there was feverish speculation about life after death, and it turned apocalyptic during the Roman period.

Although the Torah focuses on the purpose of an "earthly" life (*Olam Hazeh* – this world), the rabbis of *Pirkei Avos* embraced the notion of an afterlife ("You know that the bestowal of reward upon the righteous will be in the time to come")[55] as a solution to theodicy (God's justice), at a time when the righteous of the Holy Land were being decimated and the wicked (the Assyrians) were prospering.

꙳

A priest, a rabbi and a Muslim terrorist all die and arrive at heaven's gate. "Welcome to heaven," the angel greets them. "In order to enter you must all pass a spelling test, but not to worry, in God's eyes all men are considered equal."

Turning to the priest, the angel demands, "Spell 'God.'"

The priest replies, "G-o-d."

"Very good, you may enter." Turning to the rabbi, the angel orders, "Spell 'Moses.'"

"M-o-s-e-s," the rabbi replies.

"Excellent, enter your eternal reward." Turning to the terrorist, the angel says, "No need to worry. Here in heaven there is no discrimination. All men are judged equally and fairly. Spell 'prorhipidoglossomorpha.'"

꒷

Are we given a glimpse of *Gan Eden*?

The Talmud is ripe with its imagery: it's a place of great joy, peace, golden banquet tables, stools of gold, lavish banquets, celebratory *Shabbosim*, and lots of sunshine. There are no business transactions, no envy, hatred nor rivalry. There is "no material substance," explains the Rambam, "only souls of the righteous without bodies, like the ministering angels!"[56]

But a closer reading of the Mishna reveals that it doesn't say "all Jews" merit a portion in the next world, but uses the term *yesh*, which means all Jews *presently* enjoy that portion of *Olam Haba*.

Does this mean there's heaven on earth?

Yes, answers the Gerer Rebbe. Almost inherently, every decent Jew is assured heavenly bliss in the here-and-now, and his deeds are blessed with the aura of heaven. This is why the actual translation is not "in" the World to Come, but "to" that world, implying that the journey has its own Divine rewards.

When the Talmud states that *all Israel* has a share in *Olam Haba*, that doesn't mean all have an equal "share." The more righteous the person, the larger the "share." And in reverse: one can lose one's allocated "share" by acting wickedly on earth.

In this merit system, one earns the way into heaven! How? This is the purpose of *Pirkei Avos*, "to make the people of Israel meritorious!"

If you want to get into heaven, make sure you've got the right key!

Man Plots, God Laughs!

> All Israel have a share in the World to Come.
> — *Mishna, Introduction*[57]

Joseph Heller, famous American novelist, decided to live forever – or die trying! However, the first-century Alexandrian philosopher Philo, determined not to get sidetracked into clouds in heaven or fires in hell, dismissed the whole idea of an afterlife: in jest he pointed to folks who acted as though they were already dead, and recalled some dead people as though they were still living!

And yet, as this Mishna contends, Jews *do* believe in some form of afterlife; but, whispers the Midrash, don't plan ahead!

As the Yiddish adage goes, "*Der Mensch tracht, Gott lacht* (Man plots, God laughs)!"

The Torah is overwhelmingly focused on life in this world, and Jewish law demands that the Jew live the *here-and-now* good life, in harmony with God and His credo, "*V'chai bahem* (Live for them [mitzvos])!" In fact, the Jew will be judged for every legitimate pleasure of life that he *fails* to enjoy!

Who can describe this mysterious World to Come?

Nobody, says Isaiah: "No eye has seen these things, except for God!"

Jews spend their lives heading towards a destination they know little about, which is why the Mishna's Rabbi Jacob quickly adds: "One hour of good deeds *in this world* is more beautiful than all of life in the World to Come."

The destination is thus not as important as the journey, and the appropriate response to the philosophic question "What happens after we die?" is: it depends on how we live!

༈

An archaeologist digging in the desert in Israel uncovers a casket containing a mummy. After examining it, he calls the curator of a prestigious natural history museum.

"I've just discovered a 3,000-year-old man who died of heart failure!" the excited scientist exclaimed. To which the curator replied, "Bring him in. We'll check it out."

A week later, the amazed curator called the archaeologist. "You were right about the mummy's age and cause of death. How in the world did you know?"

"Easy. There was a piece of paper in his hand that said, '10,000 shekels on Goliath.'"

༈

It Can't Be! Sam's Here!

> Your people are all righteous; they shall inherit the land forever;
> they are the branch of My planting, the work of My hands
> [and thus, all Israel have a share in the World to Come].
> — *Mishna, Introduction*

This Mishna reassures the righteous that "they shall inherit the land forever."
Which land?

Rabbinic texts revolve around two interpretations: either *Gan Eden*, which, in short, is the idyllic spiritual realm of souls, restricted to those "who have clean hands and a pure heart," or the era of the resurrection.

Why is it not considered a reference to the Holy Land? Because Eretz Yisroel cannot be "inherited forever." Why not? This contradicts the philosophy of *Shmitta* and *Yovel*, according to which the land periodically reverts to its original owner, God.

The Hebrew prophets (Isaiah, Ezekiel) and *Tehillim* often use the term *aretz* (land) to describe "eternity," within the concept of *chaim* (eternal life); and Jewish mystics allocate the four basic elements (fire, wind, earth, water) of balance and harmony to both land and life.

Does every Jew receive a portion in the afterlife? No. So why does this Mishna ("All Israel have a share!") suggest otherwise?

Ah, that's where context comes into the picture! The next line adds the caveat.

God calls His people "My branches," in that He laid the seeds but left the growth in the hands of free will; in other words, the "afterlife," the ultimate Torah reward, is only for the worthy; entrée depends on man's actions and deeds, behavior and conduct.

⤳

Sadie goes in for a serious operation and her husband Sam stays in an adjacent room to be close to her at all times. As the effects of the anesthetic slowly wear off, he comes in, holds her hand and waits patiently. A few minutes later, his wife's eyelids begin to flutter and she starts coming to.

"Is this heaven? Am I truly in *Olam Haba*?" Sadie starts to murmur, semiconscious – until she suddenly sees her husband and says, "No, it can't be! Sam's here!"

⤳

Heaven Help Us!

> Rabbi Yaakov[58] said: This world is like an entrance chamber [*prozdor*][59] before the World to Come; prepare yourself so that you may enter the banquet hall.[60]
>
> — *Mishna 4:21*

This Mishna attempts to put man in perspective: life is simply a waiting room before meeting God; thus, it should be spent in preparation, in mitzvos, good deeds and repentance.

"I am exiting [this life] through one door," said the Ba'al Shem Tov, "and entering through another!"

But the minute we look for clues as to the nature of this World to Come we come up empty-handed or teased with tantalizing imagery.

At least we can ask: who gets to go?

The pious? Obviously! The charitable? Naturally! The clowns? Yes, in fact "the clown may be the first in God's heaven," says the Talmud, "if he has helped to alleviate the condition of human life!"

And to get there? "One path leads to paradise, but a thousand to hell!"

The categories of those who will go to hell is listed by Tosefos, the early French commentators, and includes "heretics, apostates, informers, deniers of Torah and resurrection, deviators from customs, promoters of sin, tyrants, and those who lay hands on the Temple." The place is obviously already crowded!

$\approx$

The rabbi is furious when he passes by a *treif* restaurant and sees several congregants inside. He barges in and screams, "Yankele, do you want to go to heaven?"

"Yes, I do," he replies in shame.

"Then leave this restaurant right now!"

The *rav* then turns to Pinchas. "Do you want to go to heaven?"

"Of course, Rabbi."

"Then leave now!"

The *rav* turns to the next member of the group. "Hey Beryl," he yells, "don't you want to go to heaven?"

"Ah, no, Rabbi. I don't."

"What's wrong with you? When you die you don't want to go to heaven?"

"Oh, you mean when I die! Sure! I thought you were getting a group together to go right now!"

$\approx$

The Line to Heaven

> Hillel said: One who acquires words of Torah acquired
> himself a share in the World to Come.
>
> — *Mishna 2:8*

By using the term "acquire," Hillel stresses the concept that Torah doesn't come easily or naturally.

Although it is a labor of love, it also acts as a catalyst for a life of good deeds so rewarding that it will bring the afterworld paradise to the here-and-now.

This is why the daily blessing is worded carefully as *la'asok b'divrei Torah*, to "engage in" the words of the Torah, instead of the generic *lilmod Torah*, to learn Torah.

But how does the study of Torah unite the Jew to God or eternity?

In a concept known as *achdus hamaskil v'hamuskal*, the Rambam patiently describes how a bond develops between what Rav J.B. Soloveitchik calls "the knower and known, the subject and the object of knowledge."

Unity of thought, knowledge and purpose, explains the Rambam, cements the ties of friendship (*chaver l'dei'a*) until "the finitude [merges] with infinity," a doctrine of love known as *achdus ha'ohev ve'ha'ahuv*.

Thus the Mishna teaches: "acquiring" words of Torah, via a shared objective and activity, leads to the common inheritance *morasha kehillas Yaakov* (for the entire community of Israel) of a peaceful World to Come.

❧

Shmuli arrives in heaven and joins hundreds of other new arrivals. An angel addresses the crowd: "Welcome, welcome. I want all the men to form two lines. One for those who domineered over their wives on earth, and one for those who were dominated by their wives."

After some shuffling, two lines are formed. The line of men dominated by their wives stretches as far as the eye can see. In the other line stands Shmuli, alone.

Finally, God appears and angrily addresses the long line: "You men should be ashamed of yourselves. I created you in My image, put you in charge of the earth and all its inhabitants, and it turns out you led a life ruled by your mates!"

God then turns to Shmuli with pride, and says, "Tell Me, my courageous son, how did you manage it?"

"Actually," Shmuli replies, "I'm only standing here because my wife told me to!"

❧

Boldfaced, Shamefaced!

Yehuda ben Tema said: The boldfaced are destined to *Gehinnom* [hell], and the shamefaced are destined to the World to Come; may it be Your will that the Temple be built speedily in our days, and that You grant us our share in Your Torah.[61]

— *Mishna 5:24*

What is shamefaced?

It defines the argumentative and the arrogant, the conceited and the haughty ones. But aren't these negative traits? Yes. So why is ben Tema sending them to the World to Come?

The *Sefer Hamussar* says it's OK to be "aggressive" in heavenly attitudes, just not on this earth!

The fact is, however, that Judaism has very little to say about "hell" or "heaven."

The Hebrew words *olam* (world) and *he'elem* (hidden) are formed from the same root, an implication that it was up to mankind to find the key of sanctity that opened the world to *Olam Haba*, the World to Come.

In Torah times the "afterworld" was just one place, known as *Sheol* ("pit"), and was not divided into heaven (*Gan Eden*) and hell (*Gehinnom*); originally, the Torah's system of reward and punishment, justice and mercy, were all this-worldly, in *this* life, and not postponed to any future "after."

So what happened?

A cruel Jewish history intervened and more faith was needed, especially with the sight of the righteous suffering, and the triumph of the wicked.

The change in philosophy was gradual; it finally became "belief" around the time of the Maccabeans, as Jews, trying to stay sane in an insane world, became convinced that judgment and justice must be meted out in some other world.

꒜

A gang of New Yorkers is approaching the pearly gates of heaven and the angel doesn't know what to do, so he runs to God and asks Him for advice.

"Just do what you normally do with that type. Redirect them down to hell."

The angel goes to carry out God's order but soon reappears yelling, "God, they're gone! They're gone!"

"Who, the New Yorkers?"

"No! The pearly gates!"

꒜

Deeds of the Body, Not of the Spirit

> Rabbi Eleazar[62] of Modiin said: One who desecrates sacred
> objects, disgraces the festivals, shames his fellow in public,
> annuls the covenant of our forefather Abraham, interprets
> the Torah not according to Jewish law — even if he has Torah
> and good deeds, he has no share in the World to Come.
>
> — *Mishna 3:15*

This Mishna is quite blunt: those who don't respect the sanctity of certain elements that are central to God will be denied the ultimate place of sanctity (heaven); and even if you're a Torah student and a Jew of otherwise good *middos*, it will help you not!

Isn't this unfair? Aren't Torah study and mitzvos weighed in when judgment is passed?

Yes, according to the eleventh of Rambam's thirteen fundamental Principles of Judaism; but Rabbi Elazar was convinced: even the most learned Jew, if he desecrates, disgraces, shames, annuls (i.e., refuses to be circumcised or interprets the Torah incorrectly), simply cannot claim to be leading a life of holiness.

And the mitzvos performed by such a person? Do they "count" for anything?

Of course – but they are "good deeds" of the body, not the spirit!

꘎

At the gates of heaven a doctor, nurse and HMO executive are asked to list the good deeds they did on earth.

"I have devoted my entire life to the sick and needy," replies the doctor.

"Great," says the angel, "go on in."

"I have supported the doctor," adds the nurse, "and tended to the needs of hundreds of patients."

"Wonderful. Go on in with the doctor."

"I was the president of a very large Health Maintenance Organization," says the HMO executive, "and was responsible for the health care of millions of people all over the country."

"Ah, OK...you can go on in – but you can only stay two nights!"

꘎

AUTHORITY AND COMMUNITY

Suppose you were an idiot. And
suppose you were a member of
Congress... But I repeat myself!

— *Mark Twain*

Authority and Community

One generation plants the trees, the next gets the shade!

The challenge of social justice within a civilized society began with a question thousands of years ago: "Am I my brother's keeper?"[63]

Jewish law and tradition revolves around humanizing. A community's noble duty lies toward the weak and the persecuted, the lonely and the sick, the widow and the orphan, the traveler ("stranger") and those in need. Why? Because "I, the Lord, love justice!"[64]

To deny this responsibility is, in effect, to deny being Jewish.

The question is: who should run the community?

The Talmud preferred a system called *shiva tovei ha'ir*, wherein "seven leaders of the town" oversaw the *kehilla*'s affairs. This was derived from the Biblical precedent: when there was no king in Israel the leadership was performed by "an assembly from all the tribes."[65]

In a famous *Ashkenaz teshuva* (Ashkenazic responsa), eleventh-century scholars Rabbi Eleazar ben Yitzchak and Rabbi Yehuda Hakohen established the principle of majority rule (*rov*) in politics.[66] Their model was the fact that a *beis din* decision only required a majority opinion.[67]

Rabbi Solomon Ibn Adret (*Rashba*), thirteenth-century Spanish Talmudist, was convinced that communities should be governed by majority rule. The Raavia agreed that the majority has the authority to impose its will upon the minority.[68] French scholar Jacob ben Meir Tam (*Rabbeinu Tam*) disagreed and required unanimity, ruling that majority decisions cannot obligate dissenting minorities. But his own distinguished successor, Rabbi Asher ben Yehiel (*Rosh*) disagreed with him, convinced the result would be anarchy and communal chaos.

The *Chasam Sofer* was against the ideal of rule by unanimity, seeing it as a sure way towards communal paralysis, and suggested that even Rabbeinu Tam would agree that the *minhag* of a community abrogates the halacha of unity that he favored.[69]

The Torah's concept of government is apparent when the Jews enter the Holy Land and are ordered to "appoint a king" satisfactory to God.[70]

The Jews are demanding: "Appoint a king to lead us, such as all the other nations have!"[71]

Samuel, the exemplary humble prophet-judge and son of two prophets (Elkana and Chana) is reluctant and asks God what to do. God, as the ultimate King of the Jews, feels rejected but doesn't reject the request. Ambivalent and skeptical, God adds a warning that such a realm is fraught with danger. Kings tend to exploit, wielding power to acquire wealth, wives and horses (a status symbol in the ancient world): "[A king] will take your daughters to be cooks and bakers. He will take the best of your fields and vineyards and olive groves…and you yourselves will become his slaves!"[72]

The scare tactics don't work. The Jews still wanted a king and a king they got.

God's enthusiasm for a monarchy was so lukewarm, however, that the early Torah scholars decided its establishment was not binding Jewish law. The Torah permits it, wrote Ibn Ezra, but doesn't command it; Abarbanel was an anti-monarchist and preferred to be governed by a republic. But the Rambam brushed their opinions aside and asserted that it was a Torah command to appoint a king.[73]

The general consensus comes from Samuel's famous phrase, *"dina d'malchusa dina* (the law of the land is the law)!"[74] stapled to a warning from Rabbi Chanina, the *s'gan hakohanim*, deputy high priest, that Jews "pray for the welfare of the non-Jewish government, since, were it not for the fear of it, men would swallow each other alive!"[75]

With God's direction, Samuel anoints Saul, from the tribe of Benjamin. Does Saul perform his kingly duties well? No. God directs him to annihilate the evil empire of Amalek. Saul is too merciful, and ignores pleas from Heaven ("Be not too righteous!") as he allows the Amalekite king, Agag, to go free. And Jews continue to suffer today because of Saul's misplaced compassion.

Even the righteous can stumble in leadership.

꙳

At a packed city council meeting in Tel Aviv an elderly Jewish man is sitting in the back heckling the mayor as he speaks. Finally the mayor can't take it anymore. He turns to the heckler and says, "You think you know best? Why don't you stand up and tell us all what good you have ever done for this city!"

"Well, Mr. Mayor," he says, getting up, "I voted against you in the last election!"

꙳

Rule by Piety or Royalty?

> Be careful with authorities, for they do not befriend
> a person except for their own sake.
>
> — *Mishna 2:3*

"The care of human life and happiness," wrote Thomas Jefferson, "and not their destruction, is the first and only object of good government!"

Jefferson probably read this Mishna, one that shows extreme skepticism of government, authority and career politicians (the more civil service, the less civil the servants!) – a continuation of our Sage's previous suspicion to "despise high position," and a healthy lesson learned straight from the Torah when "a new [but well-entrenched tyrant] king arose over Egypt, who didn't know Joseph!"[76]

The Heavens obviously prefer rule by piety to rule by royalty; they look to an educated judge shorn of pretensions and pomposity, and a king of humility, restraint and dignity approved not by the people but by God. (Perhaps the Yiddishists had this in mind in their disdain for elections, which, they say, bring out new thieves to run against old crooks!)

And since the welfare of God's Chosen depends upon the welfare of a strict law-and-order government, the Jews offered sacrifices for its success at the Temple – the precursor to today's God-Bless-the-Queen type Shabbas prayers.

☞

Chaim is unable to decide on a career, so his worried parents devise a plan to test him. They put $10, a *chumash*, and a bottle of whiskey on the kitchen table, and then hide in the cupboard.

"If he takes the cash he'll be a businessman," the father whispers to his wife, "and if he takes the *chumash* he'll be a rabbi."

"What if he takes the bottle of whiskey?"

"Then, I'm afraid our son will be a drunkard."

Chaim comes home, walks into the kitchen, and first flips through the *chumash*, then immediately slips the $10 and whiskey bottle into his pockets and leaves.

"Oy, oy!" the father says as he slaps his forehead, "it's even worse than I ever imagined."

"What do you mean?" his scared wife asks.

"Our son's gonna be a politician!"

☞

It's Good to Be King!

Be careful with authorities; they do not stand
by a person in his time of need.

— *Mishna 2:3*

Does Jewish rule favor decentralized authority? Yes.

In the Torah portion on justice and judges (*Shoftim*), the branches of judicial and legislative power in government are divided, the administrative duties being broken into two categories of magistrate (*shofet*) and official (*shoter*), with a justice system that is clearly decentralized ("establish courts in *all* communities, *throughout* your tribes"), which is the forerunner for today's *beis din* structure.

Despite this Mishna's cynical attitude towards government, respect for government has always been part of Jewish ethics, as articulated by Proverbs ("My son, fear God and the king"), by Jeremiah ("Seek the well-being of the city…for in its peace shall you have peace"), by Ezra (who asked the Jews to pray for Cyrus), the Apocrypha (which records how Jews made a sacrificial offering for the ruling king), by Philo (who speaks of prayers for the Roman emperor), and, in modern times, by a British chief rabbi (Jakobovits) who presented the Queen with a framed copy of the Jews' "royal prayer" from five generations of British kings and queens.

According to the Rambam, "A Sage gave more value to a country than a king," but for the Yiddishists, pragmatism ruled: Be sure you have the backing of your equals before you stir your superiors!

⇝

A Washington politician and a Czech consul are walking in the woods, when suddenly they bump into two huge bears, one male, one female.

As the unfortunate consul is being eaten by the male bear, the politician runs back into town, and tells the sheriff's office about his Czech friend. The sheriff grabs his gun and they both run back to find the bears still lurking.

"He's in that one!" yells the politician, pointing to the male bear.

The sheriff immediately shoots the female bear.

"Whatdya do that for! I said he was in the other one!"

"Exactly…and would you believe a politician who told you that the Czech was in the male?"

⇝

Government Guide

> Rabbi Chanina[77] said: Pray for the welfare of the government, for if people were not afraid of it, a person would swallow his fellow live.
>
> — *Mishna 3:2*

This Mishna diverges substantially from the more moralizing and spiritual themes of *Pirkei Avos*, but this remarkable saying – a reflection of anxiety, paranoia and concern – still offers important, practical "stay-alive" advice.

The first-century rabbinate was worried about the overwhelming presence of a ruling Roman power, yet Rabbi Chanina was adamant: Jews had to take an active interest in public matters.

But where does this exaggerated literary imagery ("swallowing one another") come from?

After Habakkuk said that God had "made men like the fish of the sea," the rabbis of the Talmud noted that it is in the nature of fish that only the fittest survive (i.e., the larger *swallow* the smaller ones).

Rabbi Chanina assumes that, since man's basic nature is arrogance, if left unchecked, one would consume (i.e., "swallow") his fellow man through the chaos of social anarchy.

To "pray for the welfare of the government" is derived from Jeremiah's cry to his brethren that they be good, law-abiding citizens whilst in Babylonian exile (the seventy offerings at the Temple constituted a prayer on behalf of the seventy non-Jewish nations).

This reveals two things: first, that *even* an abhorred occupying temporal power rules by fiat of God, for reasons unknown, but for the ultimate good of Israel (even King David prayed for his enemies!); and since Rome and Assyria were instruments of God, the next lesson was this: get involved in civic service – *even* if that meant praying for the welfare of the detested Roman Empire.

❧

Three kindergarten boys are bragging how great their fathers are.

Chaim says: "My father can run so fast that when he fires an arrow, he can run and get there before the arrow!"

Moishie says: "That's nothing! My father's so fast that he can shoot a gun and get there even before the bullet!"

"Big deal!" says Beryl, "My father's a civil servant working for the government, and he's so fast that he stops working at 4:30 p.m. and is already home by 3:45!"

❧

Bless the Throne?!

Shemaya[78] said: Do not become intimate with the ruling power.

— *Mishna 1:10*

Is there a "Divine right of kings"? No.

It was assumed that kings, like Oscar Wilde, could resist everything but temptation. Collecting wives, horses and wealth was not an option for the king who, as God's representative, was, although neither scholar nor priest, still obligated to engage in regular Judaic study.

And more: not only did the king have to personally write (or commission) two copies of the Torah, but he was ordered to take the second Torah with him everywhere, in order to "read from it all the days of his life."[79]

God leaves nothing to chance: given the possibility of power to corrupt a leader, the king must be "armed" at all times with God's law, as a reminder of God's supremacy and of his own fallibility. The de facto assumption is that given the opportunity, a leader is liable to become corrupt or at least to have the desire to use his power for questionable purposes.

And yet, even if you see a US president, who is not technically a "king," but an elected official, Jewish law requires that you pronounce a blessing over him; in fact, any leader, including a government minister, according to *Radbaz*, who has the power and authority to make decisions that affect the Jewish community is considered a "king."

What about anti-Semitic leaders? Are we obligated to bless them? No. Why not?

Tyrants lose their moral authority when they disregard the laws of God and become immediately ineligible for any such Divine blessings.

🦅

Yankele wanted $100 to buy a new bike, so his mother told him to pray to God for it. So he prayed and prayed for two weeks, but nothing turned up. He then decided to write to God requesting the money. When the postal authorities received the letter addressed to God, they forwarded it to the president. The president was so touched by the young boy's request that he sent him five dollars, as a token gift.

When Yankele got the letter, he was very thrilled to receive the five dollars and decided to write a thank-you letter to God:

Dear God,

Thank you very much for the money. I noticed that you had to send it via Washington. As usual, they deducted $95.00 for themselves.

🦅

Hermits and Holiness

> Hillel[80] said: Do not separate yourself from the community.
>
> — *Mishna 2:5*

The message of this Mishna is that hermits and holiness don't mix; or, as the poet John Donne said, "No man is an island entire of itself!"

Hillel wanted Jews to identify with the community, to strengthen unity and solidarity, to share in its "weal or woe"!

Is there a specific mitzva that the Jew involve himself in communal matters? No, nevertheless, the Rambam doesn't hesitate to define anyone who distances himself from other Jews as being outside the Jewish pale!

But what if the community is corrupt?[81]

Ah, says Rabbi Yonah, then the Jew must live in solitude, a directive not shared by many a Chassidic rebbe: "Those who think they can live without others are wrong, but those who think that others cannot survive without them are even more in error!"

"When the community is suffering, one may not say, 'I will go to my house, eat and drink, and I will be fine,'" which is in direct contradiction to the Golden Jewish Rule and the most famous of all ethical mitzvos, "*V'ahavta l'reiacha kamocha* (love your neighbor as yourself)!"[82]

This five-word directive was embraced by Rabbi Akiva who declared it the "fundamental principle of the Torah (*zeh klal gadol ba'Torah*)"; meanwhile the Midrash defines those who leave the community as "wicked sons," and Ibn Ezra, the twelfth-century author of *Shiras Yisroel*, is brutally poetic: "The wolf grabs the sheep that strays from the flock!"

Larry shows up at the synagogue on Rosh Hashana and tries to walk into the sanctuary but the usher stops him and asks him for his ticket. Larry protests, "I just need to talk to Barry for a moment."

The usher insists Larry needs to have a ticket. Larry stresses that he didn't come to take part in the Rosh Hashana services and he only needs to talk to Barry for a second. "To tell you the truth, it's about a business matter."

The usher still says no. Larry pleads, "I'll come right back out." The usher hems and haws and finally relents, saying, "Okay, just for a minute, but don't let me catch you davening!"

But Not Too Wide!

Yose ben Yochanan[83] of Jerusalem said: Let your house be
open wide, and do not talk excessively with women.[84]

— *Mishna 1:5*

Mankind is divisible into two great classes: hosts and guests, wrote Max
Beerbohm, echoing Yehoshua ben Chanania's observation: the poor does more
for the host than the host for the poor!

Rabbi Yehoshua arrives at this stunning conclusion – that the benefit is derived by the giver (host) and not the receiver (guest) – from the Torah expression
"And I will *take* [not *give*] a loaf of bread," implying that the one who *gives* is really
receiving the opportunity to do a mitzva of kindness.

This Mishna gives us the "Open House" concept for the poor and needy, but
warns that just because your door is always open to the public, don't start getting
too familiar with the women of the neighborhood.

This doesn't reduce the supremacy of the wife, chosen by God to be the *akeres
habayis* (cornerstone of the home); it only warns that this mitzva of hospitality
and openness to others should not interfere with the sanctity of a Jewish home.

Does this mean that one cannot talk to the neighbor's wife? No, but it does
mean that one should not talk to the neighbor's wife *excessively*, especially about
trivial issues.

As a *gezeira* (preventive measure) to avoid *aveira* (sin), our Sages frown on
"idle speech and insignificant chatter" with *anybody*, defining this as *bitul Torah*,
a wasteful "negation of Torah learning."

The Yiddishists were, as usual, cynical: House guests and fish spoil on the
third day!

☙

One day the *rav* hears Sadie, a neighbor he dislikes, at his front door, so he hides
in his study. An hour later he slowly opens his door, hears nothing, assumes she's
gone, and yells out to his rebbetzin, "Has that horrible old bore gone yet?"

However, she was still there, so the quick-thinking rebbetzin yells back, "Yes,
dear, she went a long time ago! But Sadie is here now!"

☙

Mine and Mine!

> There are four types of people. One who says "what's mine is mine and what's yours is yours" – he is of average character; one who says "what's mine is yours and what's yours is mine" – he is unlearned; one who says "what's mine is yours and what's yours is yours" – he is pious; one who says "what's yours is mine and what's mine is mine" – he is wicked.
>
> — *Mishna 5:13*

This Mishna is about attitude, the approach one takes towards others.

The last three are straightforward, but the first-mentioned – the one who neither gives nor takes – has attracted attention from Torah scholars who wish to define the "wickedness" in this mindset.

Some say he is "average wicked" – i.e., neither totally evil nor totally good, merely a crude shadow of a good guy! However, our Sages abhor this attitude and link it to the obnoxious ways of the cruel folks of Sodom. The person who does not give is at risk of becoming one who always takes.

This self-centered mentality ("what's yours is mine and what's mine is mine") led the Sodomites to pass laws of hatred – e.g., a ban on all visitors, effectively eliminating any vestiges of hospitality.

In contrast to the "wicked" approach, the pious individual is generous, asking for nothing in return. The expression *chassid* is derived from this approach, for it describes the Jew who does more than required by Jewish law.

The key moral in this Mishna is adaptability. When working with others one needs to be flexible and giving, in both time and possessions.

"Be pliable like a reed," advises the Talmud's Eleazar ben Shimon, "not rigid like a cedar!" – or as the Yiddishists put it: a rope drawn too taut is apt to break!

⤚

A mother is preparing pancakes for her three- and five-year-old sons. When the boys begin to argue over who will get the first pancake, she sees an opportunity for a moral lesson in generosity and sharing.

"*Kinderlach*! If Abraham were sitting here, he would say, 'Let my brother have the first pancake – I can wait.'"

"Mum's right," the older one says to his younger brother: "You be Abraham!"

⤚

Selfishness, the Only Real Atheism!

Rabban Gamliel ben Yehuda[85] said: Anyone who works for
the community should work for the sake of Heaven.

— *Mishna 2:2*

This Mishna's message? Help out those around you in a selfless, noble way.

According to Yehiel Michael Epstein, seventeenth-century kabbalist-author, it is only when all Jews are together as a community that the whole Torah can be fulfilled!

Jeremiah went a step further: communal activity is as meritorious as studying Torah! The *Tiferes Yisroel* ruled that collecting charity, if done "for the sake of Heaven," was not a waste of Torah study time.

When Titus's Roman warriors destroyed Jerusalem, they found no fewer than twenty-four different Jewish factional groups fighting amongst themselves, each arguing that they, and *only* they, had the right path to ensure *kiyum ha'umah* (the survival of the [Jewish] people."

"They fought with each other," records the historian Josephus, "doing everything their besiegers could have desired, [ceasing only when] Roman horses waded in Jewish blood up to their noses, the blood flowing in streams to the Mediterranean [a mile away]!"

Only one surviving faction, Yochanan ben Zakkai's group, was left standing in this unnecessary civil war; the others were never heard from again in Jewish history, nor, according to the thirteenth-century *Yalkut Shimoni*, a compilation of early rabbinical literature by Rav Shimon Hadarshan of Frankfurt, was the "sound of laughter from God," causing a saddened Eleazar Hakappar to conclude that "a quarrel-ridden house is doomed to destruction!"

The humble Ba'al Shem Tov railed against self-aggrandizement and egotism: "There is no room for God in him who is full of himself" – an echo of Yochanan's opinion that "Torah abides only in him who ignores himself!"

~≈

On *motzei* Shabbas, Ernie calls his neighbor, the town *rav*: "Rabbi, that was a fabulous *drasha* this morning on *ahavas Yisroel*, but I have a *she'eila*."

"Go ahead," the *rav* replies.

"Would you, as a teacher of *mussar*, think it right to profit personally from the misfortune of a neighbor?"

"Of course not! That would be wrong! Why do you ask?"

"Because I want you to return the $100 I gave you for being the *mesader kiddushin* [officiator] at my wedding!"

~≈

Friends Like These?

> Hillel said: Do not judge your fellow until you reach his place.
>
> — *Mishna 2:5*

This Mishna is a plea to give others the benefit of the doubt, not to rush to judgment, because no one knows the level of his own moral fortitude until tested or tempted in similar circumstances.

When Rav Ashi rebuked the notorious Menashe, King of Israel, for being an idolater, the king replied, "That's easy for you say! You lived in a time when there was no desire for idolatry!"

"Do not harshly condemn a person who succumbed to temptation," writes Rashi, echoing a similar admonition by Rabbi Yonah, "until, faced by a similar temptation, you *overcame* it!"

Rabbi Levi Yitzchak of Berdichev, a champion of Chassidism in central Poland, was famous for his ability to see only the good in others. Once he was traveling together with a group of Chassidim when they saw a Jew greasing the wheels of a cart while he was wearing his prayer shawl and phylacteries. The Chassidim castigated such irreverence, but not so Rav Levi Yitzhak. He raised his eyes heavenward and said: "Lord of the universe, what a wonderful Jew is this before us. Even while he is busy greasing the wheels of his cart, he is praying!"

Meiri, disagreeing with the traditional interpretation of "place" (i.e., wherever the person happens to be), prefers to place the "place" as a reference to one's own home. Why? Convinced that people are better behaved when away from home, Meiri thinks the best place to judge another Jew is when he's in his natural environment (i.e., in his own home).

₧

The *rosh yeshiva* was giving an impassioned *d'var Torah* at the school's annual banquet, with a mike wired for sound attached to his lapel mike. As he paced briskly across the stage, the *rav* dragged the mike cord with him, but as he moved back and forth, he kept getting wound up in the cord, nearly tripping as he pulled the wire after him.

After several rotations and jerks, a little girl in the back, confused by the *rosh yeshiva*'s antics, leaned toward her mother and whispered, "If he gets loose, will he hurt us?"

₧

Be a Mensch!

Hillel said: In a place where there are no men, endeavor to be a man [*ish*].
— *Mishna 2:6*

In this Mishna, one of Hillel's most famous sayings, the Hebrew word *ish* can either be construed as "*mensch*" or "leader."

The Torah repeatedly emphasizes the concept of *menschlichkeit* (i.e., "doing the right thing"). This attitude the *Netziv* (Rabbi Naphtali Z.J. Berlin) sees in our forefathers, making them deserving of the title *Yesharim*, that is to say conducting their lives in an "absolutely straight" manner – sometimes on an even higher moral plane than Jewish law required!

An example? Abraham, when trying to save Lot, had no halachic obligation to put himself, or his men, in a position vulnerable to attack by (much more powerful) kings.

Meanwhile, if you prefer to translate *ish* as leader, you are presented with the enormous challenge to become one if the circumstances demand it.

This is dicey; very few people have leadership qualities, and among those who do, few can necessarily "lead" responsibly ("If we all pulled in one direction," goes the Yiddish adage, "the world would fall over!").

In cases where there is a dearth of leadership, Meiri warns Jews not to suddenly develop excessive humility ("Excessive humility," states Proverbs, "is a sign of a scoundrel!").[86]

What makes a leader?

Rebbe Nachman of Bratzlav thought that "when a person is capable of smiling while being abused, he is acceptable to become a leader"; Rebbe Mendel of Kotzk concluded that "fanatics should not be leaders of Israel"; the Talmudic Sage Judah ben Ezekiel warned that leadership "shortens life."

The Midrash was blunt: "When the shepherd blunders and loses his way, his flock blunders after him!"

꤮

The new *rosh kehilla* (head of the community) was asked to give the Yom Kippur *drasha*, and as he spoke, he noticed a little ol' Jewish lady behind the curtain bowing every time he mentioned the name Satan. After the davening the perplexed leader went over to her and asked, "*Geveret* [madam], why is it that you bowed each time at the mention of Satan?"

"Well," she replied softly, "You know, politeness costs nothing, and – well, you just never know!"

꤮

Dayanim, Melamdim, Rabbonim

> The Men of the Great Assembly[87] said three things: Be deliberate in judgment, raise many students, make a protective fence for the Torah.
>
> — *Mishna 1:1*

This Mishna is a remarkable admission that things can go wrong.

In his *Kuzari*, Yehuda Halevi acknowledges this: "Among the nations of the world, Israel is as the heart amidst the organs of the body – [both] the sickest and healthiest of all!"

At a time when the quality of Torah transmission between generations was deteriorating, the *Anshei Knesses Hagedola* came out with a three-pronged antidote for survival.

Concerning the problems in the judicial system, the Sages advised, "Be deliberate in judgment"; the lowering in the level of Torah study called for the demand to "raise many students"; and to protect the violations of God's commandments came the order to "make a fence around the Torah."

A closer look at these three survival techniques reveals whom our Sages saw as being responsible for the continuity of the Jewish nation as a "holy people."

The first was directed at the *dayanim* (judges), the second at the *melamdim* (teachers) and their wealthy benefactors, the third at the *rabbonim* (rabbinic hierarchy), who were challenged to create "danger signals" (i.e., precautionary rules that warn the Jew that he is at risk of breaking Divine rules).

These three categories covered justice, education and the layman's observance of Torah; obviously, the Great Assembly saw these as being interconnected, three legs holding up one table, the lack of any one of which (especially Jewish education) could cause the entire enterprise of Judaism to collapse.

By the first century BCE, Shimon ben Shetach had no choice but to rule that all Jewish children must attend school, "for otherwise the Torah would be forgotten!"

In a startling admission, Rabbi Hamnuna actually links the destruction of Jerusalem to its neglect of the school system. Shimon bar Yochai apparently concurred, even ordering certain towns in Israel to be abandoned because they didn't maintain salaried teachers!

꩜

Five-year-old Rivki came home from her first day at kindergarten and told her mother, "It's a complete waste of time. I can't read. I can't write. And they won't let me talk!"

꩜

Small Fish in the Big Pond Theory

Rabbi Masya ben Charash[88] said: Be the tail of the
lions rather than the head of the foxes.

— *Mishna 4:20*

The seating protocol of the Sanhedrin is a reflection of this Mishna.

The greater the Sage, the closer he sat to the center; the moment a member died, everybody moved up one seat.

Thus the last empty seat was filled by the highest-ranking *rav* of a lower court, who went from being the "head of the fox" to the more desirable spot of being the "tail of the lions"!

Ben Charash cautions the Jew to focus not on where he stands in the social hierarchy but on the overall quality of that social group.

This is the little-fish-in-the-big-pond theory: far better to be a minor, humble, unassuming student amongst those great(er) in Torah.

Why? Because we benefit from role-model association, a "selfish" yet proactive attempt to wake from the torpor of our own stagnation and be infused and inspired towards self-improvement.

The *Tiferes Yisroel* notes that the Mishna has two recipes for social interaction: the first requires a nonjudgmental approach, to greet *everybody* in the street politely and respectfully; but when seeking a group, *chavrusa*, spouse, or friend, it's OK to be discriminatory in your choices and to mix with the more worthy and noble.

Isn't this the "snob" elitist factor?

No, it's self-preservation.

Loving your neighbor as yourself, Rabbi Akiva's motto, also requires choosing good neighbors ("Better a close neighbor," goes a Midrash, "than a brother far away!"); and the modern-day maxim "judge a man by his friends" is "borrowed" directly from the *Mishlei Hachachamim*: "If you want to know a man, ask who his friend is!"

☙

One year, on April Fool's Day, the rabbi receives an envelope containing a single sheet of paper, on which is written simply, "April's Fool."

He turns to his *shammas* and says, "This is the first time I've received a letter from a man who sends nothing but his signature!"

☙

CHARITY

The remarkable thing about my
mother is that for thirty years she
served us nothing but leftovers. The
original meal has never been found!

— *Calvin Trillin*

Charity

Simeon the Just, high priest at the time of Alexander the Great, included compassion as one of the three distinguishing features of Judaism; the other two are the study of Torah and Temple worship.

A basic Torah demand is that Jews be committed to helping others, summarized by the concept of *gemilus chassadim*, "acts of compassion," having established right at the beginning of Genesis that, "Yes, you are your brother's keeper!"

This led Rabbi Eleazar to *pasken* that giving charity to the needy supersedes bringing sacrifices to God at the Temple.[89] This is why the thirteenth-century *Sefer Chassidim* assigns supporting the needy a higher priority than building a synagogue, and why the Hebrew word for charity (*tzedaka*) is the same as "righteousness" and "justice."

Poverty in Eleazar's time was widespread. He and his rabbinic colleagues understood that a Jewish family bordering on starvation could not contribute to creating an atmosphere of joy that is necessary for serving God. Charity was essential. Hillel once provided a man who had lost all his money with a horse and a runner so he would not lose his dignity (when Hillel could not afford to hire a runner, he did the job himself!).

And so the Rambam formulated a hierarchy of giving, listing eight ways, each progressively more commendable. The highest? Helping the poor to become independent. How? By hiring them or teaching them a trade.

But at all times, sensitivity and speed were mandatory.

Rabbi Yannai wouldn't give a beggar money in public but only privately, so as to spare him the embarrassment. Eleazar ben Pedat warned Jews not to "postpone alms overnight," comparing it to "shedding blood."[90]

But abuses by phony beggars were not to be tolerated.

With uncharacteristic bluntness, Rebbe Nachman of Bratzlav said, "Giving charity to a poor person who does not deserve it carries no reward!"[91]

Rebbe Nachman's concern is derived from Jewish law.[92]

"One should not give a coin to a charity fund unless a [pious, upright] person like Rabbi Hanina ben Tradion is in charge of it!" The rabbis of the Talmud wanted *tzedaka* to be accountable and responsible (Jews who asked for food were not to be doubted; however, a request for clothes had to be investigated).

Does that mean that no mitzva has been fulfilled if money is unwittingly given to a "con artist"? Relax. The Talmud has a special reward for good intentions![93]

⤚

Two Jews in Chelm with no money wanted to be *mekayem* [fulfill] the mitzva of *tzedaka*, so they decided to print counterfeit $20 bills and disburse them to the needy. But, being idiots, they made a mistake and ended up printing $18 bills.

"*Nu*," asks one, "what do we do now?"

"Easy, we'll give them out in a small hick town where the locals won't know the difference."

So the two *shlemiels* drive off to a small, off-the-beaten-path town and seek out the local Jewish community. They enter a store and hand Yossi, the young attendant, an $18 bill, saying, "Hey boy, can you change this for us, please?"

"Sure," replies Yossi, "do you want two nines or three sixes?"

⤚

Open House!

Yose ben Yochanan said: Let the poor be members of your household.

— *Mishna 1:5*

This Mishna's approach to the poor and impoverished is an echo of Rav Huna's "Let all who are hungry come and eat!"

"Nowhere," notes Russian Rabbi Leib Kagan, "does the Torah say, 'Invite your guest to pray,' but it does tell us to offer him food, drink and a bed."

The Hebrew word for "poor" is *aniyim*, but some read it as *anavim*, which means "humble," suggesting that the family embrace the usually reticent stranger with sensitivity and humbleness, not haughtiness.

The virtue of *hachnasas orchim* (hospitality, literally the "bringing in of guests") is derived from the zealous performance of Abraham, Jewish history's host *par excellence,* who "sat at the door of the tent [in order to] see if there is a passerby whom he might take into his house."

Since hospitality, according to Rav Yehuda, was even "greater than welcoming the presence of the *Shechina*," it became a legal obligation to feed the poor and roll out the welcome mat (i.e., provide a bed) for the traveler; and so the community custom of *beis hachnasas orchim* arose during the Middle Ages, providing non-profit inns (also known as a *hekdesh*, "sanctuary") for the poor.

"A dish tastes best when shared with a guest," writes the nineteenth-century German scholar Daniel Sanders. This is a worldview inherited from our hospitable patriarch Abraham; a Midrash translates *eishel* from the verse "And he planted an *eishel* [orchard]" as "a guesthouse" for weary travelers, an acronym of *achilah, sh'siyah, linah,* to "eat, drink, stay overnight." The Yiddishists saw in *hachnasas orchim* an opportunity for self-advantage as well: Fill your house with guests, and you'll marry off your daughter!

꒰

Little Hesky is eager to help, so when several dinner guests arrive for Shabbas lunch he quickly runs into the kitchen, brings out a piece of apple cake, and gives it to his father – who immediately passes it on to one of the visitors.

He then runs back to the kitchen, returns with another piece, and gives it to his father – who again passes it on to another guest.

"Psst, *Tata*," Hesky whispers in his father's ear, "it's no use, all the pieces are the same size!"

꒰

Protective Fences

> Rabbi Akiva[94] said: Tithes are a protective fence for wealth.
>
> — *Mishna 3:17*

The Torah was the first to lay down the rule that charity and philanthropy, a Greek term for love of mankind, begin at home, a recognition of the human condition: only those who are content *within* have the moral stamina to extend a helping hand to others.

Jewish law urges the Jew to give anonymously, "with a friendly, joyful countenance!" so that donor and beneficiary are unaware of each other's identity (this is why the Temple had a *lishkas chasha'im*, a "chamber of secret charity," in which contributions were deposited secretly, and the poor helped themselves in similar secrecy).

In this Mishna, Rabbi Akiva adds a few more "fences," defining charity ("tithes") as a protective fence for wealth – i.e., if you are generous to others, God will repay you in kind.

And God even dares us to test Him! (charity is the exception to the rule not to test God): "Bring all your donations to the Temple storehouse and test Me, and [see] if I pour out to you blessing without limit!"

The Apter Rebbe told of an innkeeper who kept two boxes in which he placed whatever money he received in equal amounts. The innkeeper said that he once fell upon hard times and lost everything he had. His wife advised him to go to the village and seek a business partner. As he traveled, it suddenly dawned upon him to take God as his partner. From then on he gave half of his earnings to *tzedaka* and his business prospered.

Charity thus doesn't deplete our savings but increases our financial security! ("Give," instructs the Talmud, "so that *you* will become wealthy!").[95]

❧

Moishe was struggling with a way to approach God in his prayers regarding his poverty. Then, one morning, an idea dawned on him! Putting on his *tallis* and *tefillin*, he started praying, "Dear God, if you give me $20,000, I'll give $10,000 to charity, and keep only the rest for myself!"

Several weeks go by and he's still poor. So he begins his prayer, "Dear God, it is obvious that you question my integrity. So, here's the deal! Give me $10,000 and give the other $10,000 to charity Yourself!"

❧

Giving a Tenth

Rabbi Eleazar ben Yehuda (of Bartosa)[96] said: Give Him
from His own, for you and your possessions are His.

— *Mishna 3:8*

The meaning of this Mishna is self-evident: everything, including body, soul, life, success and possessions, belongs to God, and to be thankful is the order of the day.

The recipients of charity are thus viewed as couriers of God, collecting "on My behalf!" – or as the Midrash puts it: were you able to put up a *mezuzah* before I gave you a house? (The *Tiferes Yisroel* extends this concept to signify that not just the money was God's to begin with, but so are all the other "assets" of man, ranging from strength to talents to intelligence, and so forth.)

How much to "give Him" is quantified: in the ancient agrarian days of farming, the Jew gave ("tithed")[97] his first fruits to the Temple charity (10 percent to the Levites, 10 percent to the poor), his field "corners" and fallen wheat stalks to the downtrodden, and a percentage of his dough to the priests.

And more: to "give" was also traditionally measured in nonfinancial terms.

The Jew was expected to give of his time and to adapt his conduct: it was obligatory – because God clothed the naked, visited the sick, comforted the bereaved, and buried the dead – that man do the same.

The primary purpose of "giving" was not for charity's sake, but as a sign of gratitude and recognition, a reminder that everything the Jew owns is his by the grace of God ("Rejoice in all the good which God has given you!").

The aggados of *Shir Hashirim* makes the connection: "Those who feed the hungry also feed God!"

꘎

"I was just trying to feed my hungry family," the defendant tells the judge, after being charged with killing and eating an egret, an endangered bird. "I promise, Sir, I've never done anything like that before."

"I'm going to set you free," says the charitable judge, a family man with a soft heart. "I'm convinced you did it out of concern for your loved ones and not because of gluttony."

"Thank you, Your Honor."

"Before you go, I'm curious. What does egret taste like?"

"Well, Your Honor, it's not as tender as spotted owl but it's better than bald eagle!"

꘎

It's All about Attitude!

> There are four types among those who give charity: One who
> wishes to give but that others should not – he begrudges others;
> that others should give and he should not – he begrudges himself;
> that he should give and others should, too – he is a chassid; that
> he should not give nor should others – he is a wicked person.
>
> — *Mishna 5:16*

This Mishna does not describe donors and non-donors, but their *attitude*, stressing that *all* Jews are obligated to give *tzedaka*.[98]

Three types on display in this Mishna are straightforward: the pious Jew who wants everyone to give, the callous Jew who wants no one to give, and the "cheap, tightfisted" Jew who wants others to give but does not give himself. The latter, despite suffering from an inability to part with his own money, at least recognizes the importance of charity.

Meiri labels this type of Jew faithless; Rashi calls him "skeptical" because his hesitancy to stretch out his hand to others probably stems from fear for his own future financial well-being.

But what are we to make of the Jew who gives but does not want others to give? Surely this is a contradiction in moral terms?

The Mishna is describing the bizarre behavior of one who is unable to share his joy of performing mitzvos with others. This type of Jew seeks honor for himself, and one way to increase the odds, he rationalizes, is to deprive other Jews from gaining recognition for their own good deeds, hoping to depict them as "stingy" in comparison to his own magnanimity.

This explains the rabbinic adage: one can do wrong – even whilst doing right!

꣠

"Reb Yaakov," the *rav* asks the local *gevir* (rich man), "you've made so much money, why don't you give any to charity?"

"Rabbi, are you aware that my mother is dying and has enormous medical bills?"

"No," answers the *rav*, shifting in his seat.

"And rabbi, are you aware that my brother is blind and confined to a wheelchair, and my sister's husband died in a car accident leaving her penniless with three children?!"

The embarrassed rabbi begins to stammer an apology but is interrupted, "So if I don't give any money to them, why would I give to you?"

꣠

A Matter of Life and Death

At four periods (during the seven-year agricultural cycle) pestilence
increases...because of [the neglect of] the tithe for the poor; and
following Succos every year because of stealing the gifts for the poor.

— *Mishna 5:12*

This Mishna lists sins that result in the punishment of pestilence – specifically, withholding the poor's share of crop tithes.

In each of the six years before *Shmitta*, 10 percent of the harvest was allocated to the Levites, and around 2 percent for the priests (*ma'aser rishon*); and, in years one, two, four and five, another tithe was put aside (*ma'aser sheini*, or its equivalent in cash, to be spent in Jerusalem); in years three and six, an additional tithe was set aside for the poor (*ma'aser ani*, from the "corner," or "forgotten" parts of the field).

Why is Succos mentioned?

Because this, the Feast of Tabernacles, occurred at harvesting time, when the poor were often disappointed in their expectations.

It is obvious from the harsh punishment (pestilence is a form of death penalty) that this formula of giving charity is a serious concern to God. Why? Several reasons: firstly, the needy ("God's people") wait anxiously for this period, which makes their disappointment even deeper.

And, as the Yiddish proverb goes, stealing from the poor is stealing from God (in that the land and its produce belongs to Him).

And more! "Starving" the helpless poor by not sharing food and produce ("Do not steal from the weak because he is weak") increases their chance of succumbing to the epidemic of pestilence; thus, there is an enormous responsibility underlying the mitzva of *tzedaka*.

❧

"Mr. Goldenberg," says the divorce court judge, "I have reviewed this case very carefully and I've decided to give your wife $575 a week."

"That's very fair and kind of you, Your Honor," the husband replies, "and every now and then I'll try to send her a few bucks myself!"

❧

And Not a Penny More!

Rabban Gamliel said: Do not give excess tithes
by estimating [instead of measuring].

— *Mishna 1:16*

In other words, measure – don't guess!

This Mishna advocates preciseness in farming, advising Jews not to give more *ma'aser* to the priests, Levites and poor folks than required.

What's the rationale behind Rabban Gamliel's concern?

If, for example, more than 10 percent of the fruit and grain produce (as mandated) is given to the Levites, then the excess can *never* be tithed; thus, someone, *somewhere else* has been deprived of his portion. And more! The Levites themselves will find themselves eating more than their rightful share, a form of theft, "stealing" from the excess product that belongs to another.

This is an argument for discipline; everything has its (Torah) time and place.

Giving more might seem generous but, in fact, it disturbs the symmetry of God's immutability in His demands; and since estimates must inevitably lead to error, then the likelihood of accidentally giving *less* than 10 percent increases.

Does this accuracy apply to the kohanim? No. Why not? Because the *teruma* (one-fiftieth of the produce) was "approximate" to begin with.

❧

Moishie answers an ad for a job at the local charity; during the interview the recruiter asks him about his salary expectations.

"Well, I was looking for something in the $125,000 range."

The recruiter replies, "Would you also like a benefit package with five weeks of paid vacation, full pension plan, unlimited sick leave, full tuition scholarships at the yeshiva, free membership in the *shul*, and the use of a red Corvette?"

Moishie is stunned. "You must be kidding!"

"Yeah!" the recruiter says, "but you started it!"

❧

FRIENDS AND GREETINGS; LOVE AND ANGER

The trouble with having
friends is the upkeep!

— Milton Berle

Friends and Greetings; Love and Anger

A Chassidic saying: "One who looks for a friend without faults will have none!"

Moshe ibn Ezra, twelfth-century Sage, described friendship as man's greatest gift. Sholem Aleichem, "borrowing" from King Solomon,[99] preferred the bite of a friend to the kiss of an enemy. In choosing a friend, the rabbis of the Talmud suggest one "go up a step."

The English word "friend" is derived from the Old English verb *fréon*, "to love," and the Torah considers genuine friendship and bonding as a state of cultural sanctity, in that a group of comrades, or even just a simple *chavrusa* (Aramaic for a "pair of Jews") engaging in intense Torah study, are pursuing the most effective path to knowledge ("I have learned more from my friends than from my teachers!").[100]

And so the rabbis of *Pirkei Avos*, recognizing that for religious and personal growth a *chaver* is more important than a rabbi, urge us to "make [*asei*]" for ourselves a rabbi but go to great efforts to "acquire [*k'nei*] a friend."

A rabbi is a role model, a friend is an equal; a rabbi speaks to the whole community, a meaningful friend speaks specifically to you. To "acquire" doesn't mean to "buy" but to invest in.

Friendships are two-way streets; they need to be nurtured, actively. "He who finds a faithful friend, finds a treasure," gush the Yiddishists.

Rabbi Yehoshua concluded that a "good life" can be lived by avoiding "bad friends," a direction that requires the active pursuit of "good" friends. This "acquisition" is a constructive personal investment in time, emotion, and a cultivation of closeness.

In his dying (ethical) will, Rav Asher ben Yehiel, a thirteenth-century German-Spanish scholar, instructed his children: "Never be weary of making friends....

If you have a faithful friend, hold fast to him. Let him not go, for he is a precious possession."

When Honi, the legendary Talmudic miracle-worker, awoke from a sleep of seventy years, he plunged into depression because he didn't recognize a single friendly Sage in that generation. A Torah scholar standing nearby was so moved by Honi's overwhelming loneliness that he uttered the famous *vort*, "either friendship or death!"[101]

The question is obvious. If friendship is a natural human need, why do our Sages even have to tell us to "get a friend"? The answer is also obvious: the Torah's wisdom directs us to be careful and *selective* in *whom* we choose as friends. That sounds like a small price to pay for loyalty, support and moral guidance!

Honor and respect are due to all human beings, regardless of their level of wealth, learning or achievements. Rabbi Chaim of Volozhin, in his commentary on *Pirkei Avos* (*Ruach Chaim*) tells us why: because each human being, a handiwork of God (created in His image, *b'tzelem Elokim*), is intrinsically holy.

Respect for others brings self-respect. Saying "hello" is an indispensable element in creating a community. A symbol of this *derech eretz* (proper behavior, literally, "the way of the land") is the simple greeting. It matters not if your greeting goes unreturned – but it does matter if the greeting is accompanied by a frown!

Rabbi Masya ben Charash makes it an obligation to initiate the greeting, and Shammai adds, *b'sever panim yafos* (with a nice countenance) – do it with a smile and a happy demeanor. Jewish mystics see it as a form of *tzedaka*, capable of uplifting a depressed soul.

The rabbis of the Talmud called it "theft" if you didn't return a greeting, robbing the other of his dignity and self-respect.[102]

"Who is worthy of honor?" asks *Pirkei Avos*. And ben Zuma replies, "The one who honors others!" And so Rabban Yochanan ben Zakkai, the leading Sage of Israel at the end of the Second Temple period, was always the first to greet a stranger in the marketplace with a cheerful and pleasant countenance.[103]

Yochanan ben Zakkai's cordial behavior prompted Rabbi Israel Salanter, the nineteenth-century founder of the mussar movement, to teach that one's facial expression, which he said belonged to the "public domain," affects the mood of others.

Every morning for sixty years, Rabbi Aryeh Levin, the great "*tzadik* of Jerusalem," made it a point on his way to *shul* to greet everyone he met on the street – especially saying good morning to the street cleaners. When he spoke to others on the phone, Rabbi Chaim Friedlander maintained a warm smile on his face, convinced that "although the listener may not be able to see my smile, he can hear my smile!"

It was love at first sight between God and the Jewish people.[104]

This emotion trickled down to the greatest Sages, motivating Rabbi Akiva to define the love-your-neighbor[105] rule as the essence of Torah.

Jewish mystics took this one step further.

The Lubavitcher Rebbe considered this mitzva as a Jew's duty "to influence, and even change, the behavior and nature of his fellow man," the philosophical underpinnings of the *kiruv* outreach movement. Rabbi Zusha of Anipoli's *ahavas Yisroel* (love of one's fellow Jew) was such that he was simply incapable of seeing anything negative in a fellow Jew.

"What's better," asked the Chassidim of Schneur Zalman of Liadi, "love of God or love of one's fellow?" "The two are the same," replied the founder of Chabad (his son, Dov Ber, settled in the town of Lubavitch, which means "Town of Love").

Remember: anger is one letter short of danger.

God hates three things: anger, drunkenness and demanding that things go only our way.[106]

When judging another, the Talmud says the clues lie in how they handle drinking, money and anger – *koso, kiso v'ka'aso* (his cup, his pocket and his anger).[107]

Anger? It "rests in the lap of fools!" An angry person? He "causes strife and sin!"[108] Even non-Jewish thinkers grasped this: "Anger begins in folly and ends in repentance," mused Pythagoras, the ancient mathematical genius.

"Anger in a house is like a worm in a plant," confides Rav Chisda. "Losing your temper is disrespectful for the Divine Presence," adds Rabba bar Huna. "Anger begins with madness and ends with regret," teaches Ibn Hasdai.

After a Midrashic observation that "anyone who is angry is like one worshipping idolatry," the rabbis of *Pirkei Avos*, with their eye on interpersonal relationships (the realm of *bein adam l'chaveiro*, literally "between man and his friend") defined indiscriminate anger as a personality disorder, a threat to one's emotional equilibrium bordering on heresy.

Its antidote was infinite patience: "Be slow to anger (*erech apayim*) and easy to pacify."[109]

If anything, Judaism recognizes human nature. And so we are not told *never* to get angry, simply not to *rush* into anger. The Rambam even compares the Jew who never gets angry to a corpse![110]

Torah linguists note that *erech* is derived from the Hebrew root "to lengthen," suggesting that he who controls his anger lives longer. The Yiddishists were blunt: You can't shake hands with a clenched fist!

"When a person gives in to anger, if he is wise, his wisdom leaves him," warns Shimon ben Lakish; "if he is a prophet, his power of prophecy leaves him; if greatness was decreed for him from Heaven, anger will cause him to be degraded!"

The first homicide in the Torah (Cain's slaying of his brother, Abel) resulted from anger. And look what happened to poor Moses, humble beyond words! After hitting a rock in anger, he is spiritually crippled forever ("When any man gives way to rage, even the Divine Presence abandons him!").[111]

By describing anger in four categories,[112] *Pirkei Avos* admits that everyone loses his temper on occasion. The degree is the key. Having declared that "rage produces nothing but rage," the rabbis of the Talmud trained themselves to be calm and gentle,[113] motivating scholars over the centuries to go to great lengths to manage their anger. King Solomon turned to learning Torah when he was about to lose his temper.

Nineteenth-century Polish Rabbi Yitzchak of Vurka would wrap himself in a special coat when he felt he was about to lose his composure, hoping that a new wardrobe would calm him down. Another *rav* made it a habit to sip water for several minutes until his anger subsided. The *bracha* he made on the water reminded him of God. One Chassidishe Rebbe would start dancing whenever he felt anger. This dance step became known as a *rikud shel mitzva*, "a mitzva dance" (because it prevented the sin of anger).

The author of the medieval text *Reishis Chochma* (The Beginning of Wisdom) suggests that anger be tempered by making such a large donation to charity that a person will think twice before getting angry again.

One *mussar sefer* (*Orchos Tzadikim*) gives three practical ideas for anger management: stay silent until you calm down, then speak in a low voice, and don't look at the source of your anger.[114]

In other words: respond privately. Go for a walk, eat some chocolate, write an angry letter to the editor – but don't send it. Remember: if you speak when you are angry, you will make the best speech you will ever regret!

⇶

Ernie and Estie have a big argument and stop speaking to each other. Then one day Ernie realizes he needs his wife's help to wake up and catch an early morning flight. However, he still won't speak to her so he leaves a note on her pillow, "Please wake me at 5 a.m. I have a plane to catch."

Next morning, he wakes to the shock that it's already past 9 a.m. He finds a note next to his bed: "It's 5 a.m. Wake up!"

⇶

Friend or Foe?

> Nittai[115] of Arbel said: Distance yourself from a bad
> neighbor; do not befriend a wicked person.
>
> — *Mishna 1:7*

This is a clarion call for good friendships and good neighbors, a recognition that guilt through association is alive and well ("Woe to the evil person *and* to his neighbor!").

Pick your friends, they say, more carefully than they pick you!

Nittai the Arbelite warns us to stay away from the "bad guys," those whose influence on our lives cannot lead to anything good. This echoes ben Sira, the Sage who lived a hundred years before him, whose philosophy was similar: "He that toucheth pitch shall be defiled!"

Interestingly, the Hebrew word used to "disattach" from a bad neighbor is *hitchaber*, from the root *chibur* (connection), which also forms the word *chaver* (friend)!

This raises an intriguing question: how can we tell who's truly a good friend?

"A real friend," wrote Walter Winchell, "is one who walks in when the rest of the world walks out!" Len Wein describes a true friend as "someone who is there for you when he would rather be somewhere else," whilst an old adage goes like this: Great friends are hard to find, difficult to leave, and impossible to forget!

Ibn Gevirol compares the lack of a good friend to an amputation ("A man without friends is like a left hand without a right!"), but the clue lies in *Divrei Chassidim*: "False friends are like migratory birds; they fly away in cold weather!"

꒘

Of course the key is to find a smart friend. Not like Izzie who hooks up with Shmuli, and they decide to go on a boat cruise which hits a rock and sinks, causing the two friends to find themselves stranded in a lifeboat. Three days go by with no food or water, until suddenly a genie appears out of a floating bottle and tells them, "I'll grant each of you a single wish."

"I wish I was home," says Izzie – and *poof*! He has disappeared.

The genie waits patiently for Shmuli to make his wish. After a few minutes, Shmuli sighs, "Gee, it's awfully lonely around here. I wish my friend Izzie was here with me!"

꒘

An Enemy You Must Pay For!

> Shmuel Hakatan [the Small][116] said: At your enemy's fall do not rejoice, and when he stumbles let your heart not be joyous.
>
> — *Mishna 4:24*

Even if one's enemy's downfall is deserved, says this Mishna, quoting one of King Solomon's proverbs, one must not gloat over his downfall.

Why not? What's wrong with gloating? Surely it's human nature?

Even the Mishna admits, "The death of the wicked is beneficial to them and beneficial to the world!"

But Rabbi Shmuel feels that the display of an angry God's power unleashed in justice should be met with awe, not joy (and perhaps a prayer that it not be directed at us, as happened to Lot's wife when she turned around to see Sodom destroyed).

This ideology can be traced to the sight of Egyptians drowning in the Red Sea, when God reproached the angels: "The creations of My hand are drowning in the sea, and you are singing!"

But though the angels were not allowed to sing, the Jews did!

Miriam led the nation in the Song of the Sea. The difference? The angels were rejoicing at the annihilation of their wicked enemy; the Jews burst out in a song of gratitude for their liberation.

Why is Shmuel described as "small"? Isn't this an insult? No; his "smallness" was not physical but a description of a humble personality.

Because of his humility, his colleagues honored his request to add to the daily *Shemoneh Esrei* a supplication (*V'lamalshinim*) asking for the destruction of heretics (that God "smash and humble the wanton sinners speedily in our days!").

But isn't this itself toying with destruction and retribution? No, Shmuel's focus lay in *kiddush Hashem*, the public restoration of God's honor, recognized through His displays of justice.

A friend, reminds the Yiddishist, costs nothing – an enemy you must pay for!

⤝

Yankele didn't like Beryl. One day the two are standing in the bank when a robber bursts in, lines up all the customers and demands that they give him all the money from their wallets. As the thief approaches Yankele, he turns to Beryl and squeezes some money into his hand.

"What's this for?"

"That's the $100 I owe you!"

⤝

Group Therapy

Rabbi Chanina ben Dosa said: If the spirit of one's fellows [*briyos*] is pleased with him, the spirit of God is (also) pleased with him.

— *Mishna 3:13*

This Mishna blurs the distinction between pleasing your fellow Jew and pleasing God; in fact, Rabbi Chanina, a mystic, equates human harmony with Godly service.

The term "spirit of" is used literally, in that when the spirit is at rest it oozes tranquillity to others; this, in turn, reduces communal stress and replaces discord with peace and unity which results in allowing the "spirit of" God a calm stillness and serene atmosphere to operate in.

Rabbi Yonah defined this type of Jew as a *kiddush Hashem*, a walking, talking public tribute to God, with the *Tiferes Yisroel* granting him the utmost reward: in return for pleasing others, God compliments him with a pleasant persona.

Several commentators note that for "others" the Mishna uses the term *briyos*, from *briya*, which literally means "significant creatures." Why? In a nod to human nature, the Mishna doesn't expect you to be good to everybody, just to those who are "*briyos*" (i.e., deserving of respect).

This is a simple, straightforward mission to Jews: if you please others (i.e., if you are a *mensch*), you please God.

The word for "neighbor" is derived from the Hebrew for "dweller."

"When one invites a king into his house, he cleanses it thoroughly first," notes Rabbi Meir of Premysl. "All the more so must he cleanse himself before Hashem will dwell within him!"

🐃

The stone maker asks the widow of Bill Strange, a lawyer, to list for him three of her husband's good qualities. "He was honest, fair, compassionate," she weeps.

A week later she comes to approve the inscription on the tombstone: "Here lies Strange, an honest, fair, compassionate man, and a lawyer."

"To tell you the truth," the stone maker says, "I think it's a bit too jumbled. It reads like there's two people buried here."

"Any suggestions?"

"Sure. Let's write, 'Here lies an honest, fair, compassionate lawyer' and then people will say, 'Hey, that's Strange!'"

🐃

God's Nachas!

Shammai [and Rabbi Yishmael] said: Receive
everyone with a cheerful countenance.

— *Mishna 1:15, 3:16*

This Mishna's pursuit of a "cheerful countenance" motivated the rabbis to urge that even a *d'var Torah* must begin with a joke.

Why? It is wise to *enjoy* what you are doing, no matter what it is; and, reminds King David, God's presence doesn't dwell in a place where there is no joy.

Shammai knew: the centrality of Sinai is the mitzva of being *sameach* (happy), and, since joy nourishes the soul, cheerful Jews are God's *nachas*! Meiri, incredibly, adds that, even if you're not in a happy mood, you should fake it!

Why? So as not to disturb the atmosphere of camaraderie evident in public friendship.

In a startling Talmud story, Yochanan ben Nappaha goes even further than Shammai: the Sage advises Jews to greet each other with warm smiles rather than with food or drink.

How does a smile fill an empty stomach?

The answer comes courtesy of those Yiddishists who, despite their cynicism, instinctively understood that good cheer is an emotionally sound and stable platform ("A smile is a small curve that sets many things straight"), a warmth that helps the Jew to function properly, as necessary as food and drink – and that the pursuit of Yiddishkeit is to be associated with joy and laughter, happiness and gratitude.

Why? Because the religion of Israel is essentially a *toras chaim*, a "law of life," intended to cultivate a happy frame of mind that pulsates with the joy of existence.

꘎

Three ascetic monks are meditating in a cave. After several years of silence, one opens his eyes, and says, "Look, what a miserable day. It's raining out there." He then closes his eyes and returns to his meditation.

A year passes. The second monk opens his eyes, and says, "Look, what a beautiful day. It's sunny out there!" He, too, returns to his meditation.

Another year passes. The third monk opens his eyes, and says, "Look, you guys are never happy! If you don't stop arguing, I'm going to find another cave!"

꘎

Be First!

> Rabbi Masya ben Charash said: Be first to greet [*makdim*] every person.
> — *Mishna 4:20*

The Mishna's use of *makdim*, "to greet," was translated by the *Toldos Yaakov Yosef* as "to give precedence"; in other words, don't wait! Take the initiative to greet another. And if you do? He will respond in kind, in *shalom* (peace).

The English-language greeting *hello* (with its variants *hallo*, *hullo*, etc.) comes from the Anglo-Saxon *hale* (as in "hale and hearty") and originally meant, "I wish you well!"

But in classical Hebrew, *sholem aleichem* means "peace be with you" – and the reply is reversed: *aleichem sholem*, "with you should [also] be peace!"

The Jewish custom to greet another Jew with a *shalom* (prounounced *sholem* by Yiddish-influenced Ashkenazim) *aleichem* was originally intended to extend the concept of God between brethren, since *shalom* is one of God's Names ("God is *shalom*, His Name is *shalom*, and all is bound together in *shalom*!").

Thus, its correct meaning is not "peace be upon you" but "God be with you" – a prayer that all Jews be met and blessed with Divine Presence.

In his commentary on *Pirkei Avos*, the thirteenth-century Rabbi Yonah urged the host to treat poor guests with "a happy face"; meanwhile, Meiri sees the mitzva of greeting in reverse: not only should you love your fellow, you should become beloved by him. How? Simply by being friendly!

Abbaye was always sensitive to a "hello" that was soft-spoken, designed not to turn anybody away, not "even the idolaters in the street!" Yochanan ben Zakkai made it a point, no matter how busy or preoccupied he was, to be the first to greet another Jew affably, seeing it as a twofold gesture: it warms and reinforces the recipient's self-worth, and it gives the greeter an opportunity to be a *mensch*!

⤙

Bernie was running down the street, greeting everybody with a hello and telling them he was looking for an accountant, asking each one, "Can you help out?"

"No," said most people.

"Hi!" Bernie says to another guy, "*Sholem aleichem*! Listen, I'm looking for an accountant."

"Didn't you just hire an accountant a short while ago?"

"Yeah! That's the guy I'm after!"

⤙

Aaron's Fan Club

Hillel said: Be of the students of Aaron, loving peace and pursuing peace, loving people and bringing them closer to Torah.

— *Mishna 1:12*

Aaron's resumé is impressive and would make any headhunter drool: the older brother of Moses, co-leader of the Exodus, high priest, wearer of special golden robes, the only Jew in his generation allowed to enter the Holy of Holies, mystic communicator with God.

The virtues are obvious, but where did Aaron get the reputation as a seeker of and paradigm for peace?

The clue lies in an early manuscript (*Avos d'Rav Nassan*) that describes Aaron's inspiring approach to *sholem tzvishin Yidden* (peace among Jews).

Unwilling to rush in to reprimand or scold, he would take his time and use the weapon of patience, subtly befriending the warring parties; once their trust and friendship was won, the rest was easy.[117]

Aaron's specialty? Marriage partners!

So "great is peace between husband and wife" that Shimon ben Gamliel equated those who brought about *shalom bayis* as having brought about peace on the entire Jewish people (this is why thousands of grateful Jewish wives named their children "Aaron").

Consider the scene of his death: *all the children* of Israel cry for him for thirty days, a nationwide tribute and grief that didn't take place after the deaths of his brother (Moses) or sister (Miriam).

How did Aaron accomplish what he did?

Because of his self-image: he saw himself not as a distant leader, superior and above-it-all, but as one of the people, a communal servant, humble spokesman, a national unifier!

The Mishna doesn't expect any of us to actually reach Aaron's heights, so the best Hillel could hope for was that we become "students" of Aaron.

꒰

The shtetl *rav*, seeking to keep the peace with his hostile gentile neighbors, invites the local priest to his *Pesach seder tisch*, and offers him some of his favorite hot, pure, homemade horseradish.

The *galach* takes a big spoonful and suddenly clutches his throat and slinks off his chair. His face turning red, the priest gasps, "Rabbi, I've heard many ministers preach hellfire, but you are the first one I've ever met who actually passes out samples!"

꒰

Keep Cool!

> Rabbi Eliezer ben Hyrkanos said: Do not anger easily.
>
> — *Mishna 2:15*

This Mishna's insight is universal.

"To rule one's anger is well; to prevent it is still better," noted Tryon Edwards, even as the famous man of words, Daniel Webster, preached, "Keep cool! Anger is not an argument!"

Said the Koretzer Rebbe: "I conquered my anger long ago, and placed it in my pocket. This way I don't allow it to consume me. And if I need it, I take it out."[118]

Today's anger, they say, is better spent tomorrow!

Hatred and strife have been around since the days of Cain and Abel (the motive behind the Torah's first homicide is Cain's rage at being offended), which is why Rabbi Yonah approaches anger as a powerful yet normal part of a human's DNA.

In fact, Moses' entrée onto the stage of Jewish history occurs in a moment of anger (on seeing an Egyptian beating an Israelite), and anger at his people's constant whining about a lack of water causes him to strike a rock, as a result of which he forfeits his dream of entering the promised land ("Through anger, heroes fall!" would have been the headline of the time!).

It is this episode that motivated the Talmud to point to rage as "causing wisdom to depart from the wise and prophecy to depart from the prophet"!

This Mishna uses its words carefully, advising others not to *avoid* anger but just to temper their temper.

This ability for self-control, to bite one's upper lip before exploding in blind rage, frustration and fury, is a true reflection of one's character.

So is there an explicit prohibition against anger in the Torah?

No, yet Judaism still considers hot tempers and violent passions destructive vehicles that snatch away wisdom and weaken the soul.

❦

Bernie and his wife are having a family argument and, in a desperate attempt to make amends, he offers his wife a two-week vacation in France. She declines. He then offers her a brand new car. She declines. He then offers to renovate her kitchen.

"No!" she screams, "that's not what I want!"

"So, what do you want?!"

"A divorce!"

"Oh," Bernie says, "I hadn't planned on spending that much!"

❦

Anger Management

There are four types of temperaments. One who is quick to become angry and quick to calm down – his gain is outweighed by his loss; one who is slow to become angry and slow to calm down – his loss is outweighed by his gain; one who is slow to become angry and quick to calm down is pious; one who is quick to become angry and slow to calm down is wicked.

– Mishna 5:14

This Mishna focuses on temper, the loss of which, notes Rabba bar Huna, is equated with disrespect for God.

Chassidim have an expression (*rikud shel mitzva*) that describes a form of dancing intended to release anger as a mitzva; meanwhile the Sfas Emes thought that the true sign of a *tzadik* was his ability to control his anger at times when it is justified.

Whenever he felt angry, Rabbi Chaim of Volozhin would repeat, over and over, a Torah verse (*Ein od milvado*, "There is nothing else besides God") which distracted him towards only positive thoughts.

This Mishna, by listing certain types of angry folks, acknowledges that everyone gets angry at some time or other – even the "pious"; in fact, Rabbi Yonah thinks that anger is even necessary under certain circumstances (e.g., Phineas's anger, despite leading to a double homicide, is actually *rewarded* by God!).

The Rambam, a realist, compares the person who never gets annoyed to "a corpse"! – yet he agrees with the Maharal: those who are *always* angry suffer from a form of instability, a spiritually crippling status, guaranteed to lead to sin.

❧

It's two o'clock in the morning and the phone suddenly wakes up Shmuli and his wife. "Wrong number!" he growls and slams down the phone. It rings again, and again he screams, "Wrong number!" and hangs up in a fit of anger.

When it rings the third time, he softly says, "One extra large slice, cheese and tomatoes, garlic bread on the side. Pickup in twenty minutes."

"What was that?" his wife asks.

"I took his order," a much calmer Shmuli replies, "we can go back to sleep now!"

❧

Cosmetic Perjury

> Any love which is dependent on something, when
> the "something" ceases, the love ceases.
>
> — *Mishna 5:19*

Which "something" – which external factor – motivated this Mishnaic warning?

After Amnon, son of King David, sinned with his sister, under the guise of "love," the rabbis of the king's court *paskened* (ruled) that no man should be left alone with a woman.

Rabbi Yonah is suspicious of "self-love" that emerges from an attraction to "something else" (i.e., money, *yichus* [illustrious lineage], power, prestige, education, vanity, etc.), which he calls not love but self-interest. The Rambam defines these desires, which are not grounded in mutual respect, as "temporary, superficial needs."

They blur reality, says the *Tiferes Yisroel*, and thus, have "no future."

The Torah's focus on a person's inner esthetics is one reason why Jewish law frowns upon the shallowness of cosmetic surgery, described as "cosmetic perjury" by Rabbi Eliezer Waldenberg.

This does not mean that no effort should be made to look one's best.

In London, in the late nineteenth century, a disappointed husband told the judge that he didn't realize until the morning after his wedding (when his wife removed her makeup) that she was not the *sizkeit* (sweetness) he courted but a *miskeit* (ugliness), and asked the court for damages from her father based on "her real, and not her assumed, countenance."

He won.

❧

Miriam gets a job as a phone salesperson for a mortgage refinancing company. She places her first call. "Sir, are you interested in taking out a second mortgage on your home?"

"No, thanks, I just paid off my first mortgage, all cash."

"Would you like to consolidate all your debts?"

"No, thanks, I don't have any debts."

"How about freeing up cash for home improvement?"

"No, thanks, I just remodeled my house and paid all in cash."

Miriam thinks for a few seconds and then asks, "Hey, maybe you're looking for a wife?"

❧

Kalla My World

Our forefather Abraham was tested with ten trials and withstood all of them; this shows the love our forefather Abraham had [for God].

— *Mishna 5:4*

Love is like butter, goes the Yiddish adage – it's good with bread! But King David sang a different tune: "The world is built by love!"

Yochanan Twerski from Podolia writes: "Each goose is a swan in the eyes of its lover!" Of course, then there's the opposite view, cynically captured by the Yiddishists: All cats love fish, but few of them will enter the water!

But this Mishna refers to a different type of love: the love of God for the first Jew, whose top grade in ten formidable trials (climaxing with the *akeida* [binding] of Isaac) molded him into the suitable progenitor of the Jewish people.

It's no coincidence that the number of trials Abraham faced equals the previous number of "utterances" that created the world, and the future number of commandments at Sinai.

There are no complaints departments in the life of Abraham: he does not protest at a destiny that requires leaving his "father's house" for a distant and vaguely identified "land that I will show you"; nor when told his descendants will be enslaved for four hundred years; nor when confronted by a terrible famine in his land of destination, forcing him to descend to the licentious peninsula of Egypt; nor when that country's king, enthralled by his wife Sarah's beauty, makes advances to her; nor when he is suddenly thrust into a regional conflict with four marauding kings (the cause for which remains unknown) in order to rescue, without thought of personal benefit, his brother's captive son Lot, an odd, tragic figure.

And yet, to *kvetch* and complain *is* a Jewish custom – no matter the level of zealousness.

※

The new rabbi has been at his job for a year and is visiting his former *rosh yeshiva*.

"*Nu*, how's it going?"

"Great! In one year I've enrolled fifty families. And they are all active, involved, zealous!"

"Wow! That's *nachas*! Imagine! Fifty active families!"

"Yes," replies the new rabbi quietly, "all fifty are active, involved, zealous – twenty-five are active *for* me and twenty five are actively acting *against* me!"

※

Beauty and the Beholder

Rabbi Meir[119] said: Do not look at the jug, but at what is in it.
— *Mishna 4:27*

Rabbi Meir urges us to go beyond surface impressons, to look at the individual, not the birth certificate – especially when admiring a woman, the Torah wants men to appreciate not just the creation, but also the Creator; not just the product, but also the Manufacturer.

Rough exteriors often hide good people, and conversely, evil sometimes parades in the finest wardrobe.

That is why Jews say a special *shehechiyanu* prayer of admiration called *birkas nehenin*, "blessing of enjoyment," whenever we encounter rainbows, flowers, wisdom or anything reflective of the beauty of God's presence – to which Yiddish folklore adds: Better to talk to a woman and think of God, than to talk to God and think of a woman!

The Talmud supports the popular aphorism that "beauty is in the eye of the beholder," but cautions that, on the Richter scale of qualities in choosing a wife, "beauty" should not be the number one criterion.

King Solomon, in his poetic "Ode to the Woman of Valor," sung by a husband to his wife on Sabbath eve, asks, "Who can find a woman of valor?" and adds that "charm is false and beauty is vanity!"

An old Sinatra song goes, "Love and marriage go together like a horse and carriage," however, the Torah is not naïve.

Love, despite the slogan, does not conquer all, warn our rabbis, knowing full well that love fades and cannot alone sustain a marriage; thus the first and foremost purpose of marriage is…companionship, which is why the Torah's ideal marital component is *yichud*, an unshakable team loyalty of "togetherness."[120]

❧

Dovid decides to sell some of his stuff and puts an ad in the local paper:
"Complete set of Encyclopaedia Britannica, 45 volumes; College Edition Webster's Dictionary; Thesaurus. All in excellent condition. No longer needed… recently married; wife knows everything."

❧

LAW AND ORDER

"Pull my tooth, the whole tooth
and nothing but the tooth!"

— *Judge to dentist*

Law and Order

After linking the destruction of the First Temple and the subsequent Babylonian exile to failures of justice, the rabbis of *Pirkei Avos* warn, "The sword comes into this world because of justice delayed and justice denied!"

But the first thing to know about a Torah judiciary is that law and order, the basic ingredients of a civilized society, begin at home: "Judge every person favorably," urges Yehoshua ben Perachia, the benefit-of-the-doubt advocate of *Pirkei Avos*.

Here we have the Torah's attitude about attitude.

Justice is considered to be one of the three pillars of the world (the other two, according to Rabban Shimon ben Gamliel, are truth and peace)[121] but judging is not just about the dry facts, statistical evidence, circumstantial details. It requires a mindset of sensitivity, patience, compassion. Absent mercy and tolerance, the law itself becomes merciless and intolerant. (Abraham Lincoln took note and concluded, "I have always found that mercy bears richer fruits than strict justice!")

This is why the Great Sanhedrin, the highest court in the land, was physically placed in the Chamber of Hewn Stone near the altar on the Temple Mount. It was a reminder to the Jewish judiciary that mercy and compassion must be given equal consideration in the spiritual dock of civil law between man and man, just as it is outlined in the Torah between man and God.

The *Toldos Yaakov Yosef* points out the fact that the verse "Judges shall you place for yourself in all of your gates…"[122] uses the singular "for yourself [*lecha*]," implying that each Jew is first obligated to judge (and correct) himself, *before* judging others.

It is no coincidence that the Torah portion containing this verse (*Shoftim*, "Judges") is always read on the first Shabbas of the month of Elul, the season of introspection, a time when forgiveness of others is the most potent form of justice.

This habit of evaluating one's own behavior first, says Rabbi Simcha Bunim from Peshischa, is a prerequisite to being able to "judge others fairly." And it cannot be a passive exercise; complacency and justice are enemies.

"*Tzedek, tzedek tirdof* (Righteousness, righteousness thou shalt pursue)"[123] is not just an active command to chase justice with fervor, but a reminder that its pursuit is as important as its implementation, if not more so. And its implementation must be free of corruption, if absolute trust in the Jewish judiciary is to be maintained.

The third-century Babylonian Mar Shmuel, *rosh beis din* and *rosh yeshiva* in Nehardea, excused himself from a hearing because one of the parties had once allowed the Sage to go first over a narrow footbridge. Mar Shmuel was concerned that even this traditional act of *derech eretz* might influence his decision.

Remember: "It is better," goes the Yiddish adage, "to suffer an injustice than to commit one!"

꙳

Moishie is nervously awaiting the verdict in his criminal trial when the phone rings.

"Hello?"

"The verdict is in," says his lawyer, "justice has triumphed!"

"Appeal at once!" Moishie replies.

꙳

Judging Jewish Judges

Shimon ben Shatach[124] said: Examine witnesses thoroughly, and
be careful with your words, lest through them they learn to lie.

— *Mishna 1:9*

Rabbi Shimon addressed his (legal) advice not to the average Jew but to the judges of Israel, warning them that their participation in *mishpat*, the Judaic legal system, had to be fair, thorough and careful, and that their courtroom behavior and demeanor were reflective of the laws and justice of the scrupulous God they represented.

And what are the prerequisites of a Jewish judge? It depends on whom you ask!

The Talmud's Yochanan lists six: stature, wisdom, good appearance, maturity, familiarity with seventy languages and "a knowledge of sorcery"! – but the Rambam lists seven: "Wisdom, humility, fear of God, disdain of gain, love of truth and fellow man, a good reputation."

A judge must be *dan din emes l'amiso*, which literally means, "one who judges a true judgment to its truth."

Truth (defined by the Rambam as knowledge of God) was called "the seal of God," truthfulness of utmost importance; and when asked what one has to do for "truth to flourish," the *Chidushei Harim* replied, just "bury falsehood!" which became the inspiration for David to sing, "Truth grows out of the earth!"

Every judge who reaches a *truthfully* correct verdict is considered a partner with God in the creation of the world!

And when asked to define disaster, Eleazar ben Shimon, a second-century *Tanna*, linked it to "the kind of judges we have," a conclusion that caused Yochanan ben Nappaha to wail, "Woe to the generation that judges its judges!"

"Examine witnesses thoroughly" – what great advice.

❧

Lawyer (in court): Did you kill the victim?

  Defendant: No, I did not.

  Lawyer: Do you know what the penalties are for perjury?

  Defendant: Yes, I do. And they're a heck of a lot better than the penalty for murder!

  Lawyer: Are you married?

  Defendant: No, I'm divorced.

  Lawyer: And what did your husband do before you divorced him?

  Defendant: A lot of things I didn't know about!

❧

Mission Impossible

Rabbi Yishmael ben Yose[125] said: One who withdraws himself from serving as judge spares himself hatred, robbery and unnecessary oaths.

— Mishna 4:9

Although justice is a central concept of Judaism (the Torah insists that courts be established in every city of Israel), this Mishna cautions Jews to avoid becoming judges, sensing that it is a thankless, almost impossible task.

Who then should judge? Only those who aspire not to judge, but who are willing to do so when there is no other person available and worthy of the job; and even then, they have to be superhuman in their conduct and character, which is why Shimon bar Yochai thanked God for not making him a judge.

The Torah is aware that judges, despite performing a Divine mission, are as human as the rest of us, and to rise to the level of seeking truth is a Herculean task for a mere mortal. So the Mishna's advice is: don't judge alone, but share the burden with other judges – which is why a typical Jewish court consists of at least three judges.

The Torah itself made "judging your neighbor with righteousness" a positive command. Philo, the first-century Alexandrian Torah philosopher, was of the opinion that the judge is himself on trial; the *Zohar* accuses him of "sinning" if he doesn't "look for merits in the accused," and the Talmud suggests that, during a trial, he "should visualize a sword suspended over him, and *Gehinnom* [hell] gaping under him"!

No wonder ben Sira concluded that one should "seek not to be a judge"!

❧

"Isn't it true," the prosecuting attorney bellowed at Michel, a witness, "that you accepted five thousand dollars to compromise this case?"

Michel was silent, staring out the window as though he hadn't heard the question.

"Isn't it true that you accepted five thousand dollars to compromise this case?" the lawyer repeated.

Again, Michel didn't respond. Finally, the judge leaned over and said, "Sir, please answer the question."

"Oh, I'm sorry," Michel apologized, "I thought he was talking to you!"

❧

Imagine! Law without Lawyers!

> Rabbi Tzadok[126] said: Do not act as a lawyer (in judgment).
> — *Mishna 4:7*

This Mishna reveals a startling fact: the original Jewish court system had no place, *nor* patience, for "professional" attorneys.

Why? Because the parties themselves presented their own case, and witnesses were examined directly by the judges.

So why do we have so many lawyers today?[127] – and why do we have so many, many lawyer jokes? (What's black and brown and looks good on a lawyer? A Doberman. A lawyer's creed? A man is innocent until proven broke! Did you hear about the attorney who specialized in personal injury cases and decided to expand his practice to include libel claims? Now he has a law firm that adds insult to injury! An old lady walks into a lawyer's office and asks what his rates are. "It's $50 for three questions," he replies. "Isn't that awfully steep?" she asks. "Yes, and what's your third question?")

The opposition towards the "profession" eroded when litigants became (*Jewishly*) inarticulate, unable to present their own case.

And so the *beis din* adhered to a Rambam maxim ("One should accept the truth from whatever source") and then reluctantly began to allow spokesmen, just as God appointed Aaron as Moses' spokesman (not his lawyer!) in addressing Pharaoh.

It was then inevitable: the spokesmen, learned in Jewish law in order to be effective, became "lawyer-spokesmen," despite the axiomatic fact that the *dayanim* (judges) already knew the law.

Where does the prohibition on a non-Torah judiciary come from?

Although it is not included in the traditional 613 mitzvos, its legitimacy is derived from the Torah verse "And these are the ordinances which you shall place before them [*lifneihem*]," with the inference that "before *them*" refers to qualified Jewish justices. So does this mean that Jewish lawyers cannot represent Jewish clients in the general court system? No; the prohibition is directed to the litigant, not the lawyer!

❧

Abie thought his legal bill was too high, so he called his lawyer to send him an itemization of charges. The statement included this explanation:

"I was walking down the street and saw Abie, my client, on the other side. So I walked to the corner, waited to cross at the light, then quickly caught up to the client, only to discover it wasn't him – $150."

❧

God as Judge, Witness and Litigant!

> Rabbi Eleazar Hakappar[128] said: The newborn will die, the
> dead will come to life, the living will be judged – so that
> they know, make known, and become aware that He is God,
> Fashioner, Creator, Judge, Witness, Litigant.
>
> — *Mishna 4:29*

This daunting Mishna has one simple message: man is helpless in the face of fate and God's power.

Each one of us is propelled to his or her destiny of birth, life, death, resurrection – a cycle that operates beyond our control and often against our will.

"Life is like a taxi," observes Lou Erickson, "the meter just keeps a-ticking whether you are getting somewhere or just standing still." According to Abraham Lincoln, "It's not the years in your life that count, it's the life in your years!"

And so Jewish tombstones are inscribed with the only facts of one's life over which one has no control: name, date of birth, date of death.

To help mitigate this fate, Rabbi Yonah urges a lifestyle over which we do have some say: the pursuit of "good deeds" (mitzvos).

"Anyone who judges others favorably," notes the Talmud, "will be judged favorably in Heaven," an echo of the general rabbinic principle that the Heavens reward and punish "measure for measure" – i.e., be patient and understanding with others, and God will be patient and understanding with you.

The psychology behind this Mishnaic directive is obvious: by recognizing the innate goodness in others, perhaps we'll see it in ourselves as well!

In other words, always accentuate the positive, because it is pleasant to go through the day with an optimistic outlook that sees everything in a favorable light.

This makes for a happier disposition and, as God is sure to notice, puts a smile on your face – and what could be better than that?

❧

After examining her husband, the doctor tells Suzy, "No need to worry. I've checked everything possible, and he's fine – he just thinks he's sick."

A week later, the doctor follows up with a phone call, "*Nu*, how's he doing today?"

"Much worse, doctor! Now he thinks he's dead!"

❧

Angel for the Defense

> Rabbi Eliezer ben Yaakov[129] said: One who fulfills one
> mitzva acquires for himself a single defending angel; one who
> commits one transgression acquires one accusing angel.
>
> — *Mishna 4:13*

This Mishna introduces the concept of defending and accusing angels, who exist to execute God's will as part of His process of justice.

And yet we know very little about angels, prosecutorial or otherwise – in fact, there are so many different categories that it's hard to keep up with them; we have the *malachim* (messengers), *irinim* (watchers), *cherubim* (literally, "mighty ones"), *chayos* (holy ones), *ofanim* (literally, "wheels"), *sarim* (princes), *seraphim* (fiery ones), and so on.

The Rambam argues that "angels" (from the Greek *ángelos*) are simply metaphors for the laws of nature; the Midrash claims that one angel does not perform two missions, nor is one mission performed by two angels.

Are they anonymous?

Most are, but some have names – for instance, Michael, the preeminent angel and guardian of Israel who "holds the keys to Heaven"; Raphael, who heals; and Gabriel, who "prosecutes" Job and others before the "Divine tribunal."

How many angels are there?

I don't know, but there must be a lot because, according to the Talmud's Jonathan ben Eliezer, "From each of God's utterances an angel is born!"

A guy was taken to Mercy Hospital of the Angels for emergency surgery. After the operation, a nun appeared by his bedside, "Hi, I'm Senior Sister of the Mercy of Angels, and I want you to know you're going to be just fine. We do need to know, however, how you intend to pay for your stay here. Are you covered by insurance?"

"No."

"Can you pay in cash?"

"I'm afraid not, Sister."

"Well, do you have any close relatives?"

"Only my sister, but she's just a humble spinster nun."

"Oh, I must correct you, Sir, nuns are not 'spinsters.' They are married to God!"

"In that case, just go ahead and send the bill to my brother-in-law!"

Guilty, Until Proven Innocent!

> Yehuda ben Tabbai[130] said: When the litigants are standing before you they should be in your eyes as guilty; when they are dismissed from before you they should be in your eyes as innocent.
>
> — Mishna 1:8

This Mishna twists the traditional innocent-until-proven-guilty concept and advises judges to maintain a healthy skepticism towards the litigants, taking nothing for granted, assuming that *both* parties are equally guilty until one is proven otherwise.

The order to be fair and impartial to both litigants drives the Torah's moral imperative of *havei dan kol adam l'kaf zechus* (judge every person favorably) – but none is required to judge naively!

The Rambam, citing the example of Abraham arguing with God to spare Sodom and Gemora, extends this judicial philosophy to cities and countries; Rabbi Noson Tzvi Finkel explains his pleas in the context that only the wickedness be destroyed, not the people (on the basis of *Tehillim*'s "*Chotim lo ne'emar* [destroy sin, not sinners!]").

But even God closes the door of repentance on defendants who display a stubborn nature called *kaved lev* (literally, "heavy heart"), a self-generated "hardening" behavior that drains the heart of feelings of compassion for others (*à la* Pharaoh).

It is this motto of morality that made it unnecessary for God to list every potential prohibition in the *Aseres Hadibros* (the Ten Commandments).[131]

"What the law does not forbid, let shame forbid," reflected Seneca in his *Troades*. In several moving poems the Ramban explains how God, cognizant of the vulnerability of human nature, created scales of justice right in the human heart, in order that mankind may instinctively tell the difference between good and evil.

꘎

Frankie, in court on a public disorder charge, pleads "Not guilty!"

The prosecution then asks, "Is it true that on November 12th last year around midnight you committed an act of gross indecency with a one-legged female dwarf whilst waving a flag on the roof of a car in your underwear and traveling over 100 mph through the center of Manhattan in a snowstorm?"

Frankie thinks for a minute, and says, "What was the date again?"

꘎

Capital Punishment

> Rabbis Tarfon and Akiva said: If we had been among the Sanhedrin, no one would ever have been executed. Rabban Shimon ben Gamliel responded: Such an attitude would increase bloodshed in Israel.
>
> — *Mishna*[132]

This Mishna reveals disagreement, which still continues today, on the pros and cons of capital punishment.

Rabbi Tarfon and Rabbi Akiva opposed it; other rabbis (e.g., Shimon ben Gamliel) were for it; but Rabbi Eleazar ben Azariah reveals that a Sanhedrin which executes one person in *seventy* years is a "murderous" one! (In the modern State of Israel, established in 1948, only one execution has been carried out: that of Adolf Eichmann.)

What explains the infrequency of the death penalty if it's allowed by God?

Jewish judges were meticulous and stringent in weighing admissibility, testimony and evidence, and no fewer than twenty-three judges had to be satisfied as to the certainty of guilt before imposing a death sentence.

And even then, the method of execution, ordered Rabba ben Avuha, had to be "humane" (i.e., quick, according to Rashi); this sensitivity led one rabbi to frown upon high platforms for hanging, because the fall would lead to "disfigurement," and caused the Rambam to remind the court not to "destroy the dignity" of those sentenced to die.

⟿

About to pass sentence on the accused, an elderly Jewish man, the gentile judge asks him, "How old are you?"

"I am, *kein einahora*, ninety-one."

"Excuse me? What did you say?"

"I said, I am, *kein einahora*, ninety-one years old."

"Sir, the clerk can't type unusual words; please just answer the question with no embellishments," says the judge. "So, I ask you again, how old are you?"

"I told you: *kein einahora*, I'm ninety-one."

The judge is now losing his patience, and yells, "The accused will answer the question simply and plainly or be held in contempt of court!"

Finally, the Jewish defense lawyer rises and says, "Your Honor, I think I can resolve this. May I ask the question?"

"Sure! If you can get this trial moving, please, be my guest."

"Tell me," he asks his client, "*kein einahora*, how old are you?"

"Ninety-one!"

⟿

Absolute Power Corrupts Absolutely!

> The sword comes upon the world for delaying
> justice and for perverting justice.
> — *Mishna 5:11*

Many a revolution and societal chaos have erupted when ruling powers "delay or pervert" justice ("If there's no justice," writes Bachya ben Asher, "there's no peace!").

This is why the Torah places such heavy responsibility on Jewish judges, because they have it in their power to elevate righteousness or corrupt entire communities ("Absolute power corrupts absolutely!").

Adds the Midrash: enemies arrive at the door as a result of the "violation of just balances and just weights" – that is to say, in a community that has deteriorated to lawlessness.

The Mishna's use of a "sword" is not accidental: the judge is cautioned by the Torah to arrive at his decision as if a sword were upon his throat, and is relieved to hear that if he decides "truthfully" (*dan din emes l'amiso*), he becomes God's partner in Creation. A judge, remarks Philo, first-century Jewish philosopher, is required to keep in mind that when he tries a case he is himself on trial!

Any attempt to delay or distort justice is as though built on a *sheker* (falsehood), a recipe for community strife, and a distortion of the integrity of the Jewish system of law and order (the truth, say the Yiddishists, is the safest lie!).[133]

Another Midrash has a grim warning to those in charge of judicial administration: if justice is not meted out on earth, it is meted out in heaven!

Should the judge's decisions be based solely on Torah? No.

In a startling Talmud, we discover that Jerusalem was destroyed because its Jewish judges judged by Torah law. Is there another law? Yes. The Talmud then elaborates: Jerusalem was destroyed because its Jews judged *only* by [the letter of] the law of Torah!

꩜

"Is it true that you owe your neighbor a thousand dollars?" asks the judge.

"Yes, it's true," replies the defendant.

"Then, why don't you just pay him back?"

"Because then it wouldn't be true anymore!"

꩜

Stay Impartial

Yehuda ben Tabbai said: Do not act as a lawyer among the judges.

— Mishna 1:8

"There are a thousand ways to do injustice," warns Mishlei Yehoshua, "without breaking a single law!"

The lesson of this Mishna is this: when judging, stay impartial! ("Partiality in judgment," notes Proverbs, "is not good!")

Even if the arbiter is absolutely convinced he knows who is innocent, it is not his job, says the Rambam, to help that litigant argue his case or offer any opinions whilst the court is in session; even, adds the *Tiferes Yisroel*, if the judge is related to a witness and is legally allowed to help a relative, he is barred from doing so (nor are witnesses allowed to act as judges!).

Rabbi Yonah goes one step further: judges should not even be quoted by litigants who still have to appear before other judges; and Rashi warns the robed arbiter not to reveal the case's merits (nor even the final decision) to either of the parties unless both are present.

What was ben Tabbai's concern? Did he actually think Jewish judges would publicly take sides? No. But in those days the custom was to hold mock argument and rebuttal sessions and full rehearsals before the real trial began.

It is those sessions that the Mishna warns potential judges to stay away from, fearing that their legal glibness and lawyerly logic might help sway the case.

But this advice was not universal.

Jewish law encourages the sitting judge to intercede (and help "open the mouth of the speechless") if one of the victimized parties is too weak or too helpless (for instance, an orphan) to mount an effective case for himself.

❧

The judge was getting bored and frustrated by a lawyer's tedious arguments, and, despite numerous rulings to speed the trial along, the lawyer continued on. As tempers flared, the judge finally pointed to his ear and said, "Counselor, you should be aware that at this point, what you are saying is just going in one ear and out the other!"

"Your honor," replied the lawyer, "that goes without saying. What is there to prevent it?"

❧

LIFE AND DEATH

There's only one death per customer,
so it must be a real bargain!

— *Milton Berle*

Life and Death

Life is full of surprises.

The passengers of the "unsinkable" *Titanic* certainly never expected to have their leisurely cruise end in one of the most tragic of all maritime disasters. Running fitness guru Jim Fixx died of a heart attack after a run. When asked what he would do if told he only had six minutes left to live, the famous writer Isaac Asimov replied, "I wouldn't brood. I'd type a little faster!"

Mark Twain would look at the daily obituaries and if he wasn't listed there, would continue on as usual.

Death, a reality, means that life must be lived with the realization that one's days are numbered. To ensure a sense of mortality, Rabbi Eliezer, a student of Rabban Yochanan, urged Jews to "repent one day before you die."

Does that mean that Jews must live in a constant state of fear, worry, penitence? No.

On the contrary, Rebbe Nachman of Bratzlav warned his followers to be aware of sadness, which he described as a clever weapon, a sneaky ruse of the *yetzer hora* ("evil spirit") that could be mitigated by a shield of cheerfulness.

Even the arch-rationalist Rambam defined happiness as the "highest form of prayer," and ominously cautioned that "the Jew who does not rejoice deserves to be punished," basing his opinion on a Biblical verse, "Because you did not serve your God with joy!"[134]

Rabbi Eliezer simply wants to remind Jews to fill their days with significance and not *narishkeit* (foolishness), cognizant that how we spend our lives shapes our legacy – which will be up for review one fateful day (if death and taxes are certain, at least taxes only happen once a year!).

God may be the final critic, but we write and control the script.

That is why Judaism approaches the "present," in the context of a guide for morality, as nothing more than a transcended summary of the past.

In other words: life is pleasant, death is peaceful, beware the transition.

Rabbi Eliezer was fully aware that, as we grow older, our mortality haunts and taunts us.

To approach each day as though it may literally be the last is a reminder not to take anything for granted. Ripe ol' ages are not to be taken for granted. Our birth certificates do not have expiration dates on them!

When King David asked God when he would die, God replied, "On a Shabbas," but refused to say which Shabbas.[135] David was left to live life to the fullest, but only from one Shabbas to the next.

The lesson? The question "Is there life after death?" is incorrect. The more fitting question is, "Is there life after life"!

⤳

Three rabbis are waiting for their turn to speak at a funeral. One turns to the other and says, "Wouldn't it be good to know what family and friends say about us before we die! That way we might have some warning as to how to conduct ourselves before meeting our Maker."

"Good idea," replies one rabbi. "Tell me, what would you like to hear them say about you?"

"Well, I'd like to hear them say that I was a great *talmid chacham* [Torah scholar], always had a smile for everybody, and never lost my temper. How about you?"

"Well, I'd like to hear them say that I was a great family man, good husband and father, a pillar of the community in terms of *gemilus chesed* [deeds of kindness]."

They then turn to the third rabbi, "*Nu*, what would you like to hear?"

"Well, I'd like to hear them say... 'LOOK, LOOK! HE'S MOVING!!!'"

⤳

Choices, Choices, Choices!

> Rebbe[136] said: Which is the straight path that a man
> should choose for himself? That which is an honor to
> him and which also brings honor from mankind.
>
> — *Mishna 2:1*

This Mishna, cognizant of human nature, lobbies for a "straight," not a "righteous" path.

What's the difference?

The first is a road of interaction with others, a road that *pleases* God; the latter is being *like* God (i.e., copying His attitude towards mercy, compassion, holiness).

Rebbe positions "life" as a series of choices: every crossroad demands a decision, every decision has consequences.

"Morality," wrote the French thinker Leon Blum, "may consist solely of the courage to make a choice!"

Mankind's greatest privilege – and highest responsibility – is one's absolute free will and unfettered choice (*bechira*), a human component that our Sages considered even greater than the Pesach symbol of freedom. Why? Because liberty is only valuable if used properly.

"Without shame, Man would not be Man," noted Erich Heller.

In Hebrew, the character trait of feeling shame is called *baishanus*, in Yiddish, *a charpa un a boosha*; both are linked to the Hebrew word *kalon*, which appears more than sixteen times throughout Proverbs, Psalms, Prophets and Job, depicting such moral offenses as dishonor and humiliation.

All of human history, notes Rabbi Eliezer, begins with the discovery of shame.

"Living life," observed the Vilna Gaon, "is like drinking water – while quenching our thirst, we thirst for more!"

After Rebbe singles out *honor* as a quality of choice, the Mishna's ben Zoma elaborates, "Who is honored? He who honors!" – or in Yiddish terms: Honor is measured by those who give it, not by those who receive it!

꒛

The rabbi was staggering home one Purim night, obviously drunk, when he was stopped by a sentry at the gate to the ghetto.

"Where do you belong?" the guard demanded to know.

"To the army of God!"

"Doggonit," hissed the guard, "all I can say is you're mighty far from headquarters!"

꒛

"Let Thy Yea Be Yea, and Thy Nay, Nay!"

> Rabban Shimon ben Gamliel[137] said: On three things does the world endure [*kayam*]: justice, truth and peace.
>
> — *Mishna 1:18*[138]

In the second Mishna of *Pirkei Avos* (1:2), Shimon Hatzadik opines that the world stands [*omed*] on three things: on the Torah, on service (of God) and on *gemilus chasadim* (the performance of acts of kindness). In their attempt to list the highest spiritual fundamentals that keep the social order of life intact, the rabbis of the Mishna added another threesome: *din* (justice), *emes* (truth), *shalom* (peace)!

But wait! The terminology is in disagreement.

The world is not "*based*" on these, it "*endures*" on them. Is there a difference? Yes. The Hebrew word *omed* means "to stand on"; here we have *kayam*, which means "endure, last, sustain."

But what does "stand" mean? It can't be literal, because the universe does not stand anywhere.

Obviously, in the rabbinic mind, there must be a difference between "stands" and "endures." And it is this: the former implies a foundation, the latter implies a preexisting condition that needs attention to continue being there.

Without a foundational structure ("Torah, service [of God], acts of kindness") the universe cannot "stand," and without a functioning infrastructure ("truth, law, peace") it cannot be sustained.

Rabban Shimon thinks that we're reading it wrongly: he prefers "exists" to "stands" (i.e., "on three things does the universe *exist*...on truth and on law and on peace"). "Stands" implies a base on which to rely – without that, it falls. The Midrash weighs in on the side of "exists" – the universe is a steady entity from the time of Creation.

The difference is subtle, but important. If you stand on a chair, you're safe as long as the chair is upright. Move it, and see how long you "endure" in thin air!

Meanwhile, the Talmud saw a straight-line connection between Shimon's threesome: "If judgment is executed, truth is vindicated, and peace results!"

❧

Rivkie calls the police to report the disappearance of her husband. The officer asks for a photo and details, and whether there's any message they should give him if they find him.

"Yes," she says, "tell him my mother didn't come after all!"

❧

It's Not My Fault!

> Rabbi Akiva said: Everything is foreseen, yet free will is given.
>
> — *Mishna 3:19*

This Mishna echoes one of the most profound philosophical difficulties in the entire Torah: an omniscient God controls history and foresees the future (a concept known in Yiddish as *bashert*) – and yet the Jew has total freedom of choice at all times!

The two most baffling questions in Jewish thought? The suffering-of-the-righteous inconsistency, and freedom-of-will-versus-determinism.

So, are our fates entirely in our hands – or not? And if not, how can anybody be responsible or blamed for his (predetermined) actions?

The clue lies in an exit clause God has given Himself, *Hakol min Hashamayim chutz mi'yiras Shamayim*, "Everything is from Heaven (determinism) except the fear of Heaven (freedom of will)," stapled to a strict ultimatum: "I have placed before you life and good, death and evil, and you shall choose life!"

But don't the rabbis themselves hedge their bets, e.g.: "Everything is caused by Heaven *except* for catching a cold?" No. This is not an attempt to distance a serious God from the trivia of man but to emphasize cause-and-effect (e.g., Got a cold? Maybe you should've worn a coat!).

If you search the Torah for some clues, you'll only be confronted with more, not fewer, theological dilemmas. An example? God's promise to Abraham ("Your descendants will be slaves for four hundred years") *required* God to *force* Joseph into Egyptian exile, create sibling hatred, cause a famine, and then, finally, propel Jacob and his sons to Egypt – and still have the spiritual *chutzpa* to blame the Jews for *their* troubles?

And yet freedom of will somehow functions. How? We don't know. All you can do is file it under "Great Paradox of Human Existence."

⇝

Ol' Mrs. Finkelstein, when called to jury duty, is convinced she can influence the judge to let her go.

"Your Honor," she declares, "I simply cannot serve!"

"Why not?" he asks, skeptically.

"Because I am a psychic, and I can predict the future!"

"Well, in that case you are excused," says the man from the bench, to which she replies, "I knew that would happen!"

⇝

A Threesome

Shimon Hatzadik[139] said: The world is based on Torah, on service [of God], and on acts of kindness [*gemilus chassadim*].

— *Mishna 1:2*

Shimon narrows down his fundamental philosophy to "three things" – but wait: there's nothing new here!

Torah? We knew that already. Rendering service to God? Nothing new here! Acts of generosity and kindness? Ah, here we have an opening: but what *act of kindness* is the world "based on"?

Shouldn't Rabbi Shimon be more specific?

Maybe, but he isn't because *gemilus chassadim* is an all-encompassing expression that requires compassion, concern, caring, understanding and sensitivity, which is why it is considered the most important concept in Judaism, called a *shekula*, qualitatively equal to all other Sinai commandments; in fact, the entire Torah is based on *chesed* (loving-kindness), and opens (with God providing clothes for Adam and Eve) and ends (with God burying Moses) in Heaven's nourishment and support, giving Jews a moral and spiritual set of bookends for the pursuit of *imitatio Dei* (i.e., if it's good enough for God...!).

Midrashic linguists, noting that the word *adam* (man) implies "kinship, compassion, love," place *gemilus chassadim* on a level that transcends halacha; that is why, when compiling his eight degrees of charity, the Rambam places *gemilus chassadim*, helping others help themselves, at the top!

The final word goes to Moshe Leib of Sasov: "If someone asks your help, you shall act as if there is no God, as if there were only one person in all the world who could help him – only yourself!"

❧

A volunteer at Hatzolah, an emergency-response organization dedicated to *gemilus chassadim* in the field of medicine, picks up the phone and hears a Jew frantically yelling, "My wife is pregnant, and her contractions are only two minutes apart!"

"Is this her first child?"

"No, you idiot! This is her husband!"

❧

No Leg to Stand On!

[Rabbi Shimon Hatzadik and Rabban Shimon ben
Gamliel] said: The world is based upon three things.
— *Mishna 1:2, 1:18*

Life has great meaning; the trick is to find it! These two Sages agree on "three," but not on which three. Which one is right? Ben Gamliel's justice, truth and peace, or Shimon's Torah, service [of God] and *gemilus chassadim*?

Both are, argues the *Tiferes Yisroel*, although he seems to have a preference for the truth-justice-peace trilogy!

This is an argument against *sheker* (falsehood), which has no ability to endure, and an applause for *emes* (truth), which connotes integrity and completeness.

Liars were considered outcasts by Jeremiah, and the Talmud describes a lie as having no legs to stand on!

The word *emes* begins with *alef*, the first letter of the Hebrew alphabet; *mem* is the middle letter of both the *alef-beis* and the word, and *taf* the final letter of both as well, implying that "truth" is all-encompassing, starting at the beginning and continuing to its proper conclusion. In contrast, *sheker* has no such integrity; its three letters are convoluted, found at the end of the *alef-beis*.

Take a look at the word's physical structure. The three letters of *emes* appear in a straight line, suggestive of stability (the *alef* and *taf* have two legs, the *mem* has a long base). In contrast, the three letters of *sheker* are balancing themselves on only one point (in the original Hebrew script, the three vertical legs of the *shin* come together at a single point).

The Maharal, arguing that there is no chronological order to the Mishna's words of wisdom, notes Rabbi Shimon's three appear at the beginning of Creation, the origin of the world to the Divine, whereas ben Gamliel's three choices occur at its end (but he refuses to take sides on which three are more "important").

Yes, adds the *Tosefos Yom Tov*, Shimon's *Torah-avoda-chesed* are important, but without the harmony and progress of the other three, effective civilization would be in jeopardy.

꙳

The judge addresses the defendant: "Shloimy, do you understand that you have
sworn to tell the truth, the whole truth, and nothing but the truth?"

"I do."

"So, what do you have to say in your defense?"

"Well, under those limitations, nothing!"

꙳

Glory, Glory, Hallelujah

> Rebbe said: What is the proper path a person should choose for himself? Whatever brings glory to himself [before (in the Eyes of) God], and grants him glory before others.
>
> — *Mishna 2:1*

Rabbi Yehuda begins this Mishna with a fundamental question ("What are the proper criteria for living a true Judaic life?"), but then answers in an oblique manner: always conduct yourself in "glory."

This is a significant word, but what exactly does it mean?

In Hebrew "glory" is *tiferes*, which doesn't help; it can mean honor, admiration, veneration, grandeur, splendor – but no one lives in such idyllic surroundings.

We find the key to this Mishna if we read on: *before God* implies that the "proper path" in life is simply one that reflects a "glorious" concept, that of *kiddush Hashem*, acts and behavior that bring nothing but respect and esteem (i.e., glory, a good reputation) to the God of the Jews.

This is why the Talmud refers to Genesis as the "Book of the Upright" (*Sefer Hayesharim*), because its characters (our forefathers) acted in an "upright" manner.

This is known as *kiddush Hashem* (the sanctification of God's Name), preferably conducted in a state of modesty and humility, without fanfare, fanaticism or propaganda. (Its opposite is *chillul Hashem*, a term thrown around a lot in meaningless contexts, but basically it is any act or word that disgraces God, *openly*.)

But wait! Doesn't Judaism frown on those who chase glory?

A Jew once complained to the Chassidic master Rebbe Bunim: "The Talmud says that when a person runs away from glory and honor, they run after him. So how come I've run away from honors, but honors do not pursue me?"

Replied Rebbe Bunim: "The reason is that you keep looking backwards, to see if they are following you!"

꒜

During World War II, a group of American-Jewish soldiers from Texas found themselves stuck in London over Rosh Hashana. So they sauntered into the Great Synagogue for the High Holiday services, and one casually asked the *rav*, "Hey, what kind of a show do you guys have over here? Is it any good?"

"It should be. It's been running for nearly six thousand years!"

꒜

Who Knows Ten?

> Ten things were created on Sabbath eve, at twilight. They are:
> the mouth of the earth [which swallowed Korach], the mouth
> of the well [which accompanied Israel in the desert], the mouth
> of the donkey [which rebuked Bilam], the rainbow, the Manna,
> Moses' staff, the *shamir* worm, Torah script, the inscription [on
> the Tablets of the Ten Commandments] and the Tablets.
>
> — *Mishna 5:8*

This extraordinary Mishna lists a series of unique "magical" objects that God created just before Shabbas, at the end of the sixth day.

What makes these objects so different from the ones created hitherto? Or are they just random? No, nothing happens by chance: there's a reason, and our job is to ask why – even if the answer remains a mystery.

One clue lies in the fact that they are put into existence just when time turns from the mundane to the sacred, so they were the "finishing touches," the final glue that completed Creation. When that first Shabbas arrived, God's work was done.

And the *shamir*? Ah, the worm! What happened to this worm? It disappeared with the destruction of the Temple.

No sword or iron, hammers or axe, symbols of war, were allowed to be used in forming the stones of the altar, a symbol of peace, unity, reconciliation.

Thus this worm, one that produces a highly corrosive substance, was so strong and sharp that the rabbis of the Talmud claim it was used, akin to a diamond, to engrave the stone inscriptions on the high priest's wardrobe.

This force, which cut hard rock without destroying it, was a creation of God needed to help King Solomon construct God's own home, the Temple, the abode where the *Shechina* settled amongst men.

⇁

"I just made a twenty-four-hour period," God tells an angel. "It will be half-light and half-dark, and will keep repeating itself until the end of time!"

"Wow!" says the angel, "what are You going to do next?"

"Well," God replies, "I think I'll call it a day!"

⇁

Eye Spy

> Those who have a good eye, a humble spirit and a "lowly" soul are of the students of our father Abraham; those who have an evil eye, an arrogant spirit and a greedy soul are of the students of the wicked Bilam.[140]
>
> — *Mishna 5:22*

In the tradition of pure rabbinic symbolism, this Mishna praises the first Patriarch in terms of opthalmology, as a man with a "good eye," a reference not to eyesight but to his *middos*, specifically his ability as a young boy to see harmony, magnificence and beauty in the world – and the fact that he viewed *everybody* favorably (which is why he is known as the "father of a *multitude* of nations!").

The *Sfas Emes* interprets "a good eye" as a characteristic of being positive all the time; Rabbi Yonah links it to the one who is always generous; Rashi says it describes a person who is never jealous; to the Rambam it not only means that you're content with your lot but that you're always happy at the success of others.

This Mishna doesn't compare Abraham to Bilam; it only compares their disciples!

The disciples of the former are contrasted to those of the shortsighted and deceitful latter, the gentile prophet with "an evil eye and haughty mind" who was hired to curse Israel; instead, God turns his curses into blessings.

This is the source of the Yiddishist belief that eyes can be evil, which led to the introduction of the expression *einahora* (in Hebrew *ayin hora*, in English "evil eye") into the Jewish lexicon, that is to say, not wishing someone ill fortune. "Looks can kill!" My mother would often say, "*Kein einahora*," meaning that no evil eye should affect us.

"Rabbi," the admiring congregant says, "I come to *shul* every Shabbas just to hear your speeches. They're so inspiring you should write them down and publish them in a book!"

"Oh, I don't know," the rabbi replies with his typical modesty and concern about *einahora*. "My thoughts don't deserve so much attention. Perhaps they'll be published posthumously."

"I can't wait," she says, "I hope that will be real soon!"

Payback Time, with Interest!

> Rabbi Akiva said: The store is open, the Storekeeper extends credit, and whoever wants to borrow may come and borrow. The collectors make their rounds daily, and collect whether the person realizes it or not...and everything is prepared for the banquet [of Leviathan].
>
> — *Mishna 3:20*

This remarkable Mishna likens the ways of God to a business enterprise.

Rabbi Akiva gives us an imagery of a (kind and patient) shopkeeper who is prepared to dispense credit (rewards) – but who can just as quickly become a (vengeful and ominous) store owner hurling out judgment (punishment) if customers (Jews) abuse the merchandise (Torah).

The reward?

An invitation to the Mother of all Banquets (i.e., the World to Come), where the main course is a giant "sea monster" (*tannin*, "Leviathan") created on the fifth day of Creation.

It is only at this festive occasion, writes Abravanel, that God "rectifies" the rights and wrongs of this world, and both the righteous and wicked discover their ends.

Torah retribution was a magnet of discussion and debate throughout Jewish existence: those who turned their backs on God, roared Isaiah, would "be consumed!" Added another prophet (Hosea): if you sow the wind, be prepared to "reap the whirlwind!"

If you dig a pit, goes the Proverb, don't be shocked if you fall into it! – a cause and effect echo of the *Chad Gadya*'s dog that ate the cat that ate the kid!

The final word goes to the Yiddishists of Eastern Europe: God waits long – but pays with interest!

※

Ernie was being interviewed for a job as a lawyer in an investment house. "We're looking for a shrewd businessman," the investment banker says, "and a lawyer with integrity. Is that you?"

"Integrity?" Ernie replies, "Let me tell you. I'm so honest that my father lent me $15,000 for my education, and I paid back every penny the minute I tried my very first case."

"I'm impressed. What sort of case was it?"

"Ah...he sued me for the money!"

※

As Time Goes By

Yehuda ben Tema used to say: At five one should begin the study
of Torah; at ten, Mishna; at thirteen one becomes obligated to
observe the commandments; at fifteen the study of the Talmud;
at eighteen the wedding canopy; at twenty to pursue a livelihood;
at thirty strength; at forty understanding; at fifty counsel; at sixty
old age; at seventy fullness of years; at eighty spiritual strength;
at ninety bending over; at a hundred it is as if he has died.

— *Mishna 5:25*

Koheles might consider life a passage of futility (*hevel*), but this Mishna treats
the passage of life as an orderly progression and "pairs" the process of maturing
to different levels of Torah study and action.

It proposes flexibility, not continuity, in that one must be willing to change
one's habits to fit new spiritual circumstances that come with aging; Meiri adopted
this as The Parental Guide on How to Raise Children!

One whimsical Midrash has a more cynical "order" of priorities: "At one, man
is a king, fondled and doted upon by all; at two and three he is a pig, groping in
the garbage; at ten he prances around like a kid; at twenty he is a horse, preening
himself in search of a wife; after marriage, he works like a donkey to earn a living; when he has children he is brazen as a dog trying to support his family; and
at the end of his life he becomes senile and senseless as an ape!"

Ibn Gevirol put it well: "To seek wisdom in old age is like making a mark in
the sand; to seek wisdom in youth is like hammering an inscription in stone!"
This is similar to the Yiddish saying: A young tree bends, an old tree breaks! But
King David, in *Tehillim*, was clearly worried: "Cast me not off in old age; when
my strength fails, forsake me not!"

❧

Doctor: You're in good health. You'll live to be eighty.
Patient: But, doctor, I am eighty right now.
Doctor: See, what did I tell you!

❧

Mixing with Idiots

> Rabbi Dosa ben Horkinos[141] said: Sleep in the morning, wine in the afternoon, the chatter of the young, and sitting in the gatherings of the ignorant drive a person out of the world.
>
> — *Mishna 3:14*

"Don't waste your time" is the message of this Mishna, defined as sleeping late (i.e., missing the halachic time for *Sh'ma*), getting drunk (which dulls the senses), idle chatter (being distracted by the frivolity of kids), and mixing with morons (let's see, would Groucho Marx want to be a member of that club? [142]).

Is there a common denominator to these four activities?

Yes, says the *Tiferes Yisroel*, who admits that there's nothing wrong with any of these as long as they're done in moderation, which, concludes ben Sira, "prolongs life itself!"

The Midrash defines the moment when the angels realized that Adam was mortal: when he fell asleep. Another Midrash declares that the beginning of a man's downfall is sleep!

But there's another catalyst for these foolish activities: getting drunk!

After recognizing that wine was a legitimate source of *joie de vivre* (it "gladdens the heart," confesses Solomon, "and cheers both God and man"), as well as a medicinal substance, our Sages were well aware that, in and of itself, its euphoria could be destructive.

Judaism thus never sanctified wine, only its context (e.g., it becomes holy during a *seder tisch*, but not at the drinking parties of Ahasuerus; it's holy for a *Shabbas kiddush*, but not at the local pub, and so on).

Jewish mystics thus gave wine a metaphysical component, a multi-metaphoric source of Torah, Israel, Jerusalem – and, when sneaking a peek into the messianic future, they saw Judah's lush vineyards, flowing with wine!

❧

A man orders a beer in a bar and, just before he takes his first sip, a monkey suddenly appears and snatches the pint from him. "Hey," the guy yells, "who owns the monkey!"

"Moishie, the piano player," replies the barman.

So the guy walks over to Moishie the piano player and says, "Do you know your monkey stole my beer!"

"No," Moishie replies, "but if you hum it, I'll play it."

❧

Grudge, Greed and Envy!

> Rabbi Yehoshua[143] said: An evil eye (*ayin hora*), the evil inclination
> and hatred of humanity remove a person from this world.
>
> — *Mishna 2:16*

This Mishna narrows the negative qualities ("evils") of one's character down to three: an evil eye (jealousy), evil inclination (lust) and hatred of others (defined by Rashi as *sinas chinam* [baseless hatred]). These three character traits are basically the same: synonyms for selfishness.

By declaring that these character shortcomings "remove a person from the world," Rabbi Yehoshua is warning Jews that their presence is a force of destruction; meanwhile, Rabbi Israel Lipschitz, the *Tiferes Yisroel,* identifies them as the three corresponding traits that undermine the Mishna's delineation of the three foundations of the world ("Torah, service [of God], and kind deeds").

The concept of *ayin hora* first appears in the post-Biblical period ("He cast his eye on him and he died"), which is why, after Rav visits a cemetery, he believes that "Ninety-nine die because of an evil eye for each one who dies of natural causes!"

This is the source of the Yiddish expression *kein einahora*, in that we ask that no evil eye should affect the health or wealth of the Jew.

But another Mishna seems to reverse this advice: "Don't be wicked in your own eyes" (i.e., too much self-criticism and humility is unhealthy!).

These rabbis saw the "evil eye" as a metaphor for grudge, greed and envy, and relate how Alexander the Great once visited Eden and was given an eyeball. He weighed it against all his gold and silver, but the eye was heavier.

"Put some dust on it," he was told and the scales tipped in favor of the eye.

The lesson? The human eye is never satisfied; the more it sees, the more it wants, until finally the dust covers it in the grave; and so our Sages promoted its opposite, a "good eye" (*ayin tova*), in the spirit of generosity and goodwill, always seeing the best, not the worst, in other Jews.

⮷

Lenny's car is wrecked in a smash-up and his wife, Suzy, calls the insurance company. "We had that car insured for five thousand dollars and I want my money."

"Whoa, there, Suzy," the agent replies, "insurance doesn't quite work like that. We first ascertain the value of the insured article, and then we provide you with a new one of comparable worth."

Suzy thinks for a few minutes, then says, "In that case I'd like to cancel the policy on my husband!"

⮷

One at a Time

Go and see which is the good way to which a man should cleave. Rabbi Eliezer said: "A good eye"; Rabbi Yehoshua said: "A good friend"; Rabbi Yose said: "A good neighbor"; Rabbi Shimon said: "One who sees the consequences of his actions"; Rabbi Eleazar said: "A good heart." Rabban Yochanan said: "I prefer the words of Eleazar ben Arach to all of yours, for in his words yours are included."

— *Mishna 2:13*

Rabban Yochanan urges his top five students to *go out* from the *beis medrash* before giving him an answer to his question as to which was the most important *midda* (quality) to have; in other words, however pious and learned you are, you may still be distancing yourself from the folks you're supposed to be serving (i.e., what's good inside the yeshiva halls ain't necessarily good at the market stalls!).

So the foremost Torah scholars in the *beis medrash* go out amongst the common folk to help them decide how best to answer their rebbe.

And the winner is...a good heart!

Judah Halevi sang how "the heart was a harp," the Yiddishists credited the heart as having better sight than the eye, and to King Solomon it proved the presence of a happy person.

But what exactly does having a "good heart" mean?

Judaism views the heart as the primary source of emotions and desires, aspirations and inspirations; thus to "acquire a good (caring) heart" means to discipline one's sensitivities towards positive Judaic qualities.

This Mishna, after elevating a "good heart" over everything else, reveals an interesting fact: none of Rabban Yochanan's five primary disciples chose the same *midda*, proof that each person is different, with different backgrounds, ambitions, visions.

꩜

At the golf course one Sunday, Bernie's about to putt, when a funeral procession begins to roll by. He straightens up, takes his hat off, holds it over his heart, and stands silently until it passes. He then resumes his game.

"Boy," says his golf partner, "that was very thoughtful of you."

"Oh, it's the least I could do. Tomorrow, we would have been married twenty-five years!"

꩜

No Reality Like Mortality

Rabbi Eliezer said: Repent one day before you die.

— *Mishna 2:15*

"Repent one day before you die." How is this possible?

In most cases, death comes not by appointment but by surprise. Our birth certificates have no due-dates on them; so how does the Jew know *which* day is the next to last?

He doesn't; "therefore repent today!" is the obvious answer – *as though* it's the last chance. Why? In order to battle overt complacency, a false sense of permanent immortality, an assumption of living to a ripe old age, taking our days and years for granted.

King David asked when his death would take place, but God ignored the question; meanwhile Rabbi Israel Lipkin Salanter, master *mussar*-moralist, took the lesson to heart: "As long as the candle burns, I can still do some mending!"

Teshuva was created as an instrument of change, an annual Judaic summons (the Rosh Hashana-Yom Kippur cycle) to confront life head-on and confirm that it has meaning and content; it is nothing less than an exhortation not to just get "one year older and deeper in debt" but to amend, improve, change.

This reassessment and reappraisal of one's own self, known in Jewish tradition as a *cheshbon hanefesh*, "an accounting of the soul," requires looking back at ourselves in the mirror of yesterday, which is why Rosh Hashana is also known as *Yom Hazikaron*, "Day of Remembrance."

☙

"We're all in need of *teshuva!*" roared the young rabbi in his *Shabbas Shuva drasha*. "None of us are perfect yet, none of us are humble or perfect enough! Anyone in this *shul* who has known such a perfect person should stand up now!"

The Great Shul turns quiet, when suddenly modest little Mrs. Greenberg slowly rises and all eyes become transfixed on her.

"You know someone who is absolutely perfect?" asks the amazed *rav*.

"Well," Mrs. Greenberg says softly, "I didn't know her personally, but I keep hearing a great deal about her."

"Who is she? Everyone wants to know."

"My husband's first wife."

☙

Where There's a Will
(There's Always a Relative!)

> Eleazar Hakappar said: Do not let your evil inclination assure
> you that the grave is a refuge for you — for against your will
> were you created, against your will were you born, against
> your will do you live, against your will shall you die, and
> against your will shall you stand in judgment before God.
>
> — *Mishna 4:29*

Hey! Whatever happened to free will?

This Mishna only deprives one of choices over which one has no control anyway, such as birth and death, whilst acting as a reminder that one's way of life does not escape ultimate review.

On the contrary: when God demands, "Choose life!" Jews declare, "*Hakol min Hashamayim chutz mi'yiras Shamayim* (everything is from Heaven [determinism] except the fear of Heaven [freedom of will])" as a matter of pure Jewish faith.

When Franz Kafka, melancholy author and deep thinker, whined that "my ship has no rudder!" (an echo of Jeremiah's "Man's way is not his own"), he was ignorant of the true Jewish way of life.

King Solomon was aware: right and wrong are "in our hands," he declares, a conclusion that led the Talmudic sage Huna to note that we are "led in the way we wish to follow!"

"God is responsible for having created a world," wrote Rabbi Eliezer Berkovits, Holocaust-survivor-philosopher-author, "in which man is free to make history."

And what does the Rambam say about free will?

"Every person is fit to be as righteous as Moses or as wicked as Jeroboam, wise or foolish, kind or cruel...and may turn, of his own free will, to whichever side he pleases!"

꤮

"Beryl, Beryl!" the *rav* of a small shtetl yells as he bangs on the front door, "I have just heard that you have made marriage proposals to no less than three different girls in three different villages! This is outrageous! How can you do such a thing?"

"How? It's easy! I have a bicycle!"

꤮

Curb Your Envy

> Yochanan ben Zakkai said: Go out and see what is the evil path that a person should keep away from. Eliezer said, "An evil eye [*ayin hora*]."
>
> — *Mishna 2:14*

An evil eye? What does that mean?

The *Tiferes Yisroel* links *ayin hora* to jealousy, resentment, envy.

Another Mishna rabbi agrees with his colleague: "Envy, appetite and ambition lead to ruin!" adds Eleazar Hakappar. One Midrash gives a marriage tip ("Envious wives ruin their husbands!"); another Midrash comes to the rescue of envy's reputation: "Without envy, the world could not abide, for none would marry or build a house!"

The quality of envy became an irresistible target: it made the "bones rotten" (Proverbs); it "slayed the foolish" (Job); when stirred with anger it "shortens life" (ben Sira).

And there is no cure for it, adds the fourteenth-century scholar Bachya ben Asher in his *Kad Hakemach*: "When one judges everything negatively, one is not satisfied with what one has, becomes jealous of others, evaluates other people in a negative fashion, and comes to doubt one's teachers and God!"

This Mishna is a subtle reminder of the consequences of suspicion and assumption, in that one should always see the good in everything and be quick to give others the benefit of the doubt.

In 1887, when Warsaw Rav Isachar Dov Halevi Hurwitz published *Mishlei Yissachar*, he described envy as having "a thousand eyes – but none with correct vision!"

The "evil eye" metaphor is a challenge of character over cynicism, a warning that its adherence leads to an inability to make and maintain lasting friendships.

⇀

"Mendy, how come I never see you in *shul* anymore?" asks the *rav*.

"Well, Rabbi, to tell you the truth, when I go I envy those who think they know Hebrew – then they think they can learn well, they think they are better than everyone else. Frankly, the *shul* is full of hypocrites!"

"Don't worry, Mendy! There's always room for one more!"

⇀

If Not Now, When?

> Hillel said: If I am not for me, who is for me? If I
> am for myself, what am I? If not now, when?
>
> — *Mishna 1:14*

This Mishna, in just a few words, sums it all up.

Probably the most quoted words of Torah by Jew and gentile alike throughout history, expressed by Hillel, a poverty-stricken woodchopper from Babylon, they obviously hit a ubiquitous nerve.

His thought-provoking words ricochet through religion and philosophy, pop culture and book names (the brilliant Holocaust author Primo Levi entitled his memoir *If Not Now, When?*).

Meiri says Hillel is talking about the greater need for spiritual accomplishments than physical ones, whilst the Midrash reads it as a cry for outreach, a concern for others: "All Jews," sigh our Sages, in the ultimate ethics of responsibility, "are sureties for one another!"

Since no Jew can be an island unto himself, we may read this Mishna as, "And if I am [only] for myself, what am I?"

At first reading, Hillel's words sound so simple – but they're not.

These words of discipline and self-motivation are wise and profound, weighty and insightful, in ways that reveal themselves anew each time we reread them.

A morbid Koheles might read them in a selfishly perverted way ("All man's toil is *lefihu* [for himself, according to himself]"), but Rav Samson Raphael Hirsch sees Hillel's message as one of disowning selfishness, whilst both the Rambam ("If I do not rouse my soul to higher things, who will rouse it?") and Rabbi Yonah embrace it as a call to inspiration and independence: the challenge and obligation to "do the right thing" in life can fall on none other than "me"!

Hillel instinctively understood: time waits for no man (if not now, when?), and that where there is no man, become one!

⤙

Well, it was now or never! The day they had all been waiting for finally arrived! All the relatives of the richest man in the family gathered in his lawyer's conference room for the reading of his will.

"Being of sound mind," read the attorney, "I spent every last cent before I died!"

⤙

If Not Now, When?

MATERIALISM

"If I were the Czar," the wisest man
in Chelm told his wife, "I would
be even richer than the Czar!"

"Oh, yeah, how so?"

"Well, if I were the Czar, I would do a
little teaching of Torah on the side!"

Materialism

The rabbis of *Pirkei Avos* were so much in favor of a proper work ethic that Shemaya urged Jews to "love work!"

Nevertheless, income is predetermined, decreed each year on Rosh Hashana.[144]

Yet success or failure is still proportional to the effort. Thus, to make a living was a worthy pursuit, which is why the Mishna uses the term *melacha* for "work," taken directly from the Torah's definition of the productive physical labor involved in building the Temple.

And there was nothing wrong with seeking wealth as long as it was "kosher business" and halachically tithed (*ma'aser*). And more: the sense of productivity adds reality, self-esteem, dignity to one's life.

The Talmud points out that one can become wealthy quickly (Paul Getty's formula for success? Rise early, work late, strike oil!), but cannot become a Torah scholar quickly. That requires effort,[145] unlike Charlie Lamb's work ethic: "I always arrive late at the office, but I make up for it by leaving early!"

Being rich is having money; being wealthy is having time ("Fortunate is he whose labor is in Torah!").[146]

Leonardo da Vinci was against quickly found wealth ("He who wishes to be rich in a day will be hanged in a year!").

Robert Louis Stevenson, famous Scottish essayist, waxed poetic: "To be rich by rejoicing greatly in the good of others, to love with generosity of heart – these are the gifts which money cannot buy!"

At the end of one's life, no one says, "I wish I had spent more time at the office," nor do obituaries read, "The deceased made over $250,000 a year, drove a Mercedes and wore Armani suits"!

The question begs an answer: why does Jewish law focus so heavily on money and profit?

Our Sages understood human nature: it's the business transaction that tests the morality and integrity of a person. "Buyer beware" (*caveat emptor*) is not a Jewish consumer concept.

In an effort to weed out arrogance, our rabbis injected a precise spiritual bar which also challenges the Jew to think about the purpose of commerce, and not just how to make money "religiously," but how to spend the profits ethically, how to treat workers fairly, how to measure goods honestly.

And so the Talmud, centuries before Jack Benny's "your money or your life" routine, makes a startling statement: "You shall love God with all your heart, with all your soul, and *with all your wealth*!"[147]

꤮

The *gabbai* approaches a guest in *shul*, "I'd like to give you an *aliya*. What's your name?"

"Esther bas Moshe."

"No, I need *your* name."

"It's Esther bas Moshe!"

"How can that be your name?"

"Well," he replies, "I've been having serious financial problems, so everything is in my wife's name!"

꤮

Judaism has a positive attitude when it comes to wealth, assets, property. Wealth, together with long life and peace, is one of the "rewards" from God.[148] And if you then use your wealth to help others "within your gates, the stranger, orphan, and widow," you get another reward, that of God's blessings.[149]

The role model is there right at the start. The world's first Jew, Abraham, is both wealthy and generous to others with his riches.

And in order not to embarrass those in need, the Talmud declared that secret charity was "greater than Moses."[150] Putting money into a *pushke erev Shabbas* or *erev yom tov* is the equivalent of giving anonymously.

The rabbis are very direct: if you give ("tithe") to others, you are assured to get rich yourself.[151]

So what are you supposed to do to be rewarded with wealth? The criterion in the Talmud sounds simple. All you have to do is to be honest in your business dealings.[152]

Rabbi Yechiel ben Yekusiel, thirteenth-century *mussar* author (*Maʿalos Hamiddos*), includes "honestly obtained" wealth in his list of the twenty-four most important virtues.

Another *mussar* master, Rabbi Bachya (*Chovos Halevavos*), warned Jews to seek a healthy balance. An obsession with making more money, he was concerned, would lead to less Torah.

Most of the Sages, including the Rambam, were against deliberate poverty and asceticism, considered "sinful" because they are a quasi rejection of gifts from God.[153] But they also warned against the ethical trappings of wealth, namely causing jealousy (*ayin hora*), arrogance, envy.

Proverbs warns that too much luxury will lead to financial ruin ("One who loves wine and oil shall not be wealthy!").[154]

What's too much? Don't buy meat (a luxury in those days – and in these, too, for some) unless you can afford it, wrote the rabbis of the Talmud, noting that manna was bread, not meat.

In addition, don't let your children get used to wine, and don't get carried away with a fancy wardrobe[155] (although Rashi, with his eye on dignity and appearance, thinks more should be spent on clothes than on food).[156]

Rabbi Ephraim Lunshitz (*Kli Yakar*), *rosh yeshiva* in Lemberg, Poland, had a word of advice for the rich. Lie low and stay out of sight! He railed against the Jews of his time who lived in fancy homes and wore opulent clothes. The rabbi was echoing the words of the prophet Micah, to "walk discreetly!"[157]

To avoid overindulgence, the eighteenth-century rabbis of Fürth (three hundred years before Starbucks) forbade coffee because it was too expensive.

The thirteenth-century rabbis of the Rhineland ordered Jews not to wear shirts with sleeves because, in those days, these shirts were an exclusive fashion statement.

The fifteenth-century rabbis of Italy extended this clothing humility to color, and made Jews wear only black cloats with no silk sleeves.

In 1728, the rabbis imposed a ceiling on the number of musicians at a *simcha*, to keep the costs down, so the poor would not have to "keep up with the Cohens." Weddings had to end by midnight because the band charged more after the clock struck twelve.

This didn't go across well, so the *Vaad Arba Aratzos* (Councils of the Lands) changed course and allowed an unlimited number of musicians, on condition that the *ba'al hasimcha* (host) paid a community "tax" for the number of guests above fifteen, and invited at least one poor person for every ten guests.

Rabbi Yaacov Landau, chief rabbi of B'nei Brak, and Rav Eliezer Schach, head of the Ponevezh Yeshiva, frowned on excessive wasteful spending on weddings, *tena'im* (engagement parties), and bar mitzvos, and were especially concerned when they saw Jewish families borrowing money to pay for these affairs.

When the cost of housing in B'nei Brak went sky high, the Gerer Rebbe told his Chassidim to move to Ashdod or Arad rather than go into debt. And when the cost of a *shtreimel* went up, the Rebbe warned the manufacturers that he would stop wearing one unless they kept their prices affordable.

To remind its members of the concept of *histapkut bamuas*, "being content with less," Agudas Yisroel urged them to reduce the lavishness of the smorgasbord and the menu, as well as the number of guests, and to eliminate the *vort* and the Viennese table, and make do with a one-man band.

Pirkei Avos provides the final word, via ben Zoma: "Who is wealthy? One who is happy with his lot!"[158]

꩜

A young engaged couple are walking down 5th Avenue in Manhattan when they come across a jewelry store. Gazing in the window, Sorelle says, "Oh, Moe, look at that ring. It's so beautiful. I wish I could have it!"

So Moe takes a brick out of his coat pocket, smashes the window, grabs the ring and hands it to his *kalla*.

The couple continue down the Avenue and stop at a handbag store. Gazing in the window, Sorelle says, "Oh, Moe, look at that bag. It's so beautiful. I wish I could have it!"

So Moe takes a brick out of his inside jacket pocket, smashes the window, takes the bag and hands it to his *kalla*.

They continue walking and soon stop at a furrier store. Gazing in the window, she sighs, "Oh, Moe, look at that mink coat. It's so beautiful. I wish I could have it!"

"Hey! What do you think I am?" replies Moe, "made out of bricks or something!"

꩜

Eat-to-Live or Live-to-Eat?

> Hillel said: The more flesh the more worms, the more property the more worry, the more wives the more witchcraft, the more maidservants the more lewdness, the more slaves the more thievery.
>
> — *Mishna 2:8*

This is the final quote from the Sage Hillel, an insightful student of human nature.

But flesh and worms? What's that about?

In the context of Hillel's time, the "world of the flesh" was an expression of distaste for excess, overindulgence, a denunciation of "excess and gluttony."

And wives and witchcraft? What is the meaning of that?

More of the same scolding, this time against polygamy, even when it was legitimate, as rival wives would resort to such ploys as witchcraft (an art form abhorred by the Torah) to retain (or more likely, to regain) their spouse's attention.[159]

And were all maidservants "lewd"? And all slaves "crooked"?

Apparently, yes; it was impossible in those days to find a good female servant of high moral caliber, or a manservant without a penchant for thievery.

The *Tiferes Yisroel* was convinced that homes with too many servants were a magnet for scandal: these were the *nouveau riche* homes, the bastions of materialism, the "if I have a hundred, I need two hundred" syndrome!

These needs, warn both Rabbi Yonah and the *Machzor Vitry*, are not only morally degrading, but reduce one's life span as well ("We make a living by what we get, but we make a life from what we give!" reflected Sir Winston Churchill).

The lesson of this Mishna? Health is wealth!

The desire for possessions can lead to trouble and tragedy; overload leads to overkill; less is more, except for learning and living Torah; intemperate indulgence, from food to money to honor to attention, leads to ever more insatiable greed. The Mishna claims that overeating (the live-to-eat, not-eat-to-live maxim) is bad for the body, even *after* death!

そ

Dovid bumps into his lifelong friend Moishie and sees he's upset. "What's the matter? You look down!"

"Yes, I am. Just last week I had it all! Money, a beautiful house, a big car, the love of a beautiful woman, then, whooof! It's all gone!"

"What happened?"

"My wife found out!"

そ

Ya Can't Take It with You!

> One day a man greeted Yose ben Kisma[160] and said, "Rabbi, where are you from?" He responded, "I am from a large city of scholars and scribes." The man said, "Rabbi, would you be willing to dwell among us, and I will give you thousands upon thousands of golden dinars, precious stones and pearls?" He responded, "Even if you would give me all the silver, gold, precious stones, and pearls in the world, I would not dwell anywhere other than a place of Torah."
>
> — *Mishna 6:9*

The lesson behind Rabbi Yose's encounter with a friendly stranger in this Mishna is simple: in the battle between materialism and mitzvos, the latter wins hands down!

The rabbi flatly turns down a job offer for a coveted rabbinic post. Why? Because it is couched in a (highly exaggerated) language of money ("Ask whatever you wish!"); far better, the humble rabbi reasoned, to be immersed in Torah in poverty (the fish-out-of-the-sea analogy) than in a deep pool of avariciousness, wealth and greed.

"When a person departs this world," Proverbs reminds us, his wealth does not "accompany him, only his Torah study and good deeds"; at the grave, assets and estates stay behind, whilst the *neshoma* surges ahead into eternity carrying only the portfolio of the deceased's actions and deeds.

"That man is richest," notes Henry Thoreau, "whose pleasures are cheapest!" – or as the cranky ol' Jews used to say: Ya can't take it with you![161]

꩜

Heshie decides to visit his best friend Max in the hospital. "*Nu,*" he asks, "how are things?"

"*Nisht git,*" replies Max. "My wife Leah visits me three times a day."

"So what's wrong with that?"

"Every time she comes, she sits at my bedside and reads to me."

"What does she read?"

"My life insurance policy!"

꩜

Work to Learn!

Rabban Gamliel ben Yehuda said: Exertion in
Torah and work make one forget sin.

— *Mishna 2:2*

When, in the early days of the Mizrachi movement, the rabbis at a conference in Vienna in 1925 were searching for a motto to describe their ideology, they adopted the slogan *Torah Va'avoda*, Torah and Labor.

They understood that "six days shall you work…" meant that six days of human exertion were *obligatory* to earn the means to acquire food, clothing, shelter (as expressed in the term *Shabbos Shabboson*, which means cessation of cessations).

That is why the Torah, which minces no words, lumped the "six days" together as a single unit (*sheishes yomim*) as opposed to the plural (*shisha yomim*), implying that the six days be considered as *one* work unit of time, as opposed to staggered work days allowing one to decide when to work and when not.

Both Rashi and the Rambam consider it a serious halachic duty to teach one's children an *omanus*, a profession, *even* on a Shabbas. Along comes Dostai ben Yannai, a second-century Sage, with a stunning declaration: the Jew who doesn't work during the week is more likely to be a *mechalel Shabbas*, a "Sabbath violator"!

Ben Yannai's logic?

"Suppose a man sits idle all week and on the Sabbath eve discovers he has nothing to eat. He might go and fall in with a troop of bandits. Then he would be seized and taken in chains and put to work on the Sabbath. All this because he would not work on the six days!"

꒞

Moishie and Yossele pass a Baptist church and see a sign on the marquee that says:

COME ON IN AND CONVERT!

WE'LL GIVE YOU $400, ON THE SPOT!

Mo says to Joe, "Wait for me, I'm gonna try that."

Yossele paces outside for nearly an hour and then bangs on the church's big wooden door. Finally, Moishie sticks his head out a window.

"*Nu?*" says Yossele, "did ya get the money?"

"Is that all you people think about?" Moishie replies.

꒞

Kosher Business

Shemaya said: Love work.

— *Mishna 1:10*

This Mishna hones in on a proper work ethic – that one should not just tolerate work (*melacha*) but "love" it!

"When you eat the labor of your hands," sang King David, "happy shall you be!" – or as the Yiddishists put it: God performs many miracles, but he doesn't grow corn in the houses of the pious![162]

Being financially independent and self-sufficient was a great virtue to the rabbis of the Talmud: "Greater is one who enjoys [*neheneh*] what he achieves with his own hands than one who fears Heaven."

Our Sages thus elevate productivity to a moral level ("As others toil for me, I must toil for others"), and our linguists note that the same Hebrew word (*avoda*) means work and worship.

Money earned in a "kosher way" is called in Yiddish *bediente gelt*, a nod to the fact that making money is in itself no problem, so long as it is used for constructive purposes, and pursued with "clean hands and a pure heart!"[163]

Judaism does not consider money the root of all evil but simply warns the Jew to handle it with care;[164] in fact, the first question in the next world, says the Talmud, is "*Nasata v'netata be'emunah?* (Were your business dealings honorable?)" – and this is even *before* the query "Did you set aside time for Torah study?"

The lesson?

Of all the mitzvos the most important one is simply *kedoshim tiyu* (be holy), by not just obeying the letter of the law but also its spirit.

If making money the "Torah way" means making less money, then, say our rabbis, "So be it!"

⇁

"Thank you, Mr. Cohen," the factory owner says, "I wish I had twenty customers just like you."

"Gee, it's nice to hear that," replies Mr. Cohen, "but I must admit I'm surprised, because you know that I argue every bill and I'm always paying late."

"I know. But I'd still like to have twenty customers like you. The problem is, I have two hundred!"

⇁

Get a Job!

> Rabban Gamliel ben Yehuda said: Good is Torah
> study together with a worldly occupation.
>
> — *Mishna 2:2*

The Mishna begins by subordinating the centrality of Torah study to the importance of getting a job (i.e., self-sufficiency).

After pointing out that the *gematria* of *sulam* (ladder) (136) is the same as that of *mamon* (money), Jewish mystics note that the ladder of wealth has its basis on the ground and its top in Heaven; thus it's possible to make great gains (i.e., ascend) in the spiritual sense by carefully stepping on the rungs of wealth.

To earn an honest living is healthy, say our Sages, and seeking an occupation falls into the obligatory category of complying with the "ways of the land" (literally, *derech eretz*) – which the Mishna calls "a form of respect."

That is why Jewish law includes wording in the marriage contract (*kesuba*) that obligates the groom to financially support his wife; and our Sages warn fathers that teaching their sons a profession is as compulsory as teaching them Torah.

To support one's family on handouts, notes Rabbi Yonah, is antithetical to a sense of dignity, self-worth and accomplishment;[165] note how many of the Sages were tent makers, farmers, carpenters and merchants. Hillel was a woodcutter; Shammai, a builder; Rabbi Yehoshua, a blacksmith; Rabbi Chanina, a shoemaker; Rav Huna, a water carrier; Rabbi Abba, a tailor;[166] Rabbi Yose, a processor of hides, Rabban Yochanan, a sandal maker, Rabbi Yehoshua ben Chanania, a charcoal-burner, and Shammai, an engineer.

Because of the devastating effects of a lack of self-esteem and self-respect, the Mishna is blunt: "Idleness leads to madness!… Love work!" – even, if necessary, "flay carcasses in the marketplace and earn a living. He should not say, 'I am a priest, I am a great man, and such work is beneath me.'"[167]

꙳

The *rav* presents his salary check at the bank.
The teller apologizes for having to cash the check with soiled bills.
"Oh, that's OK," says the *rav*, "no germs could live on my salary anyway!"

꙳

The Bigger the Businessman, the Smaller the Jew!

> Rabbi Yonasan said: Whoever fulfills the Torah despite poverty will ultimately fulfill it in wealth; but whoever neglects the Torah because of wealth will ultimately neglect it out of poverty.
>
> — *Mishna 4:11*

Rav Yonasan warns that old habits die hard: if you neglect Torah because you're too busy accumulating assets and possessions, you'll still be too busy once you have assets and possessions (quickly got, quickly lost, goes an old Yiddish saying).

The *Tiferes Yisroel* sees poetic justice in this Mishna, concluding that neglecting Torah because of poverty is a (somewhat) legitimate reason. God will somehow provide sufficient means to make ends meet and to allow some Torah time in serenity; however, neglecting it when wealthy (i.e., the "Do-not-say-when-I-have-free-time-I-will-learn, lest-you-do-not-have-free-time" Common Excuse Syndrome) will bring poverty to your door, and any chance of further Torah learning will be lost to new and bewildering challenges.

This Mishna is intended to establish priorities and set limits; it also offers hope to the poor and impoverished – as long as they don't lose faith in the Torah way of life – and a word of warning to the rich who, in arrogance, turn their backs on Torah. "The one who persists in knocking," writes Moshe ibn Ezra, "is the one who will succeed in entering!" This is true for rich and poor alike.

But reality is reality, and poverty can be extremely debilitating; so our Sages, motivated by sympathy and understanding of stress, don't demand full-time Torah study. Nevertheless they do urge, according to the Rambam, a minimal amount each day.

So is it OK to be rich?

Sure. Judaism views wealth as a privilege (given by God) and an opportunity (to do something for the community), and disagrees with Isaac Leibush Peretz's cynical *bon mot*, "The bigger the businessman, the smaller the Jew!"

꜀

"Write down what you would do," asks the English teacher, "if you made a million dollars."

Lenny hands her a blank sheet of paper.

"Lenny!" she screams, "you've done absolutely nothing. Why?"

"Because if I had a million dollars, that's exactly what I would do!"

꜀

In the Genes?

Yose said: Let the money of your fellowman be as dear to you
as your own; and let all your deeds be for the sake of Heaven.

— *Mishna 2:17*

The lesson of this Mishna?

If you respect your own assets, then you *must* respect other people's money
and property; or as the Yiddish cynics phrase it: If you rub elbows with a rich
man, you get a hole in your sleeve!

"If you have money," wrote Sholem Aleichem, "you're wise and handsome –
and you can sing!" But does it help with your learning?

Told that a certain Jew had acquired great wealth, the Sage asked, "Yes, but
has he also acquired the days in which to spend it?"

Occupying yourself with Torah study "for its own sake," notes the Mishna's
Rabbi Meir, "makes the world worthwhile."

And not just for one's own sake!

"The sake of Heaven," a common Torah theme that rests on the original directive "Know Him in all your ways," was a favorite precept of the seventh Lubavitcher
Rebbe, in that a mundane mitzva, if not performed with deep Godly intent, remains a mitzva diluted to dreary dullness, and not on the ideal level of holiness.

When the Mishna asks, "Who is rich?" ben Zoma's answer comes *not* in financial, but in psychological, terms ("He who is content with his lot"). This is not
a tirade against ambition or drive, but a nod and a wink that fortune is at times
measured in such simple things as peace and serenity.

But the final word goes to Nachman Kasovir: since people think of business
while they're in *shul*, is it too much to ask that they think of God while they're
conducting business?

☞

"Rabbi," the congregant asks, "how come you're always talking business when I, a
businessman, am always talking about spiritual matters when not at work?"

"Ah, good question," the *rav* replies, "you have discovered one of the principles
of human nature!"

"And what principle is that, Rabbi?"

"People like to discuss things they know nothing about!"

☞

No Flour, No Torah;
No Torah, No Flour!

Rabbi Eleazar ben Azariah[168] said: If there is no flour (sustenance) there is no Torah; if there is no Torah there is no flour.

— *Mishna 3:21*

There is a classic debate between Yishmael and Shimon bar Yochai.

The former interprets the verse "You shall gather your grain" to mean that Torah study must be combined with a worldly occupation.

The latter, commenting on the command "Six days shall you work," considered employment "a positive command, in and of itself."

Yet the mystic Sage also hedged his bets, concerned by a Divine warning – "Torah shall not depart from your mouth, you shall meditate therein by day and by night" – which left him wondering, "If a man ploughs, sows, reaps and threshes… what is to become of the Torah?"

So, who won this lively debate?

According to Abaye, those who "followed Yishmael [balancing study with work], were successful, whilst the followers of Shimon [committed to Torah study exclusively] were not so successful."

Without Torah, one's mundane livelihood serves no purpose. And vice versa: if one works in order to conduct his life on Jewish principles, then his very working becomes a mitzva in the service of God.

The Mishna thus advises that "Torah is better with *derech eretz*" (i.e., gainful employment); the rabbis warn parents that if they don't teach their son a trade, they teach him thievery!

Rabbi Yosef Caro concludes that "if Torah is not accompanied by work, it will ultimately be nullified" – and yet the *Chofetz Chaim* still disagrees, supporting the full-time yeshiva-kollel lifestyle, but with a caveat: in each generation, only a few outstanding individuals merit the right of sole Torah immersion.

꥓

"I see you were last employed by a psychiatrist," said the employer to Reb Arye, the applicant who was trying to combine his Torah studies with a regular job. "Why did you leave?"

"Well," the young kollel guy replied, "I just couldn't win. If I was late to work, I was hostile! If I was early, I had an anxiety complex! If I was on time, I was compulsive!"

꥓

Taking Care of Business

> Hillel said: Those who are occupied excessively with business will not become wise in Torah.
>
> — *Mishna 2:6*

This Mishna is self-explanatory but begs the question: what if one *must* work in order to make a living?

The *Yismach Yisroel* renders the words "on six days, work may be done…" homiletically, in that the Jew who works for a living (a *baal melacha*) should work six days – but compensate by dedicating his entire Shabbas to Torah study and holy endeavor.

This Jew, who waits a whole week for Shabbas, not only consecrates the Shabbas but *also* sanctifies his mundane work week.

The Midrash, quoting Shimon bar Yochai's opinion on "six days shall you work," saw this as "a positive commandment [to work] *in and of itself*"!

Hillel is not against working for a living; he chooses his words carefully: one should not, he urges, be "occupied *excessively*" with business.

Rabban Gamliel adds that, unlike spiritual exertion that leads to spiritual success, excessive involvment in making money doesn't mean you'll automatically do well, because business success is ultimately in God's domain.

In other words, as with everything else in life, moderation is the key and self-restraint is paramount; in fact, the ordinary pursuit of making a living is mandatory in a religion that frowns on those who knowingly become charity cases and burdens on the community!

Since man does not live by bread alone, the Midrash calls those who have work "blessed"![169]

꒰

A young kollel guy is looking for a part-time job and becomes a vacuum cleaner salesman. He knocks on a door and, when it opens, in his zeal he rushes past the little ol' lady into her living room, throws a large bag of dirt all over her clean carpet, and says: "Ma'am, if this new vacuum doesn't pick up every bit of dirt, then I'll eat all the dirt!"

"Young man," she replies, "if I had enough money to buy that thing, I would have paid my electricity bill before they cut it off. Now, what would you prefer, a spoon or a knife and fork?"

꒰

HUMILITY, SPEECH
AND RESPECT

Jerry Lewis once turned to Dean
Martin and said, "I think I just
shot a perfect stranger!"

"Don't worry," Martin replies,
"No one's perfect!"

Humility, Speech and Respect

Rabbi Levitas of Yavneh lobbied for humility. The Talmud considered arrogance as bordering on idolatory.[170] The Rambam frowned on character extremes, and urged people to take the middle road (*shvil hazahav* – literally, "the golden path").[171]

There is no Sage in the past three thousand years who has not dived into the pool of *middos* and manners. The reason is obvious: bad behavior is the antithesis of all things Jewish!

Ah, but what constitutes unacceptable behavior?

Different times, different cultures, different *middos*. What is socially acceptable *here*, may not pass *there*! In *Pirkei Avos*, humility reigned supreme as the mother of manners; by the late eighteenth century in Europe, Rav Moshe Sofer thought humility itself was a form of arrogance.

Bad behavior is obvious to all present. It needs no definitive resume. The general rule? Treat *everyone* with politeness, even those who are rude to you – not because they are nice, but because *you* are!

Clarence Thomas was convinced that "Good manners will open doors that the best education cannot!" Solomon ben Yehuda ibn Gabirol muses, "Good manners sometimes means simply putting up with other people's bad manners!"

Rabbi Henach Leibowitz and Der Alter from Slobodka were convinced that manners (*derech eretz*) was not just polite etiquette but actual *halacha*.

An ancient Midrash even claims that considerate behavior precedes the Torah itself (*Kadma derech eretz es haTorah*).[172] The Rambam mandates, "One is obligated to conduct his affairs with others in a gentle and pleasing manner!"

Basic courtesy and civility were not introduced at Mount Sinai. Abraham was already a model of a *ba'al chessed* (master of generosity). That is why *middos* as a virtue is not included in the Torah's list of mitzvos, since it is the foundation of all mitzvos!

"What the world needs," wrote Oscar Levant, "is more geniuses with humility; there are so few of us left!"

The moment the Torah made humility the greatest of character traits, its adherents had no choice.

"You will not find the Torah among arrogant people (*gasei haruach*)."[173] Or, as the Yiddishists put it: Swallow your pride occasionally, it's nonfattening!

"The greater the Torah knowledge," opined J.B. Soloveitchik, "the more humble the scholar should be!" To the Rav, pride and Torah were "mutually exclusive." The term "arrogant *talmid chacham*" is an oxymoron; a haughty scholar will be punished by "forgetting his Torah knowledge."[174]

Humanity and humility are closely related words.

Moses' unique self-negation ("I am nothing!") is why he, alone amongst the prophets, was chosen to be the vehicle for God's words, the equivalent of *Time* magazine's "Humblest Man of the Century."[175]

Thus it is his humility that is at the heart of his greatness.

Since the Torah was given on a humble mountain to humble Jews, the rabbis of *Pirkei Avos* begin their first Mishna with a threesome of issues – "Be deliberate in judgment, develop many disciples, make a fence for the Torah" – that have a common theme: humility.

And, in case we still don't get the message, they list humility as one of the forty-eight prerequisites for acquiring Torah.

What's so great about being humble? asks the Malbim, who quotes Rabban Yochanan when he replies, "On the heels of humility comes fear of God!"[176]

This character trait allowed Moses, within his humility, to stand up to an Egyptian tyrant, do battle against Amalek, rise to defend his people against God Himself.

Humility is thus not the same as timidity.

It is the absence of ego, the dismissal of arrogance, the lack of a fake charisma.[177] It allows the Jew to start his mornings with the prayer *Modeh Ani*, a dose of humility and gratitude ("Thank you, God, for graciously returning my soul for yet another day!") that puts the spiritual into perspective.

❧

Rebecca is about to to get engaged and tells her parents that Harry, her beloved, is endowed with a unique sense of humility. When they finally meet, her father asks the potential groom, "Where do you live?"

"Near Brooklyn," he replies.

"Near Brooklyn?" interrupts Rebecca, "He's so modest! He owns a ten-bedroom mansion on five acres in the Hamptons!"

"So," asks the mother, "what do you do for a living?"

"Oh, I own a retail store," he answers.

"A store?" interrupts Rebecca, "He's so humble! Harry owns the Westchester Mall and all the stores on Sacks Ave! Such modesty!"

Harry suddenly sneezes and reaches into his pocket for a tissue. "Are you OK," asks Rebecca's mother, "do you have a cold?"

"A cold?" Rebecca interrupts, "Don't be silly, Mum, he's got full-blown pneumonia!"

⇗

Is sloppiness of speech caused by ignorance or apathy? I don't know and I don't care!

When Solomon became king, he asked God in a dream to grant him wisdom. When he awoke, he understood the speech of the birds and animals.[178] His first lesson in wisdom? Speech has spiritual power, as any student of Genesis knows, since God created the world itself via words ("Let there be light; and there was light!").[179]

Solomon then defined idiocy ("The voice of a fool is in many words")[180] and gave the Eastern European Yiddishists a great saying: Better to remain silent and appear dumb than to open your mouth and remove all doubt![181]

So it comes as no surprise that when the rabbis of *Pirkei Avos* try to define the differences between "a clod and a wise man," they do it in terms of speech: "There are seven characteristics that typify the clod, and seven the wise person: Wise people *do not speak* in the presence of those who are wiser than they are; they *do not interrupt* their friend's words; *they do not reply* in haste. They *ask* what is relevant, they *answer* to the point; they *reply* to questions in orderly sequence; of what they have not heard, they say, 'I have not heard'; *they admit* to the truth. The opposite of these typify the clod."[182]

When Onkelos, the genius convert who lived during the time of the Mishna, translated the Torah's "a living being" into Aramaic, he wrote it as "a speaking being."

Later, the Rambam swung his full rabbinic weight behind the concept of speech, breaking it down into no less than five categories, ranging from obligatory (*divrei Torah*), praiseworthy (words which inspire), permissible (as relating to business or necessities in life) and undesirable (trivial, wasteful talk, aka *schmoozing*, although the Talmud is quick to add that even the lesser speech of great scholars should be considered words of Torah)[183] to forbidden (cursing, false testimony, gossip). Interestingly, the Spanish Sage did not consider prayer as "speech."

Rabbi Yisrael of Husyatin never spoke when conducting his *Shabbas tisch*. Other than *niggunim*, there was total silence. His Chassidim believed that God was best served through silence.

This ideology is articulated by Shimon ben Gamliel ("I have not found anything better for oneself than silence…. Whoever talks excessively brings about sin!"),[184] and reduced to either a powerful weapon ("One who guards his mouth and his tongue guards from troubles of his soul") or a vehicle of salvation ("Death and life are in the power of the tongue!").[185]

The *Chofetz Chaim's Sefer Shmiras Halashon* is legendary, and, even as a young boy, Avrohom Yitzchok Kohn, the Toldos Aharon Rebbe, was so sparing with words that he disciplined himself to a hundred a day, excluding *divrei Torah*. To ensure *arichas s'fasayim*, "orderly speech," he walked around with a hundred small pebbles in one pocket and transferred a stone per word to the other pocket.

When he ran out of stones, he stopped talking for the day.[186]

⤳

Once, at a White House party, a woman approached Calvin Coolidge, famed for his silence, and said: "Mr. President, I made a bet I can get more than two words out of you."

He replied: "You lose."

⤳

Too Busy Doing Good to Be Good!

> Rabban Yochanan ben Zakkai said: Go out and see which is an evil path a person should avoid. Rabbi Eliezer said: A bad eye; Rabbi Yehoshua said: A bad friend; Rabbi Yose said: A bad neighbor; Rabbi Shimon said: One who borrows and does not pay back.
>
> — *Mishna 2:14*

This Mishna is a medley of potential faults, a litany of negative traits to avoid.

What's worse? A "bad eye" (defined as jealousy), a "bad friend" (who may lead you to spiritual collapse), a "bad neighbor" (no role model there!) – or someone who doesn't pay back a loan (the irresponsible)?

Rabban Yochanan, having advised his *talmidim* to choose *one good* character trait and perfect it, now challenges them to choose *one bad* trait and practice its avoidance.

The rabbis of the Talmud thought a man should be judged on the basis of his "portion, potion and passion!" The Midrash is more colorful: if you want to know someone's character, check out his "business, wine and conversation!"

One meaning of the word *middos* is measurement, signifying the Mishna's standards relating to man's behavior, defined by Yehiel Anav, the thirteenth-century poet-author (*Sefer Maalos Hamiddos*), as being "thoughtful of [*both*] God and man."

A Jew with good traits is simply called a *ba'al middos*, or in Yiddish slang, an *erliche mensch*, a guy who knows not to be so busy *doing* good that he has no time to *be* good!

Who defines "good traits"? *Pirkei Avos* is direct: it enumerates them as "generosity, humility, modesty."

M & M (*middos* and manners) are at the heart of Sinai, summarized as *mitzvos bein adam l'chaveiro*, "relationship commands" between Jews.

Eleazar ben Azariah was straightforward: without manners, no Torah; without Torah, no manners!

❧

The rabbi is giving his *Shabbas drasha* and can't help notice that one of his congregants, sitting right in the front row, is immersed in reading a book. Annoyed at the lack of manners, the *rav* interrupts his *d'var Torah*: "Philip! Reading while I'm talking? That's *derech eretz*?! What are you doing? Are you trying to learn something?"

"No, Rabbi. I am not learning anything. I'm listening to you!"

❧

As Is His Name, So Is He!

Hillel said: One who acquires a good name acquires it for himself.

— *Mishna 2:7*

In this Mishna, Hillel identifies *a good name* as something that needs to be "acquired" and can never be transferred to another!

And yet "the earned name," notes Phineas ben Hama, is "much more than the given name." Koheles notes, "Every man has three names: one his father and mother gave him, one others call him, and one he acquires himself!"

Adam gave names to the animals that define their qualities; Judaism relates to names not as mere arbitrary designations, but as clues that determine destiny and define one's persona (*k'shmo ken hu*, "as is his name, so is he").[187]

Name-giving thus became a family empowerment, a Jewish child's first life-cycle event.

Remember: it was the mothers, *not* the father (*nor* God), who bestowed names on eleven of Jacob's children; and, unlike today's custom of naming children after ancestors, the early Torah practice was to give the child a name reflective of hope, or linked to the state of the nurturing mother's mind. For example: Reuven's name is based on "seeing"; Shimon's on "hearing"; and when Rachel's second boy is born, the mother, who dies in childbirth, names him *Ben-Oni*, "the son of my distress!"[188]

So what's in a name? Plenty...

꙳

Chaim Ber, fascinated by a sign in Chinatown – "Reb Yankel Dudek's Chinese Laundry" – asks the owner, "'Yankel Dudek?' What sort of a name is that?!"

"Is name of owner," replies the old Chinese man, "me!"

"You? How did that happen?"

"Is simple. Many, many years ago when come to this country, stand in line at Documentation Center, man in front is Jewish man from Poland. Lady look at him and go, 'What your name?' He say, 'Reb Yankel Dudek.' Then she look at me and go, 'What your name?' I say, 'Sem Ting.'"

꙳

The Superior Crown

> Rabbi Shimon[189] said: There are three crowns – the crowns
> of Torah, priesthood, and kingship. But the crown of
> a good name is superior to them all.
>
> — *Mishna 4:17*

The Mishna's concept of "a crown" on the scholar or priest is obviously allegorical, for only a king actually wears one; thus the elevation of any particular position to "a crown" is to differentiate between the amateur and the "real thing."

In other words, to be crowned a scholar, rather than just being one, is a metaphoric acknowledgment of outstanding erudition, universally recognized.

But why does Rabbi Shimon talk of *three* crowns (the ones given to the Jews at Mount Sinai) and then go on to name four?

Because the "crown of a good name" – a "fourth" in sequence only, but in reality superior to all crowns – is, unlike kingships, priesthoods and scholarship, achievable by any Jew willing to strive for it (in fact, the absence of this "good-name crown" on a scholar, priest or king dilutes his other crowns!).

A "crown of Torah," according to Rashi and the Rambam, is a prerequisite for the crown of a good name ("Better than precious oil!") which, when attained, becomes "superior" to all other crowns!

The first three of these crowns are either gifts from God or result from being a link in the chain of a dynasty; only the fourth and most important, the crown of a good name, is self-earned!

✍

Not getting names right can be embarrassing. Izzie decides to go to a Catholic school and passes the entrance exam administered by the Mother Superior. A few days later she calls Father O'Connor, the dean of the school, and says, "Father, you have to do something about that new Jewish kid! He's driving me crazy!"

"What's the problem?"

"He insists on calling me Mother Shapiro!"

✍

A Klutz of a Boor

> Hillel used to say: A boor cannot fear sin, nor
> can an unlearned person be pious.
>
> — *Mishna 2:6*

What's a "boor"?

In Yiddish it's a *klutz*; in Hebrew, believe it or not, it's the same as in English, *boor*.

The term describes one who is anti-social and uncultured, lacking in etiquette, *middos*, good graces, usually unemployed (with no prospects, adds Rashi), a good-for-nothing – not exactly an asset to the wider community. A boor is so bad, in fact, that Hillel summarizes all of the above in a few short words: "He's insensitive to sin!"

"Be not simply good," wrote Henry Thoreau, "be good for something!"

Webster's Dictionary describes a "boor" as "a rude, unrefined, ill-bred person; one who is clownish in manners"; and so Jonathan ben Joseph, a second-century *Tanna*, defined the boor as "one who does not raise his sons for Torah."

Adds Meiri: a boor is like an unplowed field – neither has the chance of growth!

By assuming the *am ha'aretz* (unlearned one) has no chance of becoming pious, isn't Hillel being a bit harsh? After all, why can't an "unlearned" Jew be righteous? The truth is, he can!

The confusion lies in the fact that the term *am ha'aretz* no longer has the same meaning it used to have. Today, it's an unflattering expression, but once it used to mean exactly what it said: *am* (nation of) *ha'aretz* (the land) – a euphemism for "a simple man," lacking in *seichel* (common sense).

"God preserves the simple," sings King David, but to achieve true piety requires an intellectual curiosity to ask questions, a mind open to challenge, willing to explore the depths of Scripture – and only then does one come to a remarkable conclusion that opens the door to religiosity.

"The higher the truth," explains Rav Kook, "the simpler it is!"

⤳

At the monthly board meeting, the rabbi is trying to convince the members that the *shul* needs a new chandelier.

"Perhaps the rabbi is right," says Jerry, the town boor, "I wouldn't know. But tell me this, Rabbi: suppose we do buy a chandelier for the synagogue – who will play it?"

⤳

When in Doubt, Do Without!

> Rabbi Akiva said: Vows are a protective fence for abstinence.
> — *Mishna 3:17*

What's the difference between a vow and an obligation?

A vow is a promise *to do* something, an obligation is a promise *not to do* something!

Are a vow (*neder*) and an oath (*shevua*) the same? No. The former changes the status of an object. An example? If you "vow" not to watch television, you have made the television a forbidden object. The latter places an obligation on the person. An example? If you make an "oath" to lose weight, this obliges *you*; it does not affect the status of any food.

By announcing the virtue of a vow, this Mishna appears to contradict a direct Torah statement ("If you refrain from taking an oath, you will not bear a sin"), as well as a warning from the Talmud: "Whoever takes a voluntary oath, even if he fulfills it, is called sinful!"

And more: Rabbi Akiva seems to be suggesting that abstinence is a positive goal, despite the many rabbinic references against the life of a *nazir* (an ascetic).[190]

Eleazar Hakappar calls the *nazir* "a sinner," whilst the Talmud's Isaac is confused by the whole concept of self-denial: "Are there not enough injunctions in the law that you must impose upon yourself additional prohibitions?"

But Rabbi Akiva is making an observation, not a recommendation, articulated best by *Seder Eliyahu Rabba*: "He who denies himself a good life in this world is an ingrate!"

❧

A police officer pulls over Yankele one night after he sees him weaving in and out of traffic, and says, "Sir, I want you to blow into this breathalyzer tube."

"Sorry, officer, I can't do that. I'm an asthmatic. If I do that, I'll have a really bad attack!"

"Okay, fine. Then come down to the station to give a blood sample."

"Sorry, officer, I can't do that either. I'm a hemophiliac. If I do that, I'll bleed to death!"

"Okay, then I need you to walk this white line whilst counting to ten."

"Sorry, I can't do that either, officer."

"Why not?"

"Because I'm drunk!"

❧

Shame on You!

> Rabbi Akiva said: Jesting and lightheadedness
> accustom a person to immorality.
> — *Mishna 3:17*

Is this Mishna an argument against laughter, levity, comic relief? No. It's an endorsement of moderation and restraint in behavior, and, explains Rabbi Yonah, a warning that uninhibited "merriment" is an impediment to fearing God.

Rabbi Akiva was convinced that mockery and levity were the gateways to vulgarity and immoral activity, and that a general lax "jester-style" lifestyle was a sign of disrespect to one's self.

A Jew who lacks self-respect, Rav Aharon Kotler was convinced, is more likely to stumble into sin; thus the Rambam disqualified any Jew from being a witness in a Jewish court if his behavior showed a lack of shame (e.g., eating in public, working whilst half-dressed, etc.).

These elements of embarrassment, the Mishna's motto of morality, have the legal equivalent of "offenses involving moral turpitude," a word that is derived from the Latin *turpis*, which means "vile, foul, shameful," or from the Greek *trepein*, which means "twisted, malformed."

All of human history, notes Rabbi Eliezer, begins with the discovery of shame, the ability to sense the difference between right and wrong: "Anyone who commits a sin," observes Rabba bar Huna the Elder, "but is then ashamed of it receives forgiveness for all of his sins!"

"What the law does not forbid, let shame forbid," reflected the Roman author and politician Seneca. This was echoed in several moving poems of the Ramban whose lyrics explain how God, cognizant of the vulnerability of human nature, created scales of justice right in the human heart, in order that mankind instinctively tell the difference between good and evil.

꙳

Sammy, the boss, returns from lunch in a good mood and calls the whole staff in to listen to a couple of jokes. Everybody laughs uproariously – except Suri.

"What's the matter?" Sammy grumbles, "don't you have a sense of humor?"

"I don't have to laugh," Suri replies, "I'm leaving Friday!"

꙳

Three Sophisticated Antidotes

> The world is judged with goodness, and everything
> depends on the abundance of good deeds.
> — *Mishna 3:19*

This Mishna reiterates that God judges not in narrow strictness but in broad goodness, and that the verdict is easily mitigated with good (a word derived from "God") deeds. The Midrash adds that good deeds are not inherited; the Yiddishists prefer good to piety (and add: He who pelts you with stones, you pelt him with bread!).

But which "good deeds" is this Mishna referring to?

A quick glance at the *Musaf* prayer of Rosh Hashana reveals that the rule of Heaven can be swayed by three specific sophisticated antidotes: *teshuva, tefilla u'tzedaka* (repentance, prayer and charity).

So, when evaluating our foibles and shortcomings, do these three "remedies" annul or cancel evil decrees?

No: the verb *ma'avirin* means "to pass, lighten or mitigate" God's decree, but not avert it. To Meiri, the "goodness" is a reference to God's willingness to accept the process of *teshuva*, a near magic word in the Torah thesaurus.

The belief in its power to bring about amnesty is so strong that our rabbis claim it can even turn sinners into saints.[191]

꿈

John is sitting outside his local pub enjoying a quiet pint of beer, when a nun suddenly appears and starts decrying the evils of drink. "You should be ashamed of yourself, young man! Drinking is a sin! Alcohol is the blood of the devil!"

"How do you know this, Sister?"

"My Mother Superior told me so."

"But have you ever had a drink? How can you be so sure it's a sin?"

"Of course I've never taken alcohol!"

"Then let me buy you a drink and if, afterwards, you still believe it's evil, I'll give up drinking forever."

"That's impossible. How could I, a nun, sit here drinking in public?!"

"Well, I'll get the barman to put it in a teacup for you; then no one will ever know."

The nun agrees, so John goes inside and says to the bartender, "Another pint for me." Then he lowers his voice and whispers, "And could you put some vodka in a teacup?"

"Oh, no! It's that nun again, isn't it!"

꿈

Self-Doubts Are Self-Fulfilling!

> Rabbi Shimon[192] said: Do not consider
> yourself wicked in your own eyes.
> — *Mishna 2:18*

This Mishna is psychological: Have self-respect! Be emancipated from self-contempt! Self-debasement is not self-improvement! Never give up on yourself!

Rabbi Shimon warms of the danger of seeing oneself as a failure, of taking oneself too seriously; and Rabbi Yonah adds a warning: don't become a prisoner of your own self-image!

Pride and being content with oneself, this Mishna is telling us, are not such bad qualities if mixed with the right dose of humility; but be careful, self-doubts are sometimes self-fulfilling!

The third saying ("do not consider yourself wicked in your own eyes") is a bit obscure.

Rashi was concerned that the Jew who considers himself to be evil will have no incentive to do anything worthy.

The Rambam reads it not as "*Be not* wicked" but as "*Regard not thyself* as wicked!"

In other words, "Don't regard yourself as (wholly) wicked" (be not conceited or despairing), otherwise you'll give up any hope of *teshuva*; meanwhile, other scholars interpret it as meaning that you must not consider yourself so evil that you don't belong in the community.

Rodney Dangerfield claimed he never got any respect.

"When I was a kid I got no respect. The time I was kidnapped, the kidnappers sent my parents a note that said, 'We want five thousand dollars or you'll see your kid again!' With my dog I don't get no respect. He keeps barking at the front door. He don't want to go out. He wants me to leave! I could tell that my parents hated me. My bath toys were a toaster and a radio! Once, when I was lost, I saw a policeman and asked him to help me find my parents. I said to him, 'Do you think we'll ever find them?' He said, 'I don't know, kid. There's plenty of places for them to hide!'"

Handle with Care!

> [Ben Azzai] said: Do not be disrespectful of any person
> and do not be dismissive of any thing [*davar*].
>
> — *Mishna 4:3*

This Mishna extends the concept of respect (*derech eretz*, "the way of the world") for physical objects.

And so we handle-with-care such objects as a *Sefer Torah*, *sifrei kodesh*, *Sifrei Tanach*, a *siddur*, *machzor* and *tefillin*.[193]

Judaism confers dignity on *everything*, ranging from mankind to animals to insects to objects (e.g., covering *challas* on Friday night, leaving the earth untouched during its Sabbatical cycle), and demands that Jews treat everybody and everything with unadulterated *menschlichkeit* (decent behavior) in the pursuit of *mipnei darchei shalom* (the ways of peace).

Jewish law fills two entire Talmudic tracts with the mitzvos of *derech eretz* and declares that they preceded Mount Sinai by twenty-six generations, the span of time between Creation and the giving of the Torah.

The perfect example of the Mishna's second point ("don't dismiss anything") is David: when fleeing Saul, he carps at a cobweb, only to be saved by a cobweb whilst hiding from his mortal enemies in the hollow of a tree.

Rabbi Yonah translates *davar*, "thing," as "word," thus emphasizing the supreme care one must use with speech, leading ben Sira to define wisdom as being "known by the answer of the tongue!"

"It isn't necessary," notes Rabbi Chiya, "to tell a wise man to hold his tongue," whilst his colleague, Yehoshua ben Levi, measured the "worth" of each word ("A word is worth a *sela* [a small coin], but silence is worth two [*sela'im*]!").

So, enough said, already!

࿐

A restless Dovi sat in court all day waiting to be called for a minor traffic summons. When his name was finally called out, the judge adjourned the court to the following day.

"But why?" the frustrated Dovi snapped at the judge.

The annoyed judge snapped back, "That'll be twenty dollars for contempt of court! That's why!"

As Dovi took out his wallet, the judge said, "You don't have to pay now!"

"I wasn't going to," Dovi snapped back, "I'm just checking to see if I have enough for two more words!"

࿐

Waste Not!

> Rabbi Yose said: Let your fellow's property
> be as dear to you as your own.
> — *Mishna 2:17*

This Mishna, in another application of the Golden Rule, first talks about respect, not for people but for property, imploring the Jew to extend the appreciation and care that one shows towards one's own belongings to that of others as well.

The *Tiferes Yisroel* says this Mishna goes both ways: not only are we supposed to help our neighbors and friends to suffer no loss of their possessions, but we must also help them succeed and rejoice in their success as if it were our own.

Rabbi Yose has touched on the concept known as *bal tashchis,* the prohibition against cutting down fruit trees "when you besiege a city," a "do-not-destroy" principle which he extends to cover "anything of value" (food, clothing, utensils, etc.).

Rav Samson Raphael Hirsch elevated *bal tashchis* as the most basic mitzva of them all, a twin acknowledgment of the sovereignty of God and the limitation of our own will and ego.

To Moshe Ibn Ezra this Mishna reflects human nature ("It is easier to abolish than to establish!"), which is why the *Sefer Hachinuch*, a compilation of mitzvos by the medieval Jewish pietists, defined a lover of God as one who could not bear to waste a grain of mustard (the Talmud even applies this principle to those who "make a lamp burn faster than it should!").

꩜

Yossele goes across the hall to his neighbor Leibl's apartment and asks to borrow his broom. A few hours later Yossele returns with the broom and a small hand broom. "Mazel tov!" he says, "your broom had a baby." Leibl happily accepts the brooms.

The following week Yossele knocks on Leibl's door and asks to borrow his soup pot. A few hours later he returns with the soup pot and a small sauce pan. "Mazel tov," he says, "your pot had a baby." Leibl happily accepts the pots.

The next week Yossele knocks on Leibl's door and asks to borrow his laptop with the DVD player. Leibl is more than happy to lend it. A few hours later Yossele returns empty-handed. "My condolences," he says, "your laptop had a heart attack and died."

"What?" screams Leibl. "That's ridiculous! A laptop can't have a heart attack!"

"That's strange," says Yossele. "You didn't have any problem accepting that your broom and your pot could have babies..."

꩜

The Vague *Vort*

> Avtalyon[194] said: Sages, be careful with your words lest
> you deserve to be exiled and are exiled to a place of bad
> waters; the students who come after you will drink of these
> waters and die, and God's Name will be desecrated.
>
> — *Mishna 1:11*

In this Mishna, Avtalyon uses metaphor to warn Torah scholars against the use of uncertainty or ambiguity in their words – an intergenerational concern against a vague *vort* (written or spoken) being either taken out of context – or worse, misinterpreted or misquoted beyond recognition.

The result? A distorted and desecrated version of Judaism.

In the days of the Talmud, no budding erudite scholar could give a *d'var Torah* without permission from his mentor ("It usually takes more than three weeks," noted Mark Twain, "to prepare a good impromptu speech!"), and Torah students were carefully screened to make sure they were even suitable for entrance into the *beis medrash*.

"Man's fingers," notes the Talmud, "are shaped so that he can put them in his ears when evil words reach them!"

Clear communication was thus the weapon to shield traditional Judaism, and the key to the survival of authentic Torah.

The *Sefer Hamiddos* divides conversation into four categories: completely harmful (cursing, etc.); good and bad (good intentions, bad results); useless (permitted speech, but pointless); and meritorious (spiritual and moral talk).

By linking speech to potential *chillul Hashem*, which is an act that disgraces God openly, the Mishna underlines the seriousness of words and the need to communicate in a state of modesty and humility, without fanfare or fanaticism.

A Yiddish *vort*: More than one man has been hung by his tongue! Or, as an anonymous person once said: Since light travels faster than sound, people appear bright until you hear them speak!

⁂

When a tourist once visited a little town in Maine, he was surprised to hear no one speaking. Frustrated, he stopped a passerby and asked, "Is talking illegal here?"

"No," replied the man, "but we have an understanding: no one may speak unless he's sure he can improve the silence!"

⁂

Silence Is Golden

Shimon ben Gamliel[195] said: All my life I have been raised among the Sages, and I have not found anything better for oneself than silence.

— *Mishna 1:17*

Commenting on this Mishna, Rashi concludes that the person who stays silent at least *appears* to be intelligent (as against speaking out, which may prove the opposite!); the Gerer Rebbe was influenced by Rabban Shimon: "I have found nothing better for the body than silence!"

Miyut sicha, which means "a minimum of small talk or chatter" – *miyut* is derived from the Hebrew root meaning "little" (or "limited") and *sicha* from the root of *l'socheach* (to converse) – is a theme that runs through all rabbinic texts (and non-Jewish ones too: "The most precious things in speech are the pauses," noted the famous actor, Sir Ralph Richardson).

Jewish mysticism believes that each person is given a certain quota of words in his life; when he finishes using them, his time is up! Therefore it's best to retain (words) in order to sustain (life).

Wisdom? "Known by the answer of the tongue!"

Sense? "The one who curbs the tongue shows sense!"

Thus, notes Rabbi Chiya, "It isn't necessary to tell a wise man to hold his tongue!" whilst Koheles, as usual, is direct: "There is a time to keep silent and a time to speak!"

In his Aramaic translation of the Scriptures, Onkelos, a Sage of the period of the Mishna, translates "a living being" as "a speaking being"!

Clearly, our ability to speak is one of the most basic aspects of our humanity, distinguishing *Homo sapiens* from the rest of the animal kingdom!

꙳

Two five-year-olds are playing in a sandbox. One is Jewish, the other is Catholic. The Catholic boy says to the Jewish boy, "Our priest knows more than your rabbi!"

"Of course he does," the Jewish boy replies, "you tell him everything!"

꙳

Hazardous to One's Health

> Shimon ben Rabban Gamliel said: Whoever
> talks excessively brings about sin.
> — *Mishna 1:17*

Rabban Shimon's theme in this Mishna, borrowed from Proverbs, is a central point of Judaism: excessive speech is considered a form of verbal diarrhea that is detrimental, dangerous and hazardous to one's health.

Mundane speech? Forget it! Inconsequential gossip? A waste of time and energy. Sinful speech, gossip, slander? *Forgedaboutit*!

What three men know is no secret, goes the Yiddish adage, adding that "because of gossip, if you want to know what is happening in your own home, ask your neighbors!"

Silence was a sign of greatness, speech a gift not to be overused nor abused.

"Say little," cautions a previous Mishna, "[but] do much!" to which Rav Nosson adds, "If silence is becoming for the wise, how much more so for the foolish!" Or, as Anonymous puts it, "Man has two ears and one mouth; in order to listen more and talk less!"

The chief rabbi was invited to a private dinner in Buckingham Palace. Respecting his *kashrus* sensitivities, the Queen served a cold plate of fish, brought in by the local kosher deli. During the meal, the rabbi was sitting next to an obnoxious arrogant minister who kept peppering him with lots of sarcastic questions about Judaism. The rabbi simply continued eating until finally he turned to his dinner companion and said, "You know, back in my humble home, my rebbetzin has a mounted fish in her kitchen with a motto under it: "If I had kept my mouth shut, I wouldn't be here!"

Keep It Short!

> Hillel said: Do not make a statement which cannot be understood
> on the ground that it will only later be understood.
>
> — *Mishna 2:5*

In one of his responsa, Rabbi Moshe Isserles (the Rama) reminded his colleagues that one of the "most essential" qualities for a scholar was "to write, even an ordinary letter, in clear language"; in his *Sefer Sha'ashuim*, Yosef Zabara, the thirteenth-century scholar-satirist-physician from Barcelona, defined clarity as being able "to speak without erring, and to be brief without repeating!"

"Keep it short!" was the wisdom of the time, based on the theory that long, complicated explanations simply clog the mind and thoughts of the listener ("Let your speech be short," advises ben Sira – to which Bachya, the eleventh-century Spanish moralist, adds, "Be liberal with your wealth, not with your words!").

In fact, the Rambam compiled his *Mishne Torah* in order to present Jewish law in a succinct and precise manner.

This is why he chose to write it in clear Hebrew, in the Mishnaic style of brevity, rather than in Talmudic Aramaic, which was then only familiar to scholars (the Rambam's previous works had been written in Arabic). To keep it flowing, he even refrained, at great criticism from his peers, from detailing his sources.

He even asked his colleagues to stop writing and talking in their cryptic style, concerned that their students were being left exposed to confusion and thus more likely to arrive at wrong conclusions.

For this reason, the *Tiferes Yisroel* refused to use abbreviations in his analytical writings.

This Mishna lobbies for clarity, precision, lucidity.

"When you open your mouth," warns the Talmudic Sage Judah ben Bathyra, "make sure your words are clear!"

꙳

Sarah is expecting a baby and her doctor asks her to step on the scale.
    "So, how much do you weigh?"
    "I really don't know."
    "More or less."
    "More, I guess."

꙳

A Second Chance to Make a First Impression!

> Rabbi Yose[196] said: Whoever honors the Torah will himself be honored by others; whoever disgraces the Torah is himself disgraced by others.
>
> — *Mishna 4:8*

This Mishna is a lesson on reverence.

Rabbi Yose reflects modesty through association: by "honoring" the prestige and nobility of Torah, one achieves his own "greatness" through humility.[197]

This can be done in a variety of ways, including showing respect to Jewish books and Jewish scholars ("Go near an anointed person and you will become anointed!"); the manner in which a Jew talks to, or about, another person is reflective of his own character.

"No crown carries such royalty as that of humility!" notes Eleazar ben Judah, German kabbalist; in fact Jews wear *yarmulkes* (partly) for this reason. This "goodwill-ambassador-for-Torah" philosophy fits in neatly with a Malbim theory.

Known for his focus on Torah linguistics, this Volhynia-born rabbi concluded from the structure of God's twice-repeated fashion details of the *bigdei kehuna* (priestly garments) that not only was the *kohen*'s head covering intended to atone for haughtiness (*gasus haruach*), by way of instilling in the wearer a sense of humility before God ("cover your head, in order that the fear of Heaven be upon you!"), but that the *more* humility the position required, the *larger* the *kippa*.

And so it was! The *kohen gadol*'s head covering (*mitznefet*) *was* bigger than those (*migba'at*) worn by the plain *kohanim hedyotim*.

Doesn't it seem strange that size matters? Why should God care?

He doesn't.

It's not about dimensions; it's an individual's conscious effort to maintain a higher quality of humility, which is why *madim* and *middos*, Hebrew for "clothing" and "character traits," are etymologically related.

⇒

The *cheder* rebbe, assuming that everybody in his class knows that the right answer would be "humble" or "humility," points to little Izzie and asks, "What's the most important 'H' word in the eyes of God?"

Little Izzie doesn't miss a beat: "Handsome!"

"Handsome?"

"Yeah, whenever I see Beryl eating his lunch, that huge pastrami sandwich, I say, 'Come on, handsome over!'"

⇒

It's Humbling Being Humble

> Akavia ben Mahalalel[198] said: Consider three things and you
> will not come into the grip [*liyedei*] of sin: Know whence
> you came (from a putrid drop); whither you will go (to
> a place of dust, worms and maggots); and before Whom
> you will give justification and reckoning (God).
>
> — *Mishna 3:1*

What's the purpose of the combined imagery in this Mishna?

To establish priorities: as mere mortal human beings, we are finite and corporeal; flesh is deceptive – it will return to dust one day, and leave souls, molded only by our own actions, to stand before God.

Ben Mahalalel reminds us that our beginnings are humble, that mortality is our future ("as he came forth from his mother's womb, naked shall he return," moans Koheles), and that all souls eventually face *din v'cheshbon*, a "justification and reckoning"!

The Hebrew term *liyedei* also means "stem," in that, explains the *Tiferes Yisroel*, the very acknowledgment of these three ideas prevents the increase of sin.

Choosing his words wisely, ben Mahalalel molds a future weapon in the Judaic arsenal against pride and hubris, motivating the compilers of the *siddur* to position the modest *Modeh Ani* prayer ("I acknowledge You, God, for graciously returning my soul for yet another day") as the very first prayer of the day!

The suggestion that all Jews "know from where you have come" is shorthand for a sense of humility, a sound whose modern-day English etymology (related to the Latin *humus* – not to be confused with the Arabic *hummus* for "chickpeas"!) is intriguingly close to "human."

The word derives from the Latin *humilitas* and is defined as "the quality of being *humilis* (humble)," surely one of the least subtle words: it literally means "the earth beneath us," the most basic reduction of all form – and yet, this end-of-all-living-matter is the most important substance to make soil fertile again.

In non-Jewish terms, to "be humble" is symbolic of meekness, submissiveness, lowliness – on the pitiful order of wretched and worthless.

And in Jewish terms?

꿈

"Tell me, Abie, who made you?" asks the rebbe in his *cheder* class.

"Well, God made part of me."

"Part of you? What do you mean?"

"I mean he made me little – I growed the rest myself!"

꿈

A Dish without Salt

Rabbi Meir[199] said: Be humble of spirit before every person.
— *Mishna 4:12*

Rav Sa'adia Gaon was convinced that "the main purpose of man's creation is to break his bad *middos* (character traits)" [i.e., it's humbling being humble!].

And so the Torah – after a litany of warnings not to be too proud of ourselves or our talents (in other words, as soon as you think you're humble, *you're automatically not!*) – places humility and humbleness as an indispensable prerequisite of spirituality and buttresses it with a prelude: "Before honor is humility" (just as the lead-up to destruction is pride!).

Witty support comes from the medieval pietistic work *Sefer Chassidim*, whose author dryly comments: a mitzva performed in the absence of humility is akin to "a dish without salt!" Isaac Abuab I's fourteenth-century *Menorat Hame'or*, a true bestseller, having been printed more than seventy times, raves on about this character attribute (e.g., "Wherever one finds the might of God, he also finds His humility!").

The Midrash had already placed humility in center stage: when the curtain of Torah goes up, we are startled to see a burning bush debut in a *makom hefker* (a "place with no owner"), in the midst of nowhere.

God decides to introduce Himself to Moses in a desolate open desert. Why? To make a point, eternally: that the "loftiest may be found in the lowliest!"

The unassuming modesty of it all is stunning.

"Just as the Torah was given in [the desert of] humility," muses Rabbi Elimelech of Lizhensk, "so it must be received in humility."

Next, as the foundation of all Torah, a mount of humility (Sinai) is chosen, one lacking imposing grandeur; it is totally void, reminds the third-century Joseph ben Chiya, of any "lofty views or majestic trees."

Rabbi Akiva gets the final word: "Take your seat a little below your rank, for it is better to be asked to *come up* than to be told to *go down!*"

❧

"Say, Mel, you want to hit the golf course this afternoon?"
"Sorry, I can't."
"Why not?"
"The doctor told me I can't play."
"Oh, he's been out with you, too?"

❧

You're Not Great Enough to Be Humble!

> Rabbi Levitas[200] said: Be extremely lowly of spirit, for the end of man is worms.
>
> — *Mishna 4:4*

Rabbi Levitas of Yavneh does not mince his words, laying it out unpleasantly: "Be extremely lowly of spirit" – and by using the word *extremely* (*me'od me'od*, "very, very") the Mishna wants to make sure we get the point!

Why? Because "the end of man is worms"!

Thank God for King David, a Jew so humble that he often focused on his own failings! But at least the poet-singer of Israel was able to express the same "wormy" thoughts in more poetic lyrics: "Man is like a breath, his days are like a passing shadow!"

The Mishna's reference to the lowly, silent worm is, writes the Rambam, a deterrent to illusions of grandeur in life (in fact, Rav Levitas's warning had already been given earlier, in Koheles: "Humble altogether thy pride, for man's expectation is worms!").

And yet our Sages were mortified at phony displays of self-esteem and counterfeit humbleness ("don't pretend to be humble, you're not that great!"), and responded to any unacceptable *excess* of humility not as noble, but as an ignoble and derogatory characteristic.[201]

The Ba'al Shem Tov advised that in the pursuit of humility, which should *always* be tempered with joy, the Jew should never think *so little of himself* that he neglects to *think of himself at all*.

Try it this way: humility is not thinking *less* of yourself but thinking of *yourself* less!

❧

The top student in his yeshiva is sitting in the *rosh yeshiva*'s office seeking *smicha*.

"I know the important qualities necessary to be a community *rav*," the boy says. "I should behave humbly, act modestly, learn and teach Torah. Is there anything else I need to know?"

"Yes," replies the elderly *rosh*, "you will need to develop a high degree of imagination."

"What? I don't understand..."

"Because you'll always have to imagine that someone even cares!"

❧

Don't Be Shy!

> Hillel said: A bashful person cannot learn,
> nor can an impatient one teach.
> — *Mishna 2:6*

Many great leaders have had to juggle their successful accomplishments with a dose of humbleness. Sir Winston Churchill, whose courage saved Jews from Hitler's crematoria, mumbled, "I was not the lion, but it fell to me to give the lion's roar!"

This Mishna precludes a shy or impatient person from learning or teaching Torah.

Aren't shyness and humility the same? No. Shyness, reminds Rabbi Yonah, is counterproductive to learning because, according to Rav, it cripples the critical questioning component.

Spiritual growth requires a level of aggressiveness. And patience? Ibn Gabriol credited patience with turning misfortune to fortune, whilst the major theme running through the Mishna is the elevation of humility.

Thus Jews were taught to be as humble as Hillel, and not impatient like Shammai.

Rabbi Avraham of Strettin, commenting on the Talmudic adage "A *talmid chacham* should have only an eighth of a measure of pride," notes that it is the eighth verse of the eighth Torah portion (*Vayishlach*) which reveals the humility of Jacob who, despite a life of woe, manages to found a family and become wealthy.

At least Rabbi Chiya ben Ashi, in the name of Rav, had some *rachmanus* (compassion), allowing even a "disciple of a Sage [at least] an eighth [of pride]!" He had a point: there is a rabbinic adage that whatever the Torah forbids, it allows "a permissible equivalent."

☙

"You have such a cute baby," says the pediatrician to Mr. and Mrs. Katz on their first visit since the baby's birth.

"Oh, I'm sure you say that to all the parents," replies Mrs. Katz.

"Actually, no."

"Well," asks Mr. Katz, "what do you say to all the other parents?"

"That the baby looks just like them!"

☙

Respect All, Suspect All!

> Rabbi Eleazar ben Shammua[202] said: The honor of your student should be as dear to you as your own; the honor of your colleague should be as the fear of your Torah teacher; and the fear of your teacher should be as the fear of Heaven.
>
> — *Mishna 4:15*

Note how this Mishna restricts its advice to *your* student, *your* colleague, *your* teacher. Does that mean you don't have to honor or fear someone else's teacher or student or colleague?

Yes, and no.

Obviously one must treat others with the respect they're due; however, there is a higher burden on relationships and conduct towards your own (after all, your student is *your* student!).

The Mishna's Eliezer ben Hyrkanos taught his followers to "cherish your colleague's honor as your own" because, as Eliezer ben Isaac puts it, "Many pearls can be found in a poor man's tunic!" Indeed, the Talmud calls Jews who rise for the *Sefer Torah* but not for a great man "foolish."

Yehoshua ben Levi was much more skeptical: "Respect all, suspect all!" (a slogan adopted by the Romans: *timeo Danaos et dona ferentes*!).

One must honor a student even when he fails to honor you. Commenting on the Talmudic verse that says when a student gets angry, "it's the Torah that heats him up," Rashi is sympathetic to the student who, in his impatience, can get carried away.

Why is the honor of your student "your own"?

Rashi merges the student's accomplishments with his teacher's, and derives how a colleague should honor other colleague-teachers from the way Moses addresses Joshua ("Let *us* choose…") and Aaron addresses Moses, his younger sibling ("my master").

❧

Young Yitzi gets lost at the mall. He runs over to a policeman, crying, "I've lost my dad!"

"Don't worry, son, I'll take care of you like you're my own," the cop says. "So tell me, what's your father like?"

"Baseball and beer!"

❧

Out of This World?

> Rabbi Eleazar Hakappar said: Jealousy, lust and
> glory remove a man from the world.
> — *Mishna 4:28*

This Mishna lists three forms of selfishness so dangerous and pernicious that they are self-destructive – i.e., "drive a man out of the world"!

Is this a physical death? No, but it's a warning that these emotionally debilitating activities are so anti-social that they remove the Jew from his community, separate him from the *klal* (collective), and strain the harmony of his fellowmen.[203]

In the realm of *bein adam l'chaveiro* (between man and his fellow, i.e., human relationships), Rashi breaks these three cancerous traits into envy (jealousy among friends), lust (for money or immorality) and honor (seeking positions of authority); in contrast, Jewish mystics see the effects of these traits in the realm of *bein adam la'Makom* (between man and God, i.e., one's relationship with the Almighty) and link them to the disgrace and exile from Eden: envy (which the angels displayed for Adam), lust (Adam and Eve for the forbidden fruit) and desire (the honor given to Adam, the first man).

Any one or combination of these three, argues the Rambam, weakens one's *emuna* (faith – literally, "trust") system and prevents him from developing *seichel* (understanding); "God wants the heart!" The *Ben Ish Chai* felt pity for those who suffered from all three potent maladies because they made life unbearable and a constant source of personal strife, stress and strain; meanwhile the *rosh yeshiva* of Volozhin said the three purposefully appear in a chronological order: envy shows up in an infant, lust in teenagers, honor only later in life, in adulthood.

Is there an acceptable form of envy? Yes: the "jealousy among scholars." Why? Because it "increases wisdom"! And more! After God asks that we "Be jealous, for My sake!" the Midrash adds, "If not for envy, the world would not stand, a man would not plant a vineyard, marry a woman or build a house!"

The Vilna Gaon compared lust to drinking salty water; the more you drink, the thirstier you get – and the Talmud warns: "Starve it and it is satisfied; satisfy it and it is starved!"

꩜

Izzy is on another of his weight reduction diets and goes to see his doctor with a cucumber up his nose, a bagel shoved in his right ear, and a wine glass sticking out of his left ear.

"Doctor," says Izzy, "I'm not feeling very well."

"I'm not surprised," replies the doc, "you're not eating right!"

꩜

PEACE AND PRAYER
AND MIRACLES

Don't pray when it rains if you
don't pray when the sun shines!

— *Satchel Paige*

Peace and Prayer and Miracles

Prayer requires modesty, awe, and a sense of gratitude for the opportunity itself, whether spontaneous or at fixed times. In Yiddish it's called *davenen*, from the French *devant* (before), as in "Know before Whom you stand!" The same Latin root from which *devant* stems gives us the English word "divine."

The *Chofetz Chaim* had a unique attitude to prayer, reminding Jews: "Do not ask God for what *you* think is good, ask Him for what *He* thinks is good for you!"

There is a tradition in Jerusalem: if you go to the Western Wall on forty *consecutive* days and pray for one specific thing, it will be granted. And, although Hebrew is preferential, all individual prayers and most communal prayers can be said in any language that the person praying understands.

꩜

Mendel is trying to find a parking spot in Borough Park and is getting more and more frustrated as he drives around the block. In desperation, he turns to Heaven and pleads, "Please God, I'm running late! Please help me! If you find me a parking spot I promise that I'll stop speaking *loshen hora*, I'll learn more Torah, I'll be good to my family, I'll donate more to the yeshiva!"

Suddenly, miraculously, a great parking spot opens up right in front of him. He turns to God, "Never mind, I just found one!"

꩜

The challenge is this: how do we keep up the familiar repetition of daily prayer while retaining a sense of fresh intensity? This very question is reflected in the Hebrew verb *l'hitpalel* (to pray), wherein *l'* simply means "to," but the syllable *hit* connotes rigorous interaction (as in *l'hitametz*, "to exert oneself"). *L'hitpalel* also comes from the root *palel*, which means "to inspect," a reflexive act of personal introspection. Prayer is thus extremely personal, but it requires faith that "Someone" is eavesdropping.

This faith is empty without inspiration, a state of mind that in Hebrew is known as *kavana*, a recipe that stirs focus with intensity in order to "direct the heart" effectively. Jewish history credits Hannah, the prophet Shmuel's mother, for developing this concept of pure prayer ("Hannah, she was speaking in her heart, only her lips were moving and her voice was not heard!").[204]

Rabbi Chiya saw no reason to pray loudly as long as "you direct your heart to Heaven." Rabbi Meir added: keep it short!

Why the heart? Because of the Torah command for prayer, "You shall serve God with your whole heart" (this is why *tefilla* is called *avoda sheba'lev*, "service from in the heart").[205]

In other words, it's possible to go through the motion of prayer without praying. Does this invalidate the prayer? Yes and no. Certain parts of the *siddur* (e.g., the first line of the *Sh'ma*, the first blessing in *Shemoneh Esrei*) are null-and-void *a posteriori* if the person praying lacked the proper awareness.

Ironically, *kavana* is more likely to be present with more spontaneous, improvised prayer, as existed before the Babylonian exile when Jews composed their own prayers, a time when God was found at home as readily as in the synagogue. In fact, one of the most important prayers, *Birkas Hamazon* (the blessing after meals), commanded by the Torah itself, is hardly ever said in *shul*!

"It is easy to stand in prayer at a certain time each day," admits the fifteenth-century Rav Yitzchak Arama, "but if you do not concentrate in your heart, how is your prayer different from the mindless chirping of birds?"[206]

Prayer finds its way to the gates, but only effort turns the key.

꒰

The rabbi goes to visit Shmuli, who is dying, in the hospital. As he walks up to Shmuli's bed, the latter begins to flail about, waving his arms as if trying to speak. The rabbi leans over and quietly asks, "Do you have some last words of prayer to say?"

Shmuli nods yes, and so the rabbi takes out a pen and paper and hands it to him, saying, "Here, write it down and I'll make sure to give it to your family and pass it on to God."

Shmuli scrawls a message and stuffs it in the rabbi's hand. A few seconds later he passes away. The rabbi takes the note outside and hands it to the tearful widow, who opens it and reads, "GET OFF MY OXYGEN HOSE!!"

꒰

A Piece of Peace

Rabbi Eleazar said: *Talmidei chachamim* increase peace in the world....
Great shall be the peace of your children when taught of God.

— *Brachos 64a*

The Mishna imposes a constant 24/7 duty to love, pursue, seek, impose and strive for peace with vigor at all times, a character trait (for those few fortunate enough to possess it) that reveals unbelievable resilience, courage, forgiveness, tolerance and understanding.

But wait! How do we know this? Because, explains the patient Midrash, this is basically the only mitzva that is *not* rushing to *your* doorstep!

The question is obvious: if the *talmidei chachamim* are "arguing" on every page of the Talmud, in what sense does Rabbi Eleazar see them as being "*rav shalom,*" promoting peace?

First, their intent is pure (for the sake of Heaven), but more important is the fact, as articulated by the famed Rav Abraham Isaac Kook, that peace does not mean uniformity in opinion, but respect and tolerance of dispute.

If humility and arrogance are opposites on the *Pirkei Avos* scale of ethics, then, according to the Mishna's Hillel, one trait hovers above them both: the surreal, profound, untouchable, optimal pursuit of *shalom,* "peace," the most relentless goal of the Jewish people in its relations with others.

And the mystical Rav Kook dug further: peace does not come "whole, fully formed," but like light, descending upon us in many different hues, an "increasing, incremental peace," each appropriate to its own time, place and person.

OK. I want to start making *shalom.* Where do I begin?

The answer comes to us courtesy of Rabbi Shimon ben Eleazar: "If a man sits in his place and keeps silent, how can he pursue peace in Israel between one person and another? But let him leave his place and roam about in the world and pursue peace in Israel. *Seek* peace in your *own* dwelling place and *pursue* it in another place!"

~

When her husband and sons come home from *shul* on Shabbas, the lady of the house asks one of her young boys about the rabbi's *drasha*: "Nu, vos hot er geret? [What did he speak about?]"

"He spoke about *sholem.*"

"That's nice! What did he say about it?"

"He was for it!"

~

The Peace of the Purse!

Hillel said: The more charity,[207] the more peace.
— *Mishna 2:8*

The *Sefer Ma'alos Hamiddos* warns the wicked that there is one blessing they will never know: peace!

Hillel emphasizes this point: true peace of mind only comes to those who are compassionate to others, whose empathy drowns their pride; this outlook helped the Maharal link the Hebrew root of *shalom* (peace) to *shalem*, which means complete and perfect.

Peace, declares Isaiah, "is equal to everything," and God's ultimate comfort to the Jews of Jerusalem is that they may "dwell in a habitation of peace."

The microcosmic nature of peace within eschatological Torah thought is reflected in the description of the righteous in heaven who, accompanied by an angel, are told to "enter into peace."

Meanwhile, *Midrash Shmuel* defines charity as being the peacemaker between God and the poor.

The heaviest burden, goes an old Yiddish proverb, is an empty pocket (in modern-day slang: if your outgo is greater than your income, then your upkeep will be your downfall!).

Giving charity has been built into every Jewish community since the Biblical times of an agrarian Jewish society.

A sign over a community soup kitchen in my mother's little Polish shtetl read: "When you feed strangers, you occasionally feed angels."

In Latin, the term "charity" is derived from *caritas*, whose etymology means love and endearment. In Hebrew it encompasses compassion, good deeds and social justice – acts that fall within the general theme of righteousness. When Rabelais, the French satirist, died, his entire will read: "I owe much. I possess nothing. I give the rest to the poor," an attitude not reflective of a Torah that advises: don't give till it hurts, give until it feels good! And, as they say: If you think charity is a waste of time, don't waste your time on prayers!

❧

The tall and thin Chassidic rebbe is riding in his horse and buggy with his young son when they bump into the local minister.

"Say, Rabbi," asks the Reverend, "how come you're so thin and gaunt while your horse is so fat and sleek?"

The boy replies, "It's because my father feeds the horse and the congregation feeds my father!"

❧

Stop Praying, Already!

Rabbi Shimon[208] said: Be careful with the recitation of the *Sh'ma* and the prayers.
— *Mishna 2:18*

Why does this Mishna separately specify saying the *Sh'ma* and reciting prayers, as if they were two distinct obligations?

Because the *Sh'ma* is not a prayer *per se* but is in itself a solemn "stand-alone" duty, to be performed at the right time and right place; prayer on the other hand, was to be a "free utterance of the heart," inspirational, self-motivated, reflecting what each individual knew had to be expressed at any moment, any time, any place, and not regulated by perfunctory lip service ("When you pray," said Bunyan, "better that your heart be without words than your words without heart!")

Prayer is inherently internal – it is not the actual words of prayers but the thoughts and sincerity behind them that are being articulated; whereas the *Sh'ma* is the first prayer taught to a Jewish child (upon arising in the morning and going to sleep at night), and the last words recited prior to death.

Thus, the Torah enlarges the *ayin* and *daled* of the first verse in order to spell out *eid* ("witness"), in that by declaring the *Sh'ma*, comprised of three sections of the Torah ("Hear, O Israel," "If you listen to my Commandments" and "They shall make fringes"), Jews are testifying to the Oneness of God.

By separating it from regular prayer, Rabbi Shimon acknowledges that the *Krias Sh'ma* is the primary Judaic desire and plea, Israel's ultimate unambiguous declaration of allegiance and manifestation of faith, because of its opening verse, "Hear O Israel…the Lord is One" – which is why it can be said in any language!

※

The rebbetzin was in labor for hours and the end was not in sight, so her husband quickly put together a *minyan* and starting saying *tehillim*.

Thirty minutes later the rebbetzin gave birth to a baby, and, a few minutes later, to a second one. When the nurse told her that another baby was on its way, she quickly called her husband and screamed, "Rabbi, rabbi! For God's sake, stop *davening*! Stop *davening*!"

※

Somewhere from Ten to Two Hundred Fifty

> Ten miracles were performed in Egypt, ten at the sea, ten plagues in Egypt and ten at the sea.
>
> — *Mishna 5:5*

This Mishna breaks the number of miracles surrounding the Exodus into four sets of ten; we're familiar with the ten plagues, but what are the others?

I don't know; the Mishna is not explicit (but in the *Song by the Sea*, the Jews mention God's Name ten times in recognition of ten miracles).[209]

This means we have to turn to the Midrash, which doesn't list any other sets of "nine," but gives us a peek into such other miracles as the seabed drying and hardening to give the Jews safe passage, the waters themselves dividing into twelve pathways for twelve tribes, the sea wall suddenly losing its salty flavor and providing the Jews with fresh drinking water, a pillar of fire heating up the seabed, the wheels of Egyptian chariots falling off, the "shaking" of enemy troops in the water, and so forth.

But wait! Doesn't this contradict the Haggada itself? At the *seder tisch* aren't we reminded that there were fifty miracles at the sea, or two hundred, or even two hundred fifty?!

The Rambam, always seeking clarity, tries to bridge the two positions by breaking down all the miracles into ten different categories.

But whether it's ten or forty or two hundred fifty, from the sheer number of miracles surrounding the Exodus, we can understand why Nissan is nicknamed the "Month of Great Miracles"!

Belief in miracles is so axiomatic in Judaism that to deny them is heresy. "A miracle does not prove what is impossible," writes the Rambam in his commentary on the Mishna, "it is an affirmation of what is possible!" Nevertheless, in order not to let the Jew get carried away, we are reminded by the Talmud that "one must not rely on miracles alone."

Chaim finally gets a new pair of glasses. "I can see! I can see! It's a miracle," he tells the receptionist on the way out of the optometrist's office. "But wait, all I see are spots in front of my eyes!"

"Oh, my," she says, "have you ever seen a doctor?"

"No, just spots!"

RABBIS

A rabbi whom they don't want to drive out
of town isn't a rabbi, and a rabbi whom
they actually drive out of town isn't a man!

— *Israel Salanter*

Rabbis

When *Pirkei Avos* traces the legacy of Torah down the generations – "Moses to Joshua to the elders to the prophets to the Men of the Great Assembly" – the term *rabbi*, derived from *rav*, which means "distinguished (in knowledge)," is conspicuously absent.

Those who ran the governments of Israel-Judah were kings, prophets, the Sanhedrin, the priesthood. None were rabbis; although the members of the Sanhedrin all had *smicha*, they were addressed as judges (*dayanim*).

The title "rabbi" is nowhere to be found in the Torah.

It makes its first appearance in the Mishna, with the first Jew given this appellation being Rabban Gamliel the Elder.[210] Neither his father (Shimon) nor grandfather (Hillel the Elder) had the rabbinic prefix.[211]

But isn't Moses affectionately known as *Moshe Rabbeinu*, "Moses *our teacher*"?

Yes, but only after the fact. Never during his time was Moses called Rabbi Moses, in contrast to the second-century Akiva who was greeted as "Rabbi Akiva."

Even the commonly used term "rabbis of the Talmud" is incorrect. During the Talmudic era it was the *rabbanan* who led the community. In contrast to *rabbis*, which means "teachers," *rabbanan* means "scholars."

Rabbis taught; rabbanan led.[212]

In those days they were farmers, craftsmen, artisans, merchants, *ba'alei batim* (heads of families) endowed with *chachmei hamesorah*, "the wisdom of the tradition," despite the fact that they worked a third of the day, and studied two thirds (the farmer scholars worked all summer and studied Torah all winter).

The concept of *smicha*, a rabbinic degree granted by another rabbi, which allows the recipient to become a paid rabbi, was foreign in those days.

Writing in the twelfth century, the Rambam strongly opposed the idea of paying rabbis for rabbinic functions. In his day, they had jobs or businesses or were supported by their working wives.

Those wives are the unrecognized heroines of the rabbinic world, the "rebbetzins."

Rabbi Meir's wife, Beruria, was an expert in Jewish law; so was the rebbetzin of Eleazar of Worms, who was active in the community and publicly taught Torah to women every Shabbas afternoon. Rebbetzin Pearl Loew, wife of the Maharal of Prague, was an accomplished Talmudist.

In the late 1930s, Reb Chaim Shmuel Horowitz-Sternfeld's widow, Rebbetzin Sarale, continued to act as "Rebbe," and her daughter, rebbetzin to Reb Elimelech of Grodzisk, gave out *brachos* to her Chassidim.

꧁

The rebbetzin phones her husband in *the beis medrash*; "Reb Dovid, do you have time to talk?"

"Sorry, not now, dear, I'm in the middle of giving a *shiur*."

"This won't take long, I just want to tell you some good news and some bad news."

"I really don't have the time," the rabbi replies, "but quickly, just tell me the good news."

"OK. The air bag on your new Lexus works very well!"

꧁

Friendly Rabbis or Rabbinical Friends?

> Yehoshua ben Perachia[213] said: Make for yourself a rabbi [asei l'cha rav], acquire for yourself a friend, and judge every person favorably.
>
> — Mishna 1:6

"Make" a rabbi? "Acquire" a friend?

Doesn't this smack of buying friendship, importing rabbinic acceptability? No. These terms are terms of endearment, not corruption, meant to urge interpersonal relationships with genuine role models.

In this context, "to acquire" is not a transactional acquisition but a means "to invest in," in that lasting friendships require investments of time and effort, mutual respect and love.

Rabbi Avrohom Galanti has a unique explanation for the expression asei l'cha rav (make for/to yourself a rabbi); he wants you to have a rabbi to broaden your Torah knowledge, so that *you* can "make *yourself*" into a rabbi, and then do the same for someone else!

Meiri says the phrase "make a rabbi" applies to situations where there's no one in the community qualified to be a *rav*, thus he must be "made" (i.e., choose someone, invest money in him, and have him study how to be a competent *rav*). Why? Because "from books," notes Rabbi Chaim Soloveitchik, "one learns what *to* say; from a rebbe one learns what *not to* say!"

This Mishna considers associations with friends and rabbis crucial for moral, intellectual and spiritual growth, and recognizes a good catch: if you are lucky enough to find a humble, learned rabbi you should "cleave to the dust of his feet!"

In your search for rabbis and friends, the latter are more important. How do we know?

The Mishna uses a stronger word (k'nei, "to buy") for friends than it does for a rabbi (asei, "to make"). Why? Simple! It's harder to find a good friend than a good rabbi![214]

ꤜ

Little Abie fell asleep during the *rav*'s Shabbas *drasha*. When he woke up, he tugged at his father's sleeve, "Tatte, has the rabbi finished?"

"Yes, he's finished – but he hasn't stopped yet!"

ꤜ

Less Is More

> Rabban Gamliel[215] said: Make for yourself a
> rabbi, remove yourself from doubt.
>
> *— Mishna 1:16*

The first statement of Rabban Gamliel is deliberate: the Jew should choose only one, single rabbi mentor, not for Torah study (which can, and should, come from as many different teachers as possible), but for halachic decisions.

This Mishna's advice is to submit to one rabbi, like a family doctor; instead, today many Jews "shop around" for (usually lenient) rabbinic opinions. The Midrash adds: make sure he's both intellectually and ethically greater than you, so you'll feel comfortable following his rulings.

Rabbi Israel Lipschitz, author of a highly popular nineteenth-century Mishna commentary (*Tiferes Yisroel*), extends the obligation from personal to communal – i.e., once you have your own "personal rabbi," you must ensure that the community has a *rav* as well!

In those days a "rabbi" was chosen for different reasons – not because he was a good orator, but simply to teach Torah to the people, decide matters of Jewish law, and ensure that the community "behaves itself."

The Mishna purposefully uses the expression "remove *yourself* from doubt," a plea that one pursue and perform one's religious practices in a uniform and consistent manner.

Meanwhile, the Chassidic Rebbe Naphtali Zevi of Ropczyce, Galicia (the Ropshitzer), came to his position through Yiddish logic: "At first I did not want to be a rabbi, for a rabbi has to flatter his flock, and I thought of being a tailor. Then I saw that a tailor has to flatter his customers, and so does a shoemaker, and a bath attendant; and so I said to myself, 'Where, then, is a rabbi worse off?' And I became a rabbi!"[216]

꡸

The rabbi is going on and on in his *Shabbas Hagadol drasha* and becomes more and more annoyed at the restless audience, and the obvious lack of interest in his words. Finally, he explodes, "I don't mind you looking at your watches from time to time, but when you hold them to your ears and shake them to see if they're still working – well, that's going too far!"

꡸

Someone's Knocking on the Door!

> Yose ben Yoezer said: Let your house be a meeting place for the Sages, cleave to the dust of their feet,[217] and drink their words thirstily.
>
> — *Mishna 1:4*

The message of this Mishna is that there is no difference between serving God in or outside the home – i.e., one cannot be a Jew on the outside alone; on the day of judgment, warn the rabbis of the Talmud, even the beams of one's own house testify to one's true behavior in private!

Rabbi Yonah related to this Mishna as a call for more social interaction between lay people and rabbis, to help overcome major psychological barriers by the ordinary Jew who may have thought it was OK to go to a *shiur* in a *shul* or a sacred *beis medrash*, but in the home?...in a domestic setting?

So roll out the welcome mat and invite learned men into the family home, get to know them up close, use them as role models, be of service to them: "It is more important to be in the service of scholars than to study from them!"

By bringing "wisdom" into the house, Yose and Yose (ben Yoezer, ben Yochanan) are hoping to transform the Jewish home into a private Judaic Center for Wisdom (an analogy is provided by Rav: mixing with scholars is like entering a perfumery; one cannot help but absorb the sweet scents!).

꩜

The rabbi is horrified to see a Chinese delivery man drop off some food at the house of one of his congregants. He peeks through the window and is appalled to see a maid set up the *treif* food on the dining room table, and his congregant sitting down to eat shrimp, crabs and lobster.

The angry rabbi bursts into the house, shouting, "Yankele, *vas tist du*? [What are you doing?] You can't eat that!"

"Rabbi, did you actually see the food arrive in the house?"

"Yes, yes!"

"And did you watch closely as the maid opened the packages, prepared and served the food?"

"Yes, yes!"

"Well, then, there's nothing to worry about. The entire meal was done under strict rabbinical supervision!"

꩜

Fire in the Belly!

Rabbi Eliezer said: Be wary with the Sages' coals that you not get burnt,
for their bite is the bite of a fox, their sting is the sting of a scorpion,
their hiss is the hiss of a serpent, and all their words are like fiery coals.

— Mishna 2:15

Fire, metaphorically, is an integral component of Temple worship ("The fire on the altar shall not go out"), and many an aspiring rabbi-preacher has been told, "If you can't put fire in your sermon, put your sermon in the fire!"

Ben Sira was blunt: "According to its fuel, so will the fire be."

Shmuel Uceda, Safed-born sixteenth-century talmudist and kabbalist, writing in his *Midrash Shmuel*, was even blunter: "If you need a flame, fan it!"

This is what Chassidus calls *hislahavus* (fiery enthusiasm), the carrying out of a religious activity not as routine but with a fire in the belly – with zeal and enthusiasm, energy and excitement.

Rabbi Eliezer uses strange animalistic symbolism (they can "bite like a fox, sting like a scorpion, hiss like a serpent") when talking about his pious-kind-wise-compassionate colleagues. What gives?! Was Eliezer absent that day in *cheder* when they taught that "one who has studied Torah, see how beautiful are his ways"?[218]

The Rambam responds to this Mishna with pure pragmatism: don't get too close to your rabbi (in other words: keep a respectful distance of veneration); meanwhile, the Ramban and Rabbi Yonah, aware that (over)familiarity can breed contempt, are concerned that this "closeness" could lead to the sin of irreverence and condescension towards Torah scholars.

Jewish mystics grasp this in familiar terms; as with fire and flames, warm yourself from *aish Torah* – but only from a safe distance. Why? Because fire (like the *tzadik*) is something you can see and feel, but, to avoid getting spiritually scorched, you should not grab or touch!

⇜

The rabbi of Chelm and his student spend a night at an inn. The student asks the servant to awaken him at dawn so he can catch an early morning train. The next morning, after being awakened, the student, looking for his hat, gropes about in the darkness and accidentally seizes the rabbi's hat and places it on his own head. Once inside the train, the student glances into the mirror. Seeing the rabbi's hat upon his head, the student becomes furious. "I asked him to wake me, but instead he went and woke the rabbi," he shouts at the mirror.

⇜

Who Knows Five?

[Rabban Yochanan ben Zakkai] used to enumerate their praiseworthy qualities: Eliezer ben Hyrkanos,[219] a cemented cistern which does not lose a drop; Yehoshua ben Chanania, happy is she who bore him; Yose the Priest, a Chassid; Shimon ben Nesanel, sin-fearing; Eleazar ben Arach, like a spring which flows with ever-increasing strength.

— *Mishna 2:11*

This Mishna recognizes and celebrates diversity in ben Zakkai's five central disciples, his spiritual heirs, singling out a unique quality in each that "surpasses" all others.

This concept, which shuns universal conformity, places ben Hyrkanos and ben Arach on a pedestal of excellence to which all should aspire; and yet even they had different approaches to Torah study.

Rabbi Eliezer was the epitome of concentration and retention; Rabbi Eleazar constantly sought the independence of new frontiers of wisdom; thus the former preserved the teachings of the past, whilst the latter was concerned with the future.

Both were masters: Eliezer was known for his breadth of knowledge; Eleazar was unmatched in sharpness and creativity and had a unique probing, questioning mind. Which one is "better, superior"? Neither: there's a need for both, complementing each other, playing off each other, inspiring one another to even greater goals.

And then there is the ultimate tribute ("fortunate is she who bore him!") showered on Rabbi Yehoshua – that he gave his mother much *Yiddishe nachas*!

Yehoshua's mother was one of the most resolute, intense and devoted *Yiddishe mamas* in rabbinic texts; so determined was she to ensure her boy grow up in fidelity to a Torah life that she would place his crib near the *beis medrash*, so he would hear nothing but words of Torah in his infancy!

꒓

"Help, help!" Feigie frantically calls Hatzolah. "My two-year-old just swallowed a tiny magnet. What should I do?"

"Don't worry about it! He'll be fine!"

"Are you positive? How will I know for sure?"

"Well, just stick him to the refrigerator, and when he falls off, you'll know!"

꒓

Clothes Make the Man

> Rabbi Chiya bar Abba said (to Rabbi Assi): Why are the *talmidei chachamim* in Babylonia dressed up? Because they are not *b'nei Torah*.
>
> — *Mishna*

This Mishna is not a fashion statement but a statement on fashion: rabbinic wardrobes alone do not automatically translate into great rabbinic leaders!

Rabbi Chiya was obviously upset at some of his colleagues in Bavel who "dressed up" as scholars but who, despite their proper rabbinic attire, were professionally inadequate to wear the uniform of God (even goats, goes the Yiddish proverb, can grow beards!).

The *Tiferes Yisroel* was a bit kinder: he interprets "they" not as referring to the scholars of Bavel but to the community at large, accusing them of not recognizing nor appreciating the dignified *b'nei Torah* in their midst, thus *forcing* the true *talmidei chachamim* to don rabbinic robes to be more identifiable (similarly, today, we recognize a doctor by the coat he wears).

An obvious question: what difference does fashion make to God?

All psychologists agree: clothes not only make the man but also have a great impact on all those who come into contact with him.

"If you're dressed up on the outside," goes the old adage, "then you're dressed up on the inside" – a slogan that the Jewish mystics use spiritually, as a strengthening of inner convictions.

All religious ritual, notes Bachya ben Asher, must be conducted in a respectful, decorous manner – this includes outward presentation, which is why Jews change from weekday clothes into more festive ones on *erev Shabbas*, and why garments must be new or cleaned before each Jewish holiday. "It is unseemly," explains a patient Rashi, "to wear the same clothing in the kitchen as when pouring wine for a master!"

The *beis din* of Chelm imposes the death penalty on the local cobbler after he's been found guilty of murder.

"But," shouts out a dissenter, "he's our only cobbler. If we hang him, who will fix our shoes?"

The *rosh beis din* thinks for a few minutes, strokes his beard, and finally announces, "I got it! Here's the solution! True, we have only one cobbler, but we have two tailors. We'll hang one of them instead!"

Taking Credit? Think Again!

Rabban Yochanan ben Zakkai[220] said: If you have studied much Torah
do not take credit for yourself because you were created for this.

— *Mishna 2:9*

This is a warning in favor of humility and against too much boastful self-righteousness; the Jew *must* learn "much" Torah anyway, because that is his *raison d'être* in this world, and thus he cannot take too much credit for doing what he's supposed to be doing, *in any event*!

What is meant by "*much* Torah"?

Since Torah is in essence unlimited, the Jew must always extend himself further, upwards and onwards, to greater achievements. The Gerer Rebbe puts a lot of weight on the word "much," seeing "excess" in Torah learning as the path to modesty and the subjugation of a feeling of superiority: i.e., the more you know, the more humble you become.

This is the austere line of reasoning behind the Mishna's Antigonus of Socho: you're blamed if you don't (learn Torah) but get no credit if you do what's expected of you (in order to avoid the label of "arrogance"!).

At the age of eleven, Rav Moshe Feinstein had already learned all of *Nashim* and *Nezikin* (about thirteen hundred pages of Talmud). One day he walked into his father's study where his uncle stood up, saying, "For a boy who knows two *sedarim* one must stand up."

Rav Moshe's father immediately asked his son to leave the room and turned to his brother: "What are you doing? Are you trying to kill my boy? You'll turn him into a *ba'al ga'avah* (arrogant person)!"[221]

✺

Rabbonim need to have humility – and wit! One day a skeptic approached a rabbi and chastised him for still believing in the Torah: "Any sane person can see that the Bible contains impossible stuff!"

"Like what?" asks the humble *rav*.

"Well, for example, the tale of Bilam's donkey. How could a dumb animal speak?"

"That's easy, just think of it logically. If hundreds of human beings talk like asses, then it's perfectly possible for at least one donkey to talk like a human being!"

✺

REWARD AND PUNISHMENT

If we had no winter, the spring
would not be so pleasant!

— *Anne Bradstreet*

Reward and Punishment

A principle of Jewish faith is the spiritual cause-and-effect chain of events, coupled with the Mishnaic observation, "With the measuring stick that a person measures he is measured himself!"[222]

However, there is no denying it: the comfortable life enjoyed by some of the wicked and the suffering endured by some of the righteous present a tough theological issue.

The only way to approach issues of reward and punishment is to admit that no one knows God's master plan.

In *Pirkei Avos*, mankind's morality manual, Hillel, the greatest scholar of his generation, warns after watching a skull float down the river that violence begets violence. But he then accepts his own limitations in understanding Divine acts of retribution and admits his noncomprehension of the injustices around him.

The Maggid of Mezritch, in his explanation of the verse "Know what is above you," links the spiritual realms to conduct on earth.

The Lubavitcher Rebbe continued this theme and constantly reminded his Chassidim not to underestimate the holy in the mundane; all deeds must be "for the sake of Heaven."

The fact is that, with the exception of certain deeds rewarded by long life (honoring parents, saving a mother bird, using fair weights and measures),[223] no one knows which *specific* sin or good deed causes *specific* consequences – thus, "Be as careful with a 'minor' mitzva as with a 'major' one!"

Remember: today, we no longer have prophets. In God's world, good is not necessarily a reward, and evil is not always punishment. Human conclusions are just risky guesses.

But isn't "If you turn away [from Torah] God will close the Heavens and there will be no rain!"[224] specific? Yes, but the lack of rain in the twenty-first century of the Western world is not exactly going to drive Jews closer to God.

In its metaphoric sense, this threat ties the spiritual laws of nature to the physical acts of mankind. The lesson?

Lithuanian Rabbi Chaim Volozhiner, author of *Nefesh Hachaim*, reminds us: Mother Nature doesn't discriminate.

The Midrash also makes a startling observation: "Once the 'destroyer' is given permission to destroy, he does not distinguish between righteous and wicked!"[225]

This is why, in the context of reward and punishment, the Torah nearly always speaks in national, collective terms.

❧

Arguing over reward and punishment, Boruch lashes into his *chavrusa* (study partner): "You know, Lenny, I wish you were Saint Lenny, already!"

"Really, why?"

"Because then you would hold the keys to heaven, and let me in!"

"Boruch, Boruch...wouldn't it be better for you if I had the keys to the, you know, that *other* place – then I could let you out!"

❧

Fitting the Crime

> If some people tithe and some do not, a famine caused by
> partial drought will come; if people have determined not
> to tithe, a famine resulting from both unrest and drought
> will come; if people have determined not to separate challa
> from dough, a fully destructive famine will come.
>
> — *Mishna 5:10*

This Mishna introduces the precision of God's justice in that each punishment fits the crime; or as the Talmud puts it: a man who makes arrows is often slain by one of them!

Thus, in this "measure-for-measure" exercise, in a religion where "warning must precede punishment," failure on the part of a Jew to donate produce or put aside the "challa" portion for the nonworking priests leads to famine and drought for all.

The message is this: since prosperity is a gift from God, Jews must learn to share with others less fortunate; *kol Yisroel areivim zeh la'zeh* (all Israel is responsible one for the other). If we do not act with this collectivity in mind, God will enforce it with collective punishment.

꒝

A Jewish couple, married sixty years, tragically die in a car crash and find themselves in *Olam Haba*. On entry, they are taken to an enormous mansion with a beautiful kitchen and a huge marble master bathroom suite with a jacuzzi. As they "ooh and aah" they ask, "How much is all this going to cost?"

"It's free, you're in heaven!"

The husband sees a beautiful championship golf course. "Wow," he asks, "what are the green fees?"

"This is heaven, you play for free!"

In the club house they discover an extensive glatt kosher buffet lunch, featuring the cuisines of the world.

"Wow, how much must we pay to eat?"

"Hey, this is heaven, it's all free!"

"Well, where are the low fat and low cholesterol foods?" asks the husband.

"That's the best part! You can eat as much as you like of whatever you like and you never, ever, get fat and you never, ever, get sick. This is heaven!"

The husband turns to his wife and says, "Hey! You and your daily exercise workouts and all those tasteless bran muffins! I could've been here ten years ago!"

꒝

Why Bother?

> Antigonus of Socho[226] said: Do not be as servants who serve the
> Master to receive a reward. And let the fear of Heaven be upon you.
>
> — *Mishna 1:3*

The Mishna wants the Jew to simply serve God for no ulterior reason – not for honor, nor reward, nor a share in *Olam Haba* – just "let the fear of Heaven be upon you!"

But there's a problem with the structure of this Mishna: it tells us *not what* to do but *what not* to do ("do *not* be as servants…").

Why phrase the advice in negative, not positive, terms? And why so much ambiguity? (Rabbi Yonah thought the choice of words was unfortunate: he would have used "awe and reverence," not [austere] fear.)

Of course the Jew expects rewards if he acts as a *tzadik gamur* (completely righteous person): the Torah tells him so! However, even if the hope for reward is "Jewishly" legitimate, the Mishna frowns on this being the *motivation* for obedience.

But Antigonus's wording ("Do not be as servants…to receive reward!") was so poorly phrased that the Midrash, Rashi and the Rambam blame its confused message for causing two of his students (Tzadok and Baytos [Boethus]) to defect to such Torah-rejectionist sects as the Sadducees and Boethusians.

The lesson?

It's not what you say, but how you say it! Antigonus's *talmidim* thought, "Well then, why bother?" after their teacher gave *no positive* reason for serving God.

The tangible reward of a mitzva, this Mishna attempts to teach, *is the mitzva itself* – or, as Rabbi Eliezer implies: compare it to a choral musician motivated not by the applause but by the music itself!

❧

A nervous Rivkie is playing the violin at a solo concert at Carnegie Hall. When she finishes, the crowd goes wild, "Again! Play it again!"

Rivkie plays the entire piece a second time. "Again!" they shout, "play it again!"

Rivkie is so proud to be asked to play two encores and that the audience demands more and more, through several more repetitions.

Finally, an incredulous Rivkie asks, "Seven encores of the same piece at Carnegie Hall? It's unheard of! Am I that good?"

"No," they all shout as one, "but you'll keep doing it until you get it right!"

❧

Moral Leaders and Misleaders

> Anyone who influences the many towards merit, a sin will
> not come about through him; and anyone who brings the
> many to sin will not be given the opportunity to repent.
>
> — *Mishna 5:21*

This Mishna discusses the harsh reality of how one can influence others; goodness – and evil – are contagious. Shimon bar Yochai agrees, making the startling statement, "To cause another to sin is worse than murdering him!"

The *Tiferes Yisroel* adds a selfish motivation: if you try to influence others to do good, you prevent *yourself* from doing evil; this positive approach alone, say Rashi and Tosefos, is sufficient to keep one out of hell!

The most famous instance of "chain reaction" in Jewish history revolves around the saga of Mordechai and Esther in Shushan, capital of Persia.

The Megilla is explicit in describing Persian Jews as a community headed towards extinction; not only an *am mefuzar*, a "scattered folk among the nations," but also an *am mefuzar u'meforad*, "divided from within."

They could hide, but they couldn't run: their communal complacency is shattered the moment their king symbolically removes his signet ring and abdicates power to a rogue prime minister (Haman), the epitome of the Hebrew definition of *rasha* (wicked), because his first official proclamation is an order to kill all the Jews.

This led Rav Abba bar Kahana, a third-century Palestinian *Amora*, to make his famous observation on influence: "More powerful is the removal of a signet ring [which turned the Jews into immediate *ba'alei teshuva*, "returnees to the faith"] than all the pleas of the forty-eight prophets and seven prophetesses in Israel!"

"Who stimulates others to do good," notes Eleazar ben Pedat, "is greater than the doer!" – although the Eastern European Yiddishists had an opposite proverb: A saloon can't spoil the good, and a school won't mend the bad!

⚮

As the millionaire lay dying in a hospital bed, he felt guilty about the life he had led.

"Tell me, Rabbi," he whispers to the hospital rabbi, "if I leave $100,000 to this institution, will my repentance be assured?"

"I can't say for sure," replies the *rav*, "but it's certainly worth a try!"

⚮

Pious Fools, Wise Sinners!

> Rabbi said: Be careful with a minor mitzva as with a major
> one, for you do not know the reward for the mitzvos.
>
> — *Mishna 2:1*

Pious fools and wise sinners, labels created by Solomon ibn Gabirol, are those Jews who are tempted to pick and choose mitzvos, as if off a supermarket shelf; they caused Menachem Mendel of Kotzk to point to the Torah, warning "not to turn God's commandments into idols!"

In short: don't let motivation discriminate between your good deeds!

Mitzvos should have no material consequences, but, technically, this Mishna seems incorrect. Why?

Not all mitzvos are created equal: some *do* have bigger and better and more lucrative rewards – such as *l'ma'an ya'arichun yomecha*, the "prolonging of days" (i.e., a longer life) for honoring parents, dealing with "honest weights," and for the mitzva of *shiluach haken* (not removing unhatched eggs or baby chicks while the mother bird is still in the nest), to which Rashi adds his famous *vort*: "If for the fulfillment of such an easy mitzva God promises the reward of long life, how much greater is the reward for fulfilling the more difficult mitzvos!"

But in a startling admonition, the rabbis of the Mishna warn that Jews who associate this last mitzva "with Divine compassion must be silenced!"

Why?

"Because," explains Yose bar Zavida, "in doing so, they are representing all of God's traits as *compassion*, whereas all His commandments are *decrees*!"

This is the general rabbinic attitude: no attempt should be made to apply logic or reason for *mitzva* performance, *even* when it has an obvious moral basis!

꼿

It's Parshas Yisro, and the rabbi gives a forceful Shabbas *d'var Torah* on the Ten Commandments. When he's finished, Beryl turns to his friend and says, "Well, at least I've never made a graven image!"

꼿

No Pain, No Gain!

> Ben Hei Hei said: According to the effort is the reward.
> — *Mishna 5:26*[227]

This Mishna's basic point, penned in Aramaic, that God's system of justice places "effort" on the highest pedestal, brings hope and encouragement to all those Jews – especially late-start beginners, *à la* Rabbi Akiva – who are not the greatest nor wisest nor most pious.

Torah study may be *the* link to Heaven, but it's not how far down its road you travel that is the criterion, it's the effort you have made to pack the bags of devotion and sacrifice – and the journey itself.

Want to improve?

"First," advises Israel Lipkin Salanter, who believed in the logic of walking before running, "you should put together your house, then your town, then the world!"

Jeremiah warned against trying to reach one's capacity; Ibn Gabirol, eleventh-century scholar, defined ambition as a "bondage"; the Yiddishists were, as usual, blunt: Look for cake and you'll lose your bread!

In a speech in 1923, the *Chofetz Chaim* warned his listeners: "Ascend not too high; your faults may show!"

In order to dispel all the preconceived superficial notions of reward and punishment, the Talmud recalls the strange odyssey experience of Rav Yosef. The Sage passed away briefly and was then revived. When asked by his father to describe his afterlife experience in heaven, Yosef replied, "I saw an upside-down world. I saw upper ones below and lower ones above!"

Rav Yosef was shocked to see some of the righteous ("upper ones") of this world in less than the highest rungs of heaven, and some not-so-righteous ("lower ones") in more desirable conditions.

The son might have been shaken by "reality," but the father was not: "My son, you have seen a clear world!"

⇥

As the children lined up for lunch, there was a large pile of apples at the head of the table, with a sign that read: "Take only ONE. God is watching."

At the other end of the table was a large basket of chocolate chip cookies, over which was hand-written in a child's scrawl: "Take all you want! God is watching the apples!"

⇥

Just Passing the Time

> Exile comes to the world for idolatry, adultery, murder,
> and the working of the earth in the Sabbatical year.
>
> — *Mishna 5:11*

This Mishna makes a startling connection: it equates the three major sins (idolatry, adultery, murder) that supercede life itself to the laws of *Shmitta*.

What's so important about a Sabbatical year?

If every seventh day was holy, so was every seventh year one of special solemnity, known as *shnat shabbaton*, "year of rest," or *shnat shmitta*, "year of release."

This seventh year was devoted to three principles: cessation of agriculture (allowing the soil to "rest"), reversion of land to its original owner (undoing "forced" sales resulting from financial pressures), and the freeing of indentured slaves and their children (whose status came about either through poverty or other acts).

This concept is unique in the annals of human history: not only are rights over people (*workers*) and things (*land*) limited, but rights over ourselves are *equally* restricted, suggesting that spiritual creativity needs a state of suspended activity every few years.

Incredibly, this Mishna links the desecration of the year of rest to the very existence of a diaspora: "If the people do not let the land rest in their presence," notes the Talmud, "the land will rest in their absence!"

It's obvious from the severity of this Mishna that *Shmitta* is another significant signpost of how Time flies in the cosmic terms of Torah – and the rewards are obvious: *Shmitta* is a time of *release* (from the distorted encumbrances of civilization and commerce) that leads to *challenge* (I dare you to return in a year and build a better society!) and to realization (a well-rested earth is good for the soul).

Perhaps the crime does fit the time?

☙

The science teacher was explaining the complicated theories behind map reading. After twenty minutes of explaining such concepts as latitude, longitude, degrees and minutes, she points to Yankele and says, "Suppose I asked you to meet me for a snack at 23 degrees, 4 minutes north latitude and 45 degrees, 15 minutes east longitude...?"

"Ah..." mumbled the boy, "I guess you'd be eating alone!"

☙

And the Same to You!

> Rebbe said: Consider three things and you will not come to
> sin. Know what is above you: an eye that sees, an ear that
> hears, and that all your deeds are recorded in the Book.
>
> — *Mishna 2:1*

This Mishna narrows down the mitigation of sin to only three things, but the last one is deadly!

"Know what is above you…and that all your deeds are recorded in the Book."

To actually "know" is obviously beyond human comprehension, thus this Mishna narrows it down to this: God sees, hears and records it all.

The tradition that God keeps a "diary" comes to us courtesy of Moses ("Would that You would forgive their sin, but if not, blot me out of the book which You have written"); but according to Rabban Yochanan there are three, not one, "Books" – one each "for the thoroughly wicked, the righteous, and those in between."[228]

The most common greeting at the start of the new year, *Leshana Tova Tikatevu*, "May you be inscribed for a good year" (in Yiddish, "From your mouth to God's ear!") has only one response: *Gam tov l'mar*, basically "The same good to you!"

God's "eyes and ears"? Isn't this metaphoric? Not if you ask a child.

⤳

The family boards a train for a long trip, and Suzy puts her youngest daughter on an upper berth. The little girl cries for hours as Suzy tries to calm her down. "Don't worry, God is watching over you."

It doesn't help. Every hour or so the little girl cries out, "Mommy, are you there?"

"Yes."

"Tatte, are you there?"

"Yes, my child, I'm here."

But a fellow passenger has had enough, and starts screaming, "We're all here! Your father and your mother and your brothers and your sisters and your uncles and your aunts and your grandparents and your cousins! They're all here! Every last one of them! Now, for Heaven's sake, go to sleep!"

After a pause the girl whispers, "Mommy?"

"Yes?"

"Was that God?"

⤳

The Hinge in History

There were ten generations from Noah until Abraham.[229] This shows
how slow to anger God is, for all those generations increasingly angered
Him until Abraham came and received the reward of all of them.

— Mishna 5:3

In this Mishna God's anger climaxes with Abraham "receiving the reward of all of
them." The reward? What reward? Weren't his generation, and their predecessors
"wicked"?

Abraham understood that God's justice system made allowance even for those
who sinned, and thus, unlike Noah, he and his wife spent time and energy on
others. Noah thus acts as *the* hinge in history, between equal sets of ten generations (from Adam to Noah and Noah to Abraham) who openly defy and anger
God – the first motley world being destroyed by a watery wipeout, the second
being spared.

Why the difference in Divine punishment?

The answer lies in behavior: the former society was a quarrelsome and vindic-
tive one; the next generations lived in communal harmony, friendship, respect.
Noah's virtue is particular to *that* time and *that* place, thus his status borders not
on credit but discredit. This leads Rashi to make a startling claim: "Had Noah been
living in the generation of Abraham he would have been considered worthless!"

But wait: hasn't Rashi forgotten the chronology?

Abraham *did* live in Noah's generation, and, at age forty-eight, started his one-
man war against paganism during the construction of the tower of Babel; however, Jewish history credits Abraham because Noah's passivity had rendered him
a useless partner in his younger colleague's religious renaissance.

ༀ

Convinced that their drought was punishment, the local elders in Canaan bring
in a *kohen* from Goshen to pray for rain before the crops shrivel and die. The
whole *kehilla* gathers in the *shul* to pray. The *kohen* starts softly, then raises his
prayer in anger, then starts screaming at the Heavens. Miraculously, the rains
suddenly come pouring down and down for ten days and ten nights – until the
kohen finally stops.

"Wow!" says Izzie to his friend, surveying a landscape whose entire crop has
been washed away, leaving fields in ruins and devastation, "this guy really knows
how to pray!"

"Yep! Pity he doesn't know a thing about agriculture!"

ༀ

Who's the Boss!

> Pestilence comes to the world for death penalties ordered
> in the Torah which were not carried out by the courts and
> for the forbidden use of Sabbatical year produce.
>
> — *Mishna 5:11*

This Mishna puts "pestilence" in a separate category, for offenses whose traditional punishment (death) is outside the jurisdiction of the regular Jewish court.

How can this happen?

In times and places where, for whatever reason, the Sanhedrin or local *beis din* was unable to function; or, when the guilty went free because Jewish courts didn't have sufficient evidence or lacked witnesses, but the crime was still "punishable" by the hands of God.

But why should the misuse of *Shmitta* fruit draw in its wake such a deadly punishment?

Remember: epidemics are indiscriminate: "When destructive forces are given permission to smite, they do not distinguish between righteous and wicked!"

Breaking the laws of *Shmitta* ("Do not prune your vineyards!") was considered a theft not from man but from God Himself (the sanctified produce being reserved for *His* use, to be shared with the poor, animals, etc.), based on the principle that the "land is the Lord's" and thus we are all merely His tenants at will.

Breaking this "communal" law paves the way for a communal punishment.

This agricultural moratorium requires a leap of Judaic faith: the Jews are asked to completely stop cultivating the earth every seventh year, to harvest not bread but *bitachon*, to trust the Heavens that their sixth-year harvest will "spill over" not only into the seventh year, but also throughout the entire eighth year as they wait for a new crop to grow.

According to the Raavad, this is its fundamental purpose: a reminder of Who is still the Boss of the earth.

⤙

As a teaching prop for his class on *Shmitta*, the *cheder* rebbe asks his *talmidim* to bring something "fruity" to school the next day. Six-year-old Hannale arrives with a basket of eight fruit lollipops.

"This is great," the rebbe says, "I'll call your mommy later and thank her for these eight beautiful lollipops."

"Ah…" mumbles little Hannale, "perhaps you can thank her for twelve?"

⤙

Ten

The world was created in ten utterances. What
does this come to teach us?

— *Mishna 5:1*

This Mishna solidifies the mystic concept that Hebrew words matter; Divine "utterances" are an integral part of the transformation from unfathomable emptiness and chaos (*tohu vavohu*) to an intricate "something" (*yesh*) of balance and beauty.

The Genesis formula ("And God said...") is repeated nine times, and then once again regarding the institution of marriage.

The same expression is used, some 2,500 years later, when the Jews, three months out of Egypt, receive the most influential Jewish words still echoed in Western civilization: a beacon of universally accepted moral certainty, God's monumental "user-friendly" *Aseres Hadibros* (ten utterances).

We usually refer to the "ten" commandments, but there are actually thirteen.

Immediately after issuing the first ten, God adds three more that exclusively concern themselves with civil and criminal law (beginning with the laws of an *eved ivri*, a Jewish "bondsman" owned by another Jew).

God also surfaces not once but twice at Sinai, sending Jewish mystics into a search for the episode's hidden *shtei bechinot* (two aspects).

When the Divine Presence (*Shechina*) first descends "in the sight of all the people," the Torah text bursts with descriptive adjectives and nouns: "trembling, fear, thunder, lightning, dense clouds, loud blasts of a horn," stapled to a vivid use of verbs ("stoned, smitten") within emphatic expressions of awe, fear and death.

The second appearance, only to the "top of the mountain," is more subdued, all the fire and brimstone rhetoric conspicuous only by its absence.

Why the two entrances?

The first dramatic emergence was for the entire nation of Israel, united as a people of prophets; the next was reserved for the nation's elite – individual Jews (such as Moses and Aaron) who aspire to climb the spiritual peaks of Judaism and who are not in need of the fiery rhetoric.

༈

The number ten goes into a bar and asks the barman for a pint of beer.
"Sorry, I can't serve you," he says.
"Why not?!"
"You're under eighteen!"

༈

Think Well – And It Will Be Well!

> With ten trials did our ancestors test God in the desert.
> — *Mishna 5:6*

Do we know which "ten" trials the Mishna refers to?

The Talmud lists them, ranging from facing the Egyptians at the Red Sea, to the lack of water and food in the desert, to the two greatest "tests" of them all: the saga of a calf of gold and the drama of the twelve *meraglim* (spies).

The last episode led God to sigh that Israel "has tested Me ten times!" and is the basis of Tisha b'Av, one of three non-Biblical features in the Jewish calendar.[230]

The spies, despite being prominent "princes of each tribe," deliver a devastating intelligence report describing Canaan as "a land that devours its inhabitants," adding, with a stunning lack of confidence and pride, "We were in our own eyes as grasshoppers, and so were we in their eyes!"

Their *diba ra'ah*, "bad-mouthed" finding, came a mere fourteen months after the Exodus from Egypt, to an exhausted nation which stood a distance less than three days away from a promised land of milk and honey.

The cowardly report depressed the Jews into apathy, passiveness and a massive identity crisis. And worse: it created a warped desire to turn back the clock ("Would it not be better for us to return to Egypt?"), causing an angry God to declare, "You cried without cause; I will, therefore, make this an eternal day of mourning for you!"

The spies of Moses went with a preconceived bias: they were suspicious of God's promises and distrustful of the future.

Thus they saw what suited them; in contrast, Joshua's future scouts went with self-assurance, determined to implement God's will, and harbored no doubts as to their ultimate triumph.

As the Yiddishists would summarize: "*Tracht gut, es vet zein gut* (Think well and it will be well)!"

꙰

On a field trip to Washington's CIA Museum, little Shmuli is staring at a wall of the most wanted spies and asks the guide, "Is this really a photo of a wanted person?"

"Yes, our government wants him badly."

"Well," Shmuli says after thinking for a few seconds, "why didn't you keep him when you took his picture?"

꙰

Why Do Bad Things Happen to Good People?

Rabbi Yannai[231] said: It is not in our power to explain either the tranquility of the wicked or the suffering of the righteous.

— *Mishna 4:19*

This Mishna admits theological defeat: certain things in life are simply incomprehensible to the human mind.

Even Moses was unable to fathom why the righteous suffer, and in response to his question, God tried to placate the humble leader of the Jews by assuring him that there is ample reward for the pious in the World to Come.

The absence of adequate responses is why, in general, our Sages were never philosophers; instead they devoted themselves to *halacha*, to the pragmatic "what" God requires of the Jew, and not to the philosophical "why" it is required.

Rav Ami, a student of Rabban Yochanan, tried to explain the ultimate *mysterium tremendum*, why bad things happen to good people, by declaring *tiyuvta d'Rav Ami tiyuvta*; every death and suffering is caused by sin. It didn't work. He was rebuked by the Heavenly angels themselves.

This led the Yiddishists of Eastern Europe to proclaim as an article of faith: "In life, be careful. Ask God questions and He may insist you come up to hear the answers!"

The saintly *Chofetz Chaim* once pleaded, "When the going gets tough, look at the jewels [Torah] you are carrying," in a desperate attempt to point to the glorious past in the light of his community's grisly present.

"All who trust believe," cautions the *Emuna U'vitachon*, "but not all who believe are trusting." The *Mishlei Yehoshua*, a book of Proverbs, adds philosophically, "There are things which will not be believed until we see them, and others that are unseeable save by those who believe in them."

꒰

On the opening day of his new business, Baruch receives a bouquet of flowers but is confused by the attached card, which reads: "Deepest Sympathy."

He calls the florist who, after apologizing profusely for sending the wrong card, starts crying, "Oh, no! I accidentally sent your card to a funeral party!"

"Well, what did it say?"

"Congratulations on your new location!"

꒰

TIME AND WISDOM

A good politician needs the ability to
foretell what will happen tomorrow, next
month, and next year — and the ability to
explain afterward why it didn't happen!

— *Winston Churchill*

Time and Wisdom

Since history is only viewed through the prism of Time, and in order to ensure the upkeep of memory – *the* prerequisite to Jewish continuity and survival – the rabbis of *Pirkei Avos* demand that the past be transmitted from fathers to sons ("You shall tell [*vehiggadeta*] your son on that day"),[232] preferably, according to Isaiah, precept by precept, line by line, "here a little, there a little."[233]

God's Time begins with the end in mind; it is a cosmic master arrow that hurtles through the generations as the *a priori* means towards a predetermined utopian climax.

The end goal is messianic, defined as *the* harmonious integration of all Time, as "the most glistening jewel in the glorious crown of Judaism," as a day of "complete Sabbath," when the armies of reconciliation, equanimity and friendship finally defeat the forces of evil and wickedness.

How will we recognize when the clock strikes the hour?

Isaiah describes the moment: when "the wolf also shall live with the lamb, and the leopard shall lie down with the kid; and the calf and the young lion and the fatling together; and a little child shall lead them."[234]

The prophet wrote these soothing words during a horrific time: Sennacherib, the Assyrian emperor, and his superior army were occupying Judah, sacking every town and village (having already destroyed Israel's northern kingdom and kidnapped the ten [lost] tribes), and were about to decimate Jerusalem itself.

And yet Isaiah, despite his world being ringed by fire and enveloped by destruction, can only envisage a future of promise. His belief is dramatic yet simple: it is possible to make the future better than the present: "*Now* we are slaves. *Next year* we *will be* free!"

Judaism is thus driven forward through Time and Space by the belief in a Time after time, and the faith that there will come a day when the world will be perfected.

Meanwhile, we are to use the gift of time to perfect ourselves, and put time to productive use in the pursuit of wisdom. Directly put, the Torah's view of wisdom is this: if you ain't already got it, you ain't *ever* gonna get it! Why? Because God only gives wisdom to those who possess it already ("He gives wisdom to the wise!").[235]

In commenting on the Talmud's comparison between full and empty containers, Rashi explains that "an empty container [i.e., person] does not receive wisdom."[236] In contrast, if wisdom is given to a wise person [i.e., a full container] he becomes even wiser![237]

Yiddish folklore abounds with "wise fools," Jewish simpletons who sprout a unique brand of wisdom as if to prove that *seichel* (common sense) cannot be taught.

If wisdom is only for the wise, then what's the point of trying to becoming wiser?

The gain is in the effort, not the result. To the rabbis of *Pirkei Avos*, seeking wisdom is a character trait, a personality plus ("The wise-hearted will grasp every opportunity to do a mitzva!").[238]

The Jew who conducts himself "wisely" is a worthy recipient of Divine wisdom. If not, his wisdom "departs from him."[239]

Thus the rabbinic "beginning" of wisdom is humility ("Don't be wise in your own eyes!") and a fear of God.[240] Few are able to attain this level, but those who do are endowed with "happiness, honor, peace and love."[241] In fact, they achieve a status greater than that of the prophet.[242]

"When I was a boy of fourteen," goes the quote popularly attributed to Mark Twain, "my father was so ignorant I could hardly stand to have the old man around. But when I got to be twenty-one, I was astonished at how much he had learned in seven years."

⇌

When Meir Shapiro was appointed *rav* of Galina, he was still a very young man, and several members of the *kehilla* were vehemently opposed to his appointment.

"What fault have you found in me that you oppose me so strongly?" asked Reb Meir.

"I cannot stand such a young rabbi," his opponent answered.

"Then you may as well stop fighting; your complaint decreases with each passing day."

⇌

It's about Time!

Ben Azzai said: There is no person who does not have his
hour, and there is no thing that does not have its place.

— Mishna 4:3

The Torah's view on time is simple: it works in nobody's favor, unless imbued
with meaning; left alone, it has no opinion, no shape, and the popular adage "time
is on our side" is a myth.

Time does what time does best – it passes!

And so the obligation falls on each Jew in pursuit of a mitzva to elevate mundane time into something more special, more distinguished.

"Nothing," thundered the seventeenth-century Italian Yosef Solomon Delmedigo, "can withstand time!"

Abraham Bedersi, a thirteenth-century Torah thinker, grappled with a time
that "flew faster than the shades of the evening"; five hundred years later Benjamin Mandelstamm, the talented Hebrew-Russian author, waxed poetic: "The
present is the spinning wheel, the past the thread that is spun, the future the wool
for men to weave their years."

Mandelstamm should have been a tailor, not a thinker, faring no better than
the twentieth-century German dramatist Ernst Toller, who made no sense at all:
"No time is ever out of time!"

The precise nature of time eludes us, but we do know that time is a powerful
entity. Jewish mystics note that the difference between *chametz* and *matza* is not
the ingredients (they *both* contain flour and water), nor the method of baking
(both are cooked in an oven), but *time*: a difference of only one second turns one
into the other.[243]

❧

The Greenbergs, on a trip to Israel, come across an ancient temple in the Jordan
Valley and ask their guide how old it is.

"This temple is 1,503 years old, plus two months," replies the guide.

"Wow! I'm impressed," says Mr. Greenberg, "that's very, very accurate dating!
How do you know?"

"Well," replies the guide, "two months ago an archaeologist came by and said
it was 1,503 years old!"

❧

From Start to Finish

> Rabbi Tarfon said: It is not incumbent upon you to complete the task, but you are not free to withdraw from it.
>
> — *Mishna 2:21*

On the one hand, this Mishna tells us that it's more important to begin a task than to finish it, but Rabbi Tarfon is contradicted by such other Sages as Rav and Yose ("You started, you finish!"), Hama ben Hanina and Eleazar ben Pedat ("Who does not finish what he began is deposed"), and the author of *Seder Eliyahu Zuta*, who paints the Jew who starts but doesn't finish with the broad brush of "a sinner"!

Rabbi Tarfon is simply saying that it's not good for man to be idle, that wastage of time (*bizbuz zeman*) is a curse.

Another Mishna identifies idleness as the cause for pushing one down the slippery slope towards "madness and lewdness," and Rashi contends that the greater the effort, the greater the reward.

In the immortal words of David Belasco's fictional character in the *Return of Peter Grimm*, "We mustn't waste time 'cause that's the stuff life's made of!"

There is a startling Midrash that defines the desire "to *kill* some time" as a major sin, so grievous in fact that it "[leads] to death," implying that idleness is the Judaic equivalent of suicide.

The Maharal, a vigorous opponent of lethargy and laziness, was convinced that inactivity is incompatible with spirituality, and frequently argued that the only remedy to overcome its stifling effect is a rabbinic adage known as "*Mitzva haba'a leyadcha, al tachmitzena* (When a mitzva comes to your hand, do not let it become stale)!"

Joey is a lazy young man who, rather than looking for a decent job, is always thinking of how to get rich quick. One day he calls his friend: "Hey, Moishie! I think I've got it, the perfect idea! An invention for barber shops!"

"How does it work?"

"Well, it's a machine that you stick your head in, and it shaves you in a matter of seconds! Moishie, I'll make a fortune!"

"But that's preposterous!"

"Why?"

"It's impossible – everybody's head is shaped differently!"

"Maybe." Joey thinks for a few seconds and then yells back, "But only at first!"

The Crime of Wasted Time

> Hillel said: Do not say when I have free time I
> will learn, lest you not have free time.
>
> — *Mishna 2:5*

"When I ask a man, 'Why do you not study the Torah?'" writes the *Midor L'dor*, "and he answers, 'I don't want to,' I leave him alone...but when the answer is, 'I have no time,' I say he's a liar, because, if there is the will, there's the time!"

To live each day as though it may be the last is a rabbinic definition of wisdom (*chachma*) that has nothing to do with learning or studying, but with an appreciation of time: "*Eizehu chacham* (Who is wise)?" ask our Sages, and then provide the answer: "*Haro'eh es hanolad* (He who anticipates the future)!"

When defining the characteristics of a wise man, the Mishna lists seven, four of which revolve around the use of time ("he does not interrupt; he is not hasty to answer; he does not speak before his superior; he talks about first things first and about last things last...").[244]

Hillel's awareness of the ticking of the clock and the passing of seconds ("days should speak, years should teach wisdom") became a theme that rippled through Jewish folklore as an adjunct of wisdom, insight and common sense.

Commenting on the verse "And now, I have brought the first fruit [*bikkurim*],"[245] the rabbis saw the opening ("And *now*...") as a nod to immediacy; wasting time is a curse (*bitul Torah*), a failure that chips away at one's spiritual potential.

The moral?

Poor use of time is a crime. The Talmud relates how Nachum Ish Gam Zu once left a hungry beggar waiting until he unloaded his donkey; by the time the rabbi was finished, the poor man had died.

⤳

The question was posed to famed pianist Ignace Paderewski: "Is it true that you still practice every day?"

"Yes," confirmed the musician. "At least six hours a day."

"You must have a world of patience," continued the admirer.

"I have no more patience than the next fellow," clarified Paderewski, "I just use mine."

⤳

No Loss Like the Loss of Time!

Rabbi Tarfon[246] said: The day is short, the work is great, the workers are lazy, the reward is great, and the Master of the house presses.

— *Mishna 2:20*

This Mishna sounds a bit like Koheles: depressing, fleeting, life is urgent and short. Not to despair, however, there is a Heavenly bounty at the end ("the reward is great") – but only if one makes the right lifestyle choices ("Life and death I have placed before you, the blessing and the curse, and you shall choose life!").

With a sense of urgency, Rabbi Tarfon reminds us that there exists a Godly reward (not necessarily in this life) for learning "much Torah."

Shmuel Uceda, a sixteenth-century Safed-born Talmudist, wailed, "There is no loss like the loss of time!"

The ultimate twenty-first-century challenge is how to squeeze more than twenty-four hours out of a day, a peculiar desire that laid the mother egg of all illusions: that since time cannot be stretched, it must be compressed in brevity, faster segments, sound bites ("Around the world in eighty seconds," blares Fox TV News), nanosecond e-mails, speed dialing and speed dating, fast food restaurants, quickie book solutions ("How to Kill Time!"), and in Arkansas there's a drive-through church for those who "want to experience religion but don't want to get out of their cars."

Not so fast, whispers the rabbinic wisdom of *Pirkei Avos*, "There is a time and a place for everything" – to which we must add a cautionary note from Isaiah, "I will hasten it, but only in its time!"

But when is *its* time?

No one knows: yet all understand that failure to seize the moment leads to time wasted, obliterated, lost forever, never to return.

❧

"How was your date?" Surale asks her roommate.
"Terrible! He showed up in his 1932 Rolls Royce!"
"Wow! That's a very expensive car. It's timeless! What's so bad about that?"
"He was the original owner!"

❧

A Carpenter without Tools!

> Rabbi Eleazar ben Azariah said: If there is no Torah there is no proper conduct; if there is no proper conduct there is no Torah. If there is no wisdom there is no fear of God; if there is no fear of God there is no wisdom. If there is no knowledge there is no understanding; if there is no understanding there is no knowledge.
>
> — *Mishna 3:21*

On his death bed, Yochanan ben Zakkai reminded his *talmidim* to fear God as much as they feared each other.

"Only that much?" one replied.

"If only!" he answered.

There is no poetic vagueness in this Mishna; it is a litany of incestuous spiritual logic: to close the circle of life, Torah needs proper conduct and proper conduct needs Torah; knowledge is nothing without understanding, and understanding in the absence of knowledge is nothing!

The Mishnaic terms for knowledge and understanding are *da'as* and *bina*; the former, according to the Rambam, refers to "acquired" knowledge, the latter to the refinement of concepts via observation.

Are they linked? Yes. Knowledge is "acquired" only after facts are analyzed in a rational way (wisdom doesn't necessarily come with age – sometimes age just shows up all by itself!).

"King Solomon was wiser than everyone, even the idiot," notes the Rebbe of Berdichev. "Every idiot believes himself wiser than everyone else, and it is impossible to convince him of this fallacy. But Solomon was so wise that in his presence even the idiots had to acknowledge themselves as fools!"

⇝

David and Ernie are watching television news covering a guy about to jump from a bridge.

"I bet ya ten bucks he jumps," says David.

"Oh, yeah! I bet ya ten bucks he doesn't!" says Ernie.

Suddenly, the guy jumps off the bridge, committing suicide.

Ernie takes out his wallet and hands David ten bucks, but David refuses. "I can't take your money. I cheated you. I already watched the five o'clock news and I knew he would jump."

"Well," says Ernie, "I saw it on the five o'clock news also. I just didn't think the guy was dumb enough to jump again!"

⇝

Wise, Strong, Rich, Honored

> Shimon ben Zoma[247] said: Who is wise? He who learns
> from all people.... Who is strong? He who conquers his
> evil inclination.... Who is rich? He who is satisfied with his
> lot.... Who is honored? He who honors others [*briyos*].
>
> — *Mishna 4:1*

Who is wise, who is strong, who is rich and who is honored?

This Mishna's wisdom is stunning in its simplicity.

Want wisdom? Learn from everybody.

Why? Because the Torah's version of wisdom requires interaction with folks both smart – and not-so-smart.

Want strength?

Forget about flexing your physical muscles. Why? Because the Torah's idea of strength comes from the spirit, from willpower, restraint, controlling one's desires.

Want to be rich?

Money and wealth are means to an end, and that "end" is inner contentment, to be happy with what you have.

"True riches," writes the thirteenth-century Italian-Jewish poet-scribe Yehiel Anav, "is contentment." Ben Sira exhorted, "With little or with much, be content," an echo of ben Zoma's definition of who is rich: "He who rejoices in his lot!"

Seeking honor? Then honor others.

Why? Because they are created in God's image. But how? By treating them with respect and generosity, qualities which will then be offered in return.

In his definitions of the wise, the strong, the rich and the honored, Rabbi Shimon tries to focus the Jew on "the middle of the road," away from extremes. The key is seeing past superficiality to the true value of life.

❧

Abe, a multimillionaire, is eating in a restaurant when he suddenly starts choking on a chicken bone. He is saved by a surgeon seated at the next table. After regaining his composure, Abe turns to his savior: "God bless you! I'd like to thank you, how much do I owe you?"

"I'd be more than happy," replies the doctor, "if you gave me a tenth of the sum you were willing to give me one second before I saved you!"

❧

The Numbers Game

Rabbi Elazar ben Chisma[248] said: Astronomy and the numeric
values of Hebrew letters are the spices to wisdom.

— *Mishna 3:23*

The rabbis of the Mishna considered astronomy one of the "secrets of the Torah";
however, by the time of the Rambam, it had deteriorated into sheer superstition
(astrology), which this Sage, virtually alone amongst the rabbis of his generation,
aggressively lectured against.

It didn't take long before the rabbinic adage "*Ein mazel l'Yisroel* (Israel is not
subject to the signs of the Zodiac)" – which the Yiddishists undertood in an al-
ternate translation and turned into a popular cynical refrain, "The Jews have no
mazel (luck)" – was set aside completely.

When Sholem Aleichem's Tevye concocted the ghost of Tzeitel to fool his wife
Goldie, the ghost might have been fictitious on stage, but not to the masses of Yiddish audiences throughout Eastern Europe who "knew, positively," that if you were
born under the planetary sign of Mercury you would be "wise and radiant"; under
Venus, "rich and adulterous"; under Mars, "a shedder of blood," and so on.

Beyond astronomy, the Mishna refers to the wisdom in *gematria*, what we
call "numeric values," a formula based on the hidden wisdom of the Hebrew alphabet.

This is not just a pastime of Jewish mystics; even Rashi resorts to it: for example, when explaining how *tzitzis* remind us of mitzvos, the commentator of
commentators takes the word's numeric value (600), then adds the eight strings
of the corners plus its five knots to arrive at…613, the number of mitzvos in the
Torah!

Here's another example: the Torah tells us that Abraham had 318 skilled staff,
which also happens to be the sum of the letters in the name Eliezer; thus the "three
hundred eighteen" servants must mean Eliezer!

Is this method binding on halacha? No. It is a fascinating and enjoyable arith-
metical exercise. Try it! It's fun!

※

The rebbe decides to use a math analogy to explain a difficult page of Gemora.
"OK," he says to his class, "you take two thirds of water, one third of cholent, one
third of potatoes…"
"Wait!" one kid yells out. "That's four thirds already!"
"OK! OK! – just take a larger pot!"

※

Standing Still Is Going Backwards!

> Hillel[249] said: One who seeks a name loses his name, one who does not increase his knowledge decreases it, one who does not study deserves death, and one who makes use of the crown[250] of Torah will pass away.
>
> — *Mishna 1:13*

What Hillel is saying is this: in the absence of Torah, considered the source of life, what's the point of living?

But don't get carried away, he warns. The Jew who "uses the Crown of Torah will perish!"

Reish Lakish interprets this as a warning, similar to that against *me'ila*, the crime of misappropriation, to those who use their knowledge of Torah for their own selfish benefit.

What does "one who seeks a name loses his name" mean?

Celebrity is short-lived; ambition can be fleeting, a good name being trampled in its path ("vaulting ambition which overleaps itself!" is how Shakespeare puts it).

Rashi explains that Torah study is for its own sake – not for fame, nor fortune, nor power ("A little light," says Yosef Shlomo Delmedigo, "is precious, but too much can be blinding!" – or, as the Yiddishists put it, "To know the taste of wine, it's not necessary to drink the whole barrel!").

In other words, if you study for recognition, your "name" will elude you, for this is a fame that flees from those who seek it!

Influenced by the verse "Before a fall, greatness!" the Rambam warns that when we see a Jew's "name" (i.e., reputation) spread too far and wide (*negad sh'ma*), we know that he is soon destined to fall (*avad sh'may*)!

In his second point – if you're not increasing (your) knowledge, you're decreasing it – Hillel argues that less is not more; less is even *less*!

Standing still is not just stagnation, it's going backwards!

꩜

Walking home from *shul* one early winter morning, the well-known rabbi sees a dog in the water struggling to stay afloat. Unconcerned about his own safety, he jumps right in and, after a struggle, manages to bring the animal out alive.

"Hey," a passerby yells out, "that was brave. Are you a vet?"

"Of course I'm vet!" the rabbi shouts back, "and I'm freezing, too!"

꩜

Get Wise or Get Smart?

Rabbi Chanina ben Dosa[251] said: Anyone whose fear of sin precedes his
wisdom, his wisdom will endure; and anyone whose wisdom precedes
his fear of sin, his wisdom will not endure; anyone whose good deeds
are greater than his wisdom, his wisdom will endure; anyone whose
wisdom is greater than his good deeds, his wisdom will not endure.

— *Mishna 3:11–12*

The rarest gift anyone can possess is common sense! According to this Mishna,
wisdom alone is insufficient. Motivation is the key to whether getting wise is also
getting smart; in fact, anyone who is aware of his foolishness is already a little
wiser!

It is not fascination, curiosity, or an intellectual pursuit of Torah, but the fear
of *not* learning that is the "right" path to acquiring wisdom, the former being
too abstract, too academic, leading to a selective type of wisdom that "will not
endure."

Rabbi Chanina, in noting that actions speak louder than wisdom, advises that
practice must *exceed* knowledge; this explains why the Torah chronology at Sinai
is "We will do [practice] and [*only then*] we will hear [learn, get wisdom]."

This is a paradox: how can you "do" that which you don't "know"?

Because there is a third component, the most important, even *before* actions or
wisdom, and that is commitment; the rabbis of the Talmud note that God rewards
the Jew not only for the mitzva but also for *planning* to do the mitzva.[252]

꘎

Two Beis Yaakov girls, on their first trip abroad, are visiting Spain. One day, they
decide to do a mitzva and buy dresses for their mothers. They stroll into the
local shopping area and see a beautiful dress in a store window. They go in and
start trying on clothes to see what would best suit their mothers. Suddenly, they
realize the room has gone quiet. Shoppers are giving them dirty looks, until one
English-speaking woman whispers to them, "Pssst. This is a dry cleaner!"

꘎

TORAH AND MITZVOS

Please God! Help me get up! I
can fall down by myself!

— *Yiddish saying*

Torah and Mitzvos

The apex of all religious activity is the study of Torah for its own sake (*Torah lishma*), and the reward for doing a *mitzva* is...another *mitzva*!

The pursuit of Torah and the benefits of *mitzvos* are thus internal.

The term *mitzva* is related to *tzavta* (an association/cleaving), implying that only through *mitzvos* can one "get near to" God. This association is considered a *mitzva* in itself, the ultimate reward, notes Rav Nachum of Chernobyl, for whatever the previous *mitzva* was.

If each *mitzva* led to such a reward, the rabbis of *Pirkei Avos* didn't discriminate between a "light" mitzva and a "weighty" one.

Rav Yissaschar Dov, the Belzer Rebbe, had a different insight into the Mishna's urging that Jews "run to do (even) an 'easy'" mitzva. He considered the "running" after a mitzva suggestive of the repetitive pursuit of that same mitzva, a "chase" that would come to improve its performance.

The reward is thus not just a passive "mitzva-for-another-mitzva" but that its repeated performance will be rewarded by the eventual perfect fulfillment of the *first* mitzva.

The Gerer Rebbe agreed: the benefit lies in the mitzva chase itself, an act of desire and fear of God which was rewarded by performing the mitzva *again*, but improved by repetition.

There is another aspect to the cause and effect of a mitzva, built on the rabbinic principle "According to the difficulty is the reward!"

This means that there may be no distinction between a "light" and a "weighty" mitzva, if the former is done with minimal effort. This line of thinking places the spotlight not on the actual mitzva but on the difficulties encountered along the way.

The question is obvious: if the reward for Torah study is greater than for any mitzva, why bother with mitzvos at all? Just study Torah day and night!

This is a contradiction in terms. God's words came in wrapping paper known as *lilmod v'la'asos* (to study *and* perform), both in the context of attachment to God (*dveikus*).

To study without the intent to perform is not study but an intellectual pursuit; to perform in the absence of study is an unnecessary deficiency.

For example: it's absurd to study the laws of *lulav* during *Succos* without ever picking up a *lulav*; it compares to picking up a *lulav* without the knowledge of what to do with it.

❧

After his Shabbas *dvar Torah* on the Ten Commandments, while walking home from *shul*, the rabbi bumps into Beryl and his wife.

"*Nu*," he says, "how did you like my sermon today?"

"Oh, Rabbi, my husband and I both thoroughly enjoyed it."

"In that case, perhaps you can come to *shul* more often?"

"It's difficult," replies Beryl, "but Rabbi, at least we keep the Ten Command-ments."

"That's good to hear."

"Yes, my wife keeps six of them and I keep the other four!"

❧

Don't Try This at Home!

> This is the way of the Torah: Bread and salt will you eat,
> measured water will you drink, on the ground will you sleep, a
> life of suffering will you live, and in the Torah will you labor.
>
> — *Mishna 6:4*

This anonymous Mishna describes the philosophy of the *nazir* (ascetic Jew), recognizable by his long disheveled hair – an admission that, in the service of God, appearance mattered little – and who voluntarily vowed abstinence from such worldly pleasures as wine.

The *nazir*, from the Hebrew root "to make separate," believed that his acts of frugality, abstinence and deprivation resulted in self-sanctification, on the (incorrect) theory that wealth and material possessions were incompatible with a Torah lifestyle.

But don't try this at home!

Promoting "denial" as an ideal is a direct clash of Judaic values that demand of Jews to live and enjoy "normal" lives (i.e., balancing the material with the spiritual), a healthy philosophy that frowns on poverty and self-flagellation ("a person will one day give an accounting for everything his eyes saw which, although permissible, he did not enjoy!").

Rav Yehuda (*Rebbe*), the leading scholar of his time and compiler of the Mishna, was staggeringly wealthy yet managed to live a life of such piety and asceticism that the Talmud claims "humility" itself died with him; however Samuel, Rabbi Eleazar Hakappar and King Solomon all thought the life of the nazirite was extreme and self-destructive.

And the Rambam?

He calls ascetics "sinners" because their acts and beliefs (falsely) imply that "God is the enemy of the body!"

❧

Moishie wants to be an actor, so he moves to Hollywood and auditions for roles. For six months he tries his best, living a life of austerity while waiting to be discovered. Then one day his big break arrives. He calls home: "Mamma! I just got a role in the movies!"

"Mazel tov!" she says. "Tell me, what part is it?"

"I play the part of a Jewish husband!"

"Oh," she scowls, disappointed. "Next time, try and get a speaking role!"

❧

Torah as Necklace

> Great is Torah, for it gives life to those who live by it in this world
> and in the next world. Torah is a tree of life to those who take hold
> of it, and those who support it are fortunate; they are a graceful
> garland for your head and necklaces for your throat. In Torah,
> years of life, prosperity, honor and peace will be added to you.
>
> — *Mishna 6:7*

This Mishna uses symbolisms and metaphors to describe poetically how the wisdom of Torah not only prolongs life itself, but also has the potential to grant wealth, honor and peace (in both this world and *Olam Haba*, the World to Come).

Depicted as a graceful garland, such as the ancient Romans wore as a crown or necklace ornament (in Hebrew, throat is *garon*), the Torah is symbolized as a "tree of *life*." Why? Because a tree also lives and grows, providing both fruit and shelter to its surroundings; in the same way Torah gives life to the Jew who comes in contact with it.

But wait!

The text does *not* grant these infinite blessings to "students" of Torah, but only to "doers" of Torah; in other words, study as much as you want, but if you can't make the leap from the intellect (learning) to specific acts (mitzvos) and proper behavior (*middos*), the entire exercise is lacking.

Or is it?

The general concensus is this: continuous Torah study, regardless of the motivation, will eventually translate into "mitzvos [performed] for the sake of Heaven."

❧

Several couples are celebrating their fiftieth wedding anniversary.

"So, what do you think is the secret of a long union?" one little old Jewish lady asks Rebbetzim Greenbaum, "eating well, sleeping right, learning Torah?"

"The three most important words in a long marriage," Rebbetzim Greenbaum replies, "are 'You're probably right'" – to which Rabbi Greenbaum automatically mumbles in the background, "She's probably right!"

❧

A Company of Scorners

> Rabbi Chanina ben Tradyon[253] said: If two people sit together and do not exchange words of Torah between them, it is a company of scorners; but if two people sit and exchange words of Torah between them, the Divine Presence rests between them.
>
> — *Mishna 3:3*

Rabbi Yom Tov Lipman Heller, seventeenth-century German-born scholar-author (*Tosefos Yom Tov*), notes that this Mishna talks *not* of Jews not studying Torah, but of Jews not "exchanging" words of Torah; in other words, solitary learning is not the ideal ("Who is wise? One who learns from *all* people!").

This Mishna is one of contrasts: two Jews share words of Torah and thus merit being in the presence of God; the two others who do not, in an assault against the sanctity of time, are destined to descend into derision and ridicule.

Rabbi Chanina, having defined the latter as a *moshav leitzim* (company of scorners) involved in meaningless, mock conversations, was inspired by Proverbs to advise Jews to "cast out the scorner" amongst them and rid the world of "contention."

The Torah term for scorners (*leitzim*) is a negative one, an image of fools who laugh in the face of reality; and in modern Hebrew a clown is a *leitzan*, one who laughs inappropriately, not in humor but in contempt and disrespect.

And so King Solomon warns us to stay away from the *leitz*, defined by the Yiddishists as "a misfortune," whilst Rav Yaakov Emden is convinced: "What one fool spoils, a thousand wise men cannot mend!"

In general, Judaism has patience for the uneducated but not for the foolish!

꣓

"Oy vey," cries Izzy as he locks his car door and realizes that he has left the key in the ignition.

"Why don't we get a coat hanger to open the door," suggests Hyman, his buddy.

"Can't do that," replies Izzy, "people will think we're breaking into the car."

"OK, then let's get a penknife, cut the rubber seal around the driver's door, slide a finger in and pull out the key!"

"No, no," says Izzy, "people will think we're stupid for not using a coat hanger!"

"OK," says Hyman, "but you'd better think of something quick. It's starting to rain and your sun roof's still open!"

꣓

Consistency or Constancy?

Shammai said: Make your Torah study a fixed practice.

— *Mishna 1:15*

A Yiddish saying: "The Jew without learning is the real pauper."

When Shammai urged Jews to "fix" a time for Torah study, little did the Mishna Sage realize that his idea would, in today's age of *daf yomi*, reach near-halachic status.

Originally, after conquering Eretz Yisroel, Joshua was ordered to "delve" into Torah study "day and night," but by the time of Shammai the study of Torah had diminished to the extent that Jews were urged to at least set aside some time each day.

Is there an ideal time to "fix"?

First thing in the morning, says the *Mishne Berura*, while the mind is fresh, unencumbered, curious.

Rabbi Yishmael wants the Jew to learn Torah all day; the *Tiferes Yisroel* says there's "no minimum, no maximum," whilst Rabbi Meir Simcha of Dvinsk argues that, since each Jew has different circumstances (some rich, some poor; some working, some not; some young, some old), this is a "flexible" mitzva, depending on each Jew's situation.

Neither the Rambam nor Rabbi Yonah related to the word *fixed* as "fixed," claiming that what the Mishna is suggesting is that the idea of Torah study is not that it be "fixed" by the hands of a clock but approached as an ongoing challenge in the Jews' daily regimen.

Rav Israel Lipkin Salanter, the master of Mussar, preached consistency over constancy ("constant study is not study *all* day, but *each* day")…and when one great rabbi was asked, "What should the course of study be for a person who only has a half hour a day to learn – should he learn Bible, Talmud or halacha?" the *rav* replied, "Let him learn a half hour a day of *mussar* (manners, how to behave, etc.), for then he will change his value system – and realize that he has more than a half hour a day at his disposal to learn Torah!"

❧

A *kollel* guy turns to his *chavrusa* and asks, "Hey, what would you do if you won the lottery?"

"How much?"

"Ten million dollars!"

"Wow! For that much money," replies his friend, "I'd leave *kollel* and learn Torah for the rest of my life!"

❧

Status Symbol

> Rabbi Tzadok said: Do not make the Torah into a crown with
> which to aggrandize yourself or a spade with which to dig.
>
> — *Mishna 4:7*

This Mishna is a reminder that Torah is a gift to Israel that comes with obligations, and those who use its knowledge for personal, social or financial gain are abusing God's grant.

The expression, not to use Torah as a "spade to dig," refers to its abuse for utilitarian, especially financial, goals.

One day Rabbi Tarfon was passing through a garden and ate some leftover figs. The garden custodians saw him and beat him but stopped when he told them who he was. For the rest of his life he grieved over this incident: "Woe is me, for I have used the crown of the Torah for my own benefit!"

The Rambam worked (as a doctor) to make a living and was appalled at his colleagues who "cashed in" on their Torah knowledge, accusing them of cheapening the spiritual "product" by making the Torah look like any other "profession."

What's so negative about turning the Torah into "a crown"?

In general, this is a positive attribute for scholars ("Whoever holds back his student from serving him, it is as if he denies from him kindliness!"); but using it selfishly, as an egotistical tool to be admired or respected by others, borders on contempt or worse – hollow hero-worship!

A "crown," in the metaphoric language of the rabbis, is not a decoration but a symbol of the very essence of the wearer (i.e., the crown of a king identifies him as a genuine king, etc.); therefore, the truly pious Jew who "wears a crown" wears it as an embodiment of his total dedication to the Torah.

Thus, by honoring him we honor what he stands for!

⇝

Two Jews were arguing over who had the more pious *rav*.

"My rabbi," shouts Beryl, "is so *frum* that he fasts every day, except on Shabbas and on Yom Tov!"

"That's a lie!" yells back Shmeryl, "I saw him having a bagel just yesterday!"

"Ah ha!! That shows you how little you know! My *rav* is so humble and modest about his piety that when he eats, he only does so to hide the fact that he's fasting!"

⇝

For Its Own Sake

> Rabbi Meir said: Anyone who engages in Torah study for
> its own sake [*lishma*] merits many things; not only that,
> but the entire world is worthwhile for him alone.
>
> — *Mishna 6:1*

This Mishna elevates the concept of Torah study to a lofty ideal – that of *lishma* (literally, "for its [own] sake").

For "*its own*" sake? What does this mean?

It is a recognition that there is a difference in study for God's sake and study because of one's own interest; *Torah lishma* is thus an elevated level of dedication towards scholarship *in and of itself*, with no selfish motive of reward, status, recognition, or even intellectual stimulation, other than seeking to obtain a higher level of understanding, in order to reach a level of spirituality that brings one "closer" to God.

The *rosh yeshiva* of Volozhin wrote an entire chapter just on the definition of *lishma*, whilst the Rambam extended it to cover all the mitzvos, that they be pursued only for their own sake.

Yet selfless Torah study, more so than any other mitzva, is the most effective way to develop a passionate opportunity to "understand" the character, temperament and moral disposition of God, a prerequisite for appreciating and then, with newfound humility, sharing God's "philosophy" (i.e., values) of life.

The ideal of Torah *lishma* often led the rabbis of the Talmud to be suspicious of scholars whose conclusions were not arrived at *lishma*, even rebuking a king of Israel (David) for selfishly describing Torah study as "music" and "delight" to his ears, and crediting it with aiding him through tough times.

⇝

The *rosh yeshiva* is troubled at Beryl's lack of concentration in learning, so he's not surprised when his pupil walks into his office one day and announces that he's leaving yeshiva and going to college. Nevertheless the *rosh yeshiva* puts up a show of astonishment.

"But why?"

"In order to get degrees in philosophy, astrodynamics and nuclear physics."

"I still don't get it! What's so good about those degrees?!"

"Well, I'll be able to answer such difficult questions as 'What is existence?' 'What's the essence of matter?' and, 'Do you want fries with that?'"

⇝

A Sponge, Funnel,
Strainer and Sifter

> There are four types of students: A sponge, a funnel, a strainer and a sifter. The sponge absorbs everything; the funnel takes in on this side and brings out on the other; the strainer lets out the wine and retains the lees; the sieve lets out the flour dust and retains the fine flour.
>
> — *Mishna 5:18*

This Mishna defines students based on their ability to retain knowledge.

A "sponge student" might retain it all, but he cannot distinguish between the different types of knowledge he absorbs; what goes in the ear of a "funnel student" goes out the other; a "strainer student" discards what's significant and retains trivia; whilst the "sieve student" retains the significant material and rejects the inconsequential.

So which type is the superior student?

Actually, none of the above.

The master of Torah, according to the *Tiferes Yisroel*, is the one who listens, organizes the knowledge in his mind, and can teach it coherently to others.

"Who is great?" asks Yehuda Hanasi, "he who is not ashamed to admit he does not know!"

The concept of retaining knowledge led to a disagreement between two major Torah scholars: Rashi argues that it's not the end of the world if one retains flawed facts, whilst the Rambam considers the absorption of superficial knowledge harmful (better, he says, to be ignorant than to "know" imperfect facts).

The Midrash puts it thus: If you lack knowledge, what do you have? If you have knowledge, what do you lack?

⇝

John the atheist is hunting through the woods, when he comes upon Big Foot. Big Foot approaches him menacingly and John yells out, "God, save me!"

Seconds later, a voice rumbles down from Heaven, "I thought you didn't believe in me!"

"Well," John answers, "until a few minutes ago I didn't believe in Big Foot either!"

⇝

Be Practical, Not Theoretical!

> Shimon ben Rabban Gamliel said: Study is
> not the primary thing but action.
>
> — *Mishna 1:17*

This is the age-old Jewish version of the chicken 'n' egg question! What comes first? Is it better to study Torah, or to live Torah?

The answer?

Action speaks louder than words; the aim of the Torah is practical, not theoretical!

This conclusion comes to us courtesy of the historic Synod of Lod, and from Yehuda Hanasi, "What we do is more important than what we study," an echo of this Mishna's "Study is not the main thing but deeds…for it is by deeds that Man atones for his shortcomings."

In his *Pachad Yitzchak* on Shavuos, Rabbi Yitzchak Hutner, a leading Torah scholar of the twentieth century, saw an asymmetrical relationship between the two, in that the study of Torah "co-opts" performance and transforms the fulfillment of a mitzva into a dimension of "active study" (in other words, study has independent, and yet paramount, significance).

So what role does study or faith play, if any? They are important *only* if they lead to the right acts (mitzvos).

Yet, action not rooted in study is unsustainable. The Midrash illustrates this philosophy by a story: There were two muleteers who were enemies. One day the mule of one of them fell under its heavy load, but the other muleteer didn't care and continued to walk on. Suddenly he remembered learning the law of Exodus, "If your enemy's animal falls under his burden, you must help him." He then returned and the two men became friends. Thus, doing the right thing (action) required knowing (studying) what's the right thing to do.

That learning is more important is the reason we say a blessing (*shechalak meichachmaso liyire'av*, "Who has given a part of His wisdom to those who revere Him") when we see someone involved in Torah studies – but not when we see one involved in performing mitzvos!

৯

It's *erev yom tov*, so Sadie decides to visit the sick in hospital. After she enters the elevator, an orderly comes in pushing a complex machine that has several pipes, dials and gauges all over it.

"Man," she says, "I'd hate to be connected to that device!"

"Me, too," agrees the orderly, "it's a carpet shampooer!"

৯

Growing Old and Gray

> Yochanan ben Bag Bag[254] said: Look into the Torah, grow old and gray over it, and never move away from it, for you will find no better portion than it.
>
> — *Mishna 5:26*

That Jews should "grow old and gray" is not a curse but an acknowledgment that Torah study cannot be relegated to a single time or age; on the contrary, the Mishna designates it as a continuous reflection of values at certain stages of maturity, nominating the age of five for the study of Bible, ten for Mishna, etc.

As a result of this "infinite" body of teaching, even the greatest Jew never "completes" his studies during his entire life, approaching the process as a never-ending challenge, full of daily freshness, and convinced of one thing only: a life spent "reared on Torah" assures one of dying "with a good name."

This is the glue that held the nation of Israel together, a belief system held together by a tradition that proved unbelievably resilient in all geographic circumstances.

In his poetry ("The Torah is a deep sea, and man a vessel to draw as much as he wishes…"), Rav Yosef Hurvitz is echoing a *Zohar* concept: the Torah's rich soil can be "harvested" on so many levels that each time one opens a page of Torah, even the *same* page, one discovers a new experience, a new adventure.

In fact, the more one looks, the more one finds; the more one finds, the more one understands; the more one understands, the more one can grow.

Rabbi Eliezer inherited a thousand ships and towns, but never saw any of them because he didn't want to waste a second of Torah study; and the Talmud relates how the Sages wouldn't even interrupt their studies to say *Labriut* (in Yiddish, *Tzu gezunt*, "Good health") to a colleague who sneezed in the *beis medrash*!

❧

"Rebbe," Bentzion asks, "why do we eat kugel on Shabbas?"

"Because kugel and Shabbos have the same *gematria*."

The next day Bentzion corrects him: "Rebbe, I added it up. The *gematria* of Shabbas is greater than the *gematria* of kugel!"

"Okay! Okay! So just have another piece of kugel!"

❧

Those Who Can, Teach!

Rabbi Yishmael[255] said: One who studies Torah in order to teach is granted the ability to study and to teach; one who studies in order to "do" is granted the ability to study, teach, observe and do.

— *Mishna 4:6*

This Mishna, despite the concept of *Torah lishma*, places an "agenda" on Torah study, in that one should not make learning a superficial, abstract art but at least have an "end goal."

The Torah's value is thus not in intellectual stimulus, which can just as easily be satisfied by any disciplined scientific study, from geometry to geology, but in its God-recognized guidance for a relevant, meaningful and sanctified life.

Learning alone, according to Rabbi Yishmael, was of little value; learning to teach was the goal ("Who learns but doesn't practice Torah," warns the Midrash, "is better off never having been born!").

In presenting the Jew with two choices, study "to teach" or "to do," Rabbi Yishmael seems to prefer the latter. This is obvious: one cannot teach until and unless one "does" (or as the Yiddishists put it: Words that come from the heart enter the heart).

The lesson?

One must study in order to improve *oneself* in "doing," and then, and *only* then, should one seek to teach others.

This is not only practical advice but common sense: for no student will eagerly absorb lessons or values unless the teacher is an honest, sincere, walking, talking, real McCoy (i.e., a "doing") role model – the exact opposite of the popular adage "Those who can't, teach!"

⁓

The young *kollel* guy decides to go door-to-door teaching Torah. He rings one doorbell and it's quickly obvious that the little ol' Jewish woman is unhappy to see him.

She slams the door in his face, but the door doesn't close, it bounces back open. She tries again, but it bounces back again. Convinced that the *kollel* guy has his foot in the door to stop it from closing, she slams it with all her might to teach him a lesson – but it bounces open once more.

"Perhaps," says the *kollel* guy softly, "it would help if you move your cat!"

⁓

Not So Fast!

> Rabbi Yose said: Prepare yourself to study Torah
> because it is not an inheritance to you.
>
> — *Mishna 2:17*

This Mishna talks about attitude and is aimed at those Jews who think that, perhaps because their father or *zeida* was a great Torah *tzadik*, Torah will come easily and naturally to them.

Although the Talmud hints that, after three generations, the Torah "returns to its innkeeper," it also declares that no person is born great, and that scholarship simply cannot be passed on to children (the Yiddishists cynically add: Who comes for the inheritance is often made to pay for the funeral!).

But then the Talmud makes an interesting observation: one should be "careful" with the children of the poor, "for from them the Torah will come forth!" (another reason not to deny schooling to those who cannot afford tuition).

In approaching Torah study, each Jew faces the same uphill battle. There are simply no shortcuts. If it's not an inheritance, why then does Moses, in his summary of Deuteronomy, "command us [to observe] the Torah; it is an inheritance [*morasha*] to the Nation of Israel"?

In this context, *morasha* is more accurately translated as a "national heritage," rather than the more commonly understood sense of *inheritance* (which is expressed in the teaching that "anyone who withholds [the teaching of] a law from a student is as if he steals from the student's father's inheritance!").

Jewish mystics immediately pounce on the similarity between *morasha* and *m'orasa*, "betrothed," in that not only is Torah a possession, it is a symbolic spouse.

꒳

Shlomo's walking down a street in Miami and bumps into an old friend.

"Freddy, you look awful. What happened?"

"Well, my mother died in May and left me $15,000."

"Oh, I'm sorry to hear that."

"And then in June, my dad died and left me $50,000."

"Oh, no wonder you're depressed."

"And then just last month, would ya believe it, my aunt died and left me $70,000!"

"Wow, that's a lot to deal with. Losing three close family members in three months, that's terrible!"

"And then this month," continued Freddy, "nothing! Not even a single dime!"

꒳

Three's *Not* a Crowd!

> Rabbi Shimon said: Three who ate at one table and spoke words
> of Torah, it is as if they had eaten from the table of God.
>
> — *Mishna 3:4*

Why three?

According to the Rambam, the purpose of Torah (sometimes called "a three-part Torah") is to make peace (*shalom bayis*) in the world; and harmony usually requires a "third" person to intercede between two who are at odds.

Shtayim, the Hebrew word for two, is the only single-digit number whose name ends with a *mem*, the letter which is used to transform a pronoun from singular to plural.

A "third" also adds an element of excitement ("When all think alike," muses Walter Lippman, "then no one is thinking!").

By placing the three at "one table, eating together, speaking words of Torah," Rabbi Shimon paints the ultimate image of friendship and unity, and solidifies the concept that *divrei Torah*, "words of Torah," are only potent when discussed in a group.

What's the significance of three eating together?

The Maharal notes the similarity between *parnassa* and *parnass*; the former signifies nourishment, the latter the one who provides it, a link between one's physical and spiritual needs; the rabbis of the Talmud use the term *parnass* in describing God, in that Torah provides the Jew with nourishment!

The family table is the family altar to God (the altar was "three cubits high"), a spiritual place where *divrei Torah* must be discussed (this explains why it takes a minimum of three Jews to offer the joint Grace after Meals [*bensching*]).

꙳

Shapiro, an older gentleman, is concerned about his wife's hearing, so he decides to test her one day as she sits on the couch reading the paper. He shuffles over to the far corner and says, "Honey, can you hear me?" But there's no response.

So he comes five feet closer, and says, "Honey can you hear me?" Still no response. So he leans over the back of her chair and raises his voice, "Honey, can you hear me?"

Mrs. Shapiro puts the paper down and turns to him, "What's with you? I said 'Yes' three times!"

꙳

Caution! Error Ahead!

> Rabbi Yehuda[256] said: Be cautious in Torah study, for inadvertent
> errors in study are considered as willful transgressions.
>
> — *Mishna 4:16*

Making a mistake in Torah is a monumental mistake! Why? Because when
an error "creeps in, it stays!"

Rabbi Yonah thus argues for constant review; Meiri says this applies especially
to those who study Torah with an eye on *horaa*, to clarify halacha; and the venerable *Machzor Vitry* warns teachers that their carelessness will be judged by God
not as "inadvertent" but as deliberate.

But our rabbis also realized that to blunder was to be human; adds the Ram-
bam, "It's impossible to be human and not to err!" At least, pleads the Talmud's
Ishmael ben Elisha, "Err innocently rather than presumptuously," which is why
Judah ben Ilai defined the sins of the ignorant as "unwitting errors"!

Rav Yehuda is surprisingly tough on Torah scholars whose mistakes (in Hebrew, *shegagos*; the Jew committing the error is called a *shogeig*) are bluntly compared to intentional misdeeds, turning the very concept of innocent and unin-
tentional "errors" upside down.

Why? The Mishna expects a higher standard from Torah scholars. If they arrived at an erroneous conclusion, it was assumed that they were guiltless in intent
but guilty of neglect, complacency or, even worse, conceit – not to mention the
deterioration of their own spiritual level.

To Hillel, the contradiction in terms was obvious: the ignorant are simply not
pious!

Errors lead to ignorance, warns Nachman of the Talmud, and "ignorance admits negligence!" His colleague, Yochanan ben Nappaha, was more colorful: "An
ignorant Jew can be torn like a fish!"[257]

❧

Three months after his daughter married, the father comes rushing into the *rav's*
office demanding an immediate divorce.

"This is a very serious matter," replies the *rav*, taking down the Gemora dealing with divorce, in preparation for a decision. "What exactly is the fault of this
young man?"

"He can't play cards!"

"What?!" the *rav* screams, slamming his Gemora shut, "is that a fault? I pray
that none of our young men could play cards!"

"That's the problem, rabbi! This one *can't*, but *does*!"

❧

The Gift of Gifts!

> Rabbi Akiva said: Beloved is Israel that they were
> given a precious utensil [the Torah].
>
> — *Mishna 3:18*

Rabbi Yose ben Kisma calls the "luggage" of Torah a "precious gem!" – and when a student excitedly told the Kotzker Rebbe that he had just finished all of *shas*, the Rebbe replied, "You've done all of *shas*, but what did *shas* do to you?" – to which even the non-traditionalist Sigmund Freud had the right answer: "It was the study of Torah which kept the scattered Jews together!"

When launching his innovative *daf yomi* program, Rav Meir Shapira of Lublin quoted the story of a shocked Rabban Gamliel who witnessed Rabbi Akiva drowning from a shipwreck, only to find him later alive and healthy on dry land.

"How did you survive?" he asks Akiva, who replies, "I grabbed hold of a *daf* (a plank of wood), and with this *daf* for support, I sailed over every wave until I reached land."

Rav Shapira used this clever play on words to argue that one cannot survive the turbulence of life without clinging to a *daf* Gemora, the folio of Talmud.

Destined to shape a people's consciousness, the Jews' Torah, their "portable homeland," was wrapped tightly around their shared adventures; this was the glue that held Israel together, a sacred treatise bound by values and stapled by a tradition that proved unbelievably resilient in all geographic circumstances.

The Torah enabled entire Jewish communities to reestablish themselves after each forced uprooting. No matter where the wind blew the hapless Jew, a copy of *Shas* (Talmud, which means, "to learn") went along for the ride, a silent companion of ritual and consciousness.

❧

Yechiel, a Polish Jew, arrives in New York as an immigrant and immediately begins the process of learning English, so he will be able to communicate with others. Soon he goes on to apply for a driver's license at the DMV, where he is asked to take an eyesight test.

The optician holds up a card with the letters C Z W I X N O S T A C Z and asks him, "Can you read this?"

"Read it?" Yechiel replies, "I know the guy!"

❧

Due Diligence

> Rabbi Eleazar [ben Arach][258] said: Be diligent in the study
> of Torah; know what to answer a heretic [*apikorus*].
>
> — *Mishna 2:19*

This Mishna challenges us to be prepared to answer the argumentative challenges posed by heretics.

Why do we care? Why take a heretic seriously?

The Talmud describes a debate (more like a confrontation) between Rabbi Avohu and a heretic who "proved" that God was a priest and thus could not possibly have buried Moses. The entire back-and-forth, from both sides, is an incoherent, absurd exercise in futility, yet our Sages dutifully recorded the exchange.

Why? To show that no question must ever be ignored; ben Arach considered it a *chillul Hashem* for a Jew not to be able to answer an *apikorus* (a Jewish heretic, the term being the Hebrew equivalent of Epicurus, the ancient Greek philosopher and founder of the philosophy "Eat, drink and be merry, for tomorrow you may die!").[259]

Did this way of thinking actually attract Jews? Yes. The intelligentsia of third-century Alexandrian Jews and Jews in Judea embraced the atheism of this new "religion," accepting the anti-Torah idea that pleasure is the beginning and end of life.

The rabbis considered the Jewish heretic such a danger in their midst that they increased the number of blessings (from eighteen to nineteen) in the daily *Shemoneh Esrei* prayer to include a "blessing regarding the heretic [*Birkas Haminim*]."

❧

The rabbi, shocked to see Abe the heretic come into *shul* one Shabbas morning with a St. Bernard dog, runs over to him: "Hey! What are you doing here with a dog?"

"Rabbi, my dog came here to pray."

"Are you crazy? He can't come in here! Dogs don't pray!"

"But rabbi, this one does, watch!"

Abe nods to the dog who takes out a *yarmulke*, *tallis* and *siddur*, and starts *davening*...

The rabbi regains his composure, and coolly turns to Abe: "Maybe your dog also wants to go to rabbinical school?"

"Well, Rabbi, perhaps you can talk to him! He wants to be a doctor!"

❧

On the Road, Again!

Rabbi Nehorai[260] said: Exile yourself to a place of Torah and do not say it will come after you or that your colleagues will preserve it for you.

— *Mishna 4:18*

This Mishna may use a term (*goleh*) from the same Hebrew root as *galus* (exile), which the Torah uses to describe the forced and brutal exile of the Jewish nation – but it differs substantially in context.

If the Jew is not living in an environment of sanctity, Rav Nehorai urges him to "relocate" and settle in a Torah-friendly religious community.

So why use the provocative term "exile"?

It's a reminder: Jews must not only sometimes uproot themselves geographically but also psychologically, "exiling" themselves from old habits and beginning life anew – even in their customary surroundings.

Thus the very idea of "exile" is to feel uncomfortable, not at home, not fully settled, not yet independent: a state of wandering flux that stays incomplete until the Jew "cleaves to the dust of the feet [of the scholars] and thirstily drinks their words" – either at home or abroad.

The lesson of this Mishna?

To be proactive in the search for Torah surroundings, to spurn passivity and apathy.

In fact, this is how the exciting adventure of the Jewish people begins: with a single expression from God to Avram, *lech* (go), a proactive term that symbolizes the history of a people whose first step lies in Abraham's migration, a compelling directive to abandon an entire way of life and step forward into the unknown, unexplored, unfamiliar, "to the land that I will show you," with no road map, no navigational system, no coordinates, no Map Quest, no e-mails, no Blackberry and no cell phone!

❧

The rabbinic chaplain, who had a habit of ending all his speeches with a plea that the audience reflect upon the purpose of life, was invited to give a *drasha* in a psychiatric prison ward. He concluded each *d'var Torah* with the same rhetorical question – "After all, what are we here for?" – which left his listeners in a pensive, quiet mood.

This time, at the end of the lecture, instead of the usual reflective silence, one guy yelled out: "Well, rabbi, we don't know why *you're* here; but *we're* here because we are not all *there*!"

❧

Who Knows Ten?

> Chalafta ben Dosa of K'far Chanania said: When ten people sit and study Torah, the Divine Presence dwells among them.... How do we know this applies even to five...even three...two...one?
>
> — *Mishna 3:7*

This Mishna differentiates between the quota for praying and learning – ten for the former, no minimum for the latter; in fact, God's Presence dwells *anywhere, anyplace, anytime* even one lonely Jew sits and learns – although the rabbis of the Talmud embrace the more-the-better philosophy, in that Divinity is more strongly felt in groups than by a solitary person.

Rav Chalafta's use of "ten" is not to be confused with the quota for a *minyan*; instead, he derives it from the Torah's word for assembly (*eida*), the minimum number of a *tzibur*, the basic unit (of "completeness") for public prayer ("*davening mit a minyan!*").

Five refers to God's "band, bundle" (*aguda*), which can also mean "a handful" (i.e., five fingers). And "three"? From the minimum number of judges required to form a Jewish court.

What happened to "four"? Doesn't that count? No.

Jewish mystics see the number "four" as symbolic of "diversity, division, dispersion." Why? Because of the verse "I have scattered you like the four directions of the Heavens."

"Three"? The minimum number of judges to form a *beis din*.

And "two"? The source comes from the verse "Then those who fear God spoke to each other, and God listened and heard" – or, colloquially today: two are better than one!

꙳

The math teacher is addressing the *cheder* class, and asks seven-year-old Benny, "If there are four planes flying, and two more planes join them, how many planes are flying?"

Benny looks confused.

"What's the problem?" the teacher asks.

"Well," little Benny says, "I know that 4 + 2 = 6, but I can't figure out what the planes have to do with this!"

꙳

If There Is No Vineyard, Why a Fence?

> Rabbi Akiva said: The oral transmission is a
> protective fence around the Torah.
>
> — *Mishna 3:17*

To lessen the possibility of desecration, our rabbis added dozens of additional "Thou-shalt-nots" (*takanos*) that act as "fences" (*seyag la'Torah*) around the Torah. An example? Certain objects (cash, radios, pens, etc.) were declared *muktze* ("excluded," i.e., forbidden to be touched) on Shabbas by the logic that to touch was to use.

What's the legal basis of this extraordinary power?

"You shall take measures to safeguard that which I give you," God instructs.

But there were caveats; no "double-dipping" (*gezeira l'gezeira*) was allowed (i.e., one protective measure could not safeguard another protective measure), and, adds the *Yalkut Shimoni*, a thirteenth-century compilation of earlier rabbinical literature, "Do not make the fence more important than what it fences in, for if there be no vineyard, why a fence?"

But the Talmud is lenient in extenuating circumstances, which led such major *poskim* (halachic deciders) as Rav Shmuel Engel, in recognition of the practical and sometimes lifesaving necessities of everyday life under hostile regimes, to allow Jews to carry government-ordered identification papers on Shabbas (the *Chasam Sofer* relied on the halachic "umbrella" of *shinui* – i.e., doing something in an unusual manner to distinguish it from a weekday act – to permit the carrying of a handkerchief on Shabbas outside the *eruv* by tying it around one's wrist, which was not the usual custom of carrying.

In messianic times observing the Shabbas will become easier. Why? Rabbi Shimon explains: today, if a Jew gathers figs on Shabbas, the Jew speaks, the fig is mute; but in those times, the Jew shall become mute, and the fig will shout, "Stop! Today is Shabbas!"

❧

The rabbi is on the phone: "Dovid! I just heard that you played cards on Shabbas! You can't do that! It's forbidden! Is it true?"

"Yes, Rabbi. I confess."

"Confession is not sufficient," roars the *rav*. "*Teshuva* demands that you make a donation to a worthy cause to pay for your behavior!"

"Oh, don't worry, Rabbi. This sin has already cost me plenty!"

❧

Sleepless Nights

> Rabbi Chanina ben Chachinai[261] said: One who stays
> awake at night or travels on the road alone and leaves his
> heart open to idleness bears the guilt for his own soul.
>
> — *Mishna 3:5*

What's the connection between being awake at night and traveling alone?

Both the nighttime and deserted roads are dangerous; thus the Mishna is lobbying for Torah study as a safety shield, an armor of protection, not because the Torah acts as a bulletproof, miraculous weapon, but because the Jew immersed in its study is worthy of a higher level of Divine protection.

Rabbi Yonah advises the traveling Jew to take along an "accompaniment" (i.e., a *sefer*); the Talmud claims that night was created only for sleeping or learning Torah ("My soul is satisfied," sings *Tehillim*, "when I remember and meditate upon Thee whilst asleep"); Rashi adds the ultimate incentive: "He who adds to the nights with increased study of Torah will have his life prolonged!"

The Mishna then gives a startling warning: "Rabbi Yaakov said: One who is walking along the road and is studying [Torah], and then interrupts his studies and says, 'How beautiful is this tree! How beautiful is this plowed field!' – Scripture considers it as if he himself bears the guilt for his soul."

Apparently, when traveling one cannot interrupt one's Torah study, *even* to admire Mother Nature, which is itself an obligation for the Jew!

꠸

It's late at night and Shmuli's wagon suddenly tips over into a ditch in a desolate area. He gets out and rehitches his horse, Buddy, to the wagon, but then yells, "Pull, Nellie, pull!"

Buddy doesn't move.

He then hollers again, "Pull, Nellie, pull!"

Buddy still doesn't move.

Finally he screams, "Pull, Buster, pull!"

All of a sudden, Buddy starts pulling, and the wagon is freed from the ditch.

One of the passengers is intrigued. "How come you called your horse by the wrong name three times?"

"Well," replies Shmuli, "Buddy is blind, and if he thought he was the only one pulling, he wouldn't even try!"

꠸

Got a Headache? Study Torah!

Rabbi Yehoshua ben Levi[262] said: You will not find a
freer person than one who is involved in Torah study;
for all those who study Torah are uplifted.

— *Mishna 6:2*

Rabbi Yehoshua believed Torah had therapeutic powers and was thus the best medicine (Got a headache? Study Torah!).

The source for Torah study, not just one of the 613 mitzvos but the one that is "equivalent to all the other mitzvos," is derived from Deuteronomy: "And you shall teach it to your children."

But wait!

This talks about "teaching," not studying; and so the rabbis of the Talmud elaborate that, in order to teach Torah, one must study first (study leads to action!).

That Torah outweighs other mitzvos – including honoring one's parents, bringing peace between people, even building the Temple in Jerusalem – is incorporated in the daily prayers ("A single day devoted to the Torah outweighs a thousand sacrifices!").

When Torah scholars wrote down their thoughts, they subordinated their own names to the title of their books (e.g., *Chofetz Chaim*, instead of "by Rabbi Yisrael Meir Kagan"), preferring to be associated with scholarship rather than family surnames.

Over the centuries, the Jews' legendary love of Torah study, the most dominant feature of Jewish life, caused the leaders of Islam to honor them as the People of the Book (*Ahl al-Kitab*). In ancient times, Egyptian leader Ptolemy II, a noted bibliophile, ordered that "the Jews' book" be translated into Greek, convinced that "their laws are befitting of imitation."

This reputation led to today's Western consensus that the Jewish people, with a thirst for knowledge that expanded beyond Torah, are the most educated in the world!

❧

It's Baylie's first day at her job. She's nervous. Suddenly her boss calls on the intercom, "Fax me that report, right away!"

"OK," she says, "but please fax it right back. It's my only copy!"

❧

Born to Toil!

> Rabbi Nechunia ben Hakanah[263] said: Whoever accepts upon himself the yoke of Torah study, the yoke of government and the yoke of earning a living will be removed from him; and whoever casts off from himself the yoke of Torah study, the yokes of government and earning a living will be placed upon him.
>
> — Mishna 3:6

What is a yoke?

A piece of equipment placed around the neck of a plowing animal to help him *shlep* all his burdens.

What is the "yoke of government"? Taxes, military service, etc.

Ben Hakanah's reference to "government" must be placed in historic context: he wrote this at a time when the Jews were under the oppression of a Roman ruler who had banned Torah study.

The above Mishna, with all its intriguing "yokes," is quite straightforward: the Heavens compensate those who diligently study Torah.

The reward? An easier and less burdensome life, especially as it relates to *parnassa* (livelihood).

Psychologically, it is true: those who adopt the "yoke" of Torah ("Man was born to toil!" cried Job) are less likely to stress themselves out in the pursuit of social status, power or crass materialism.

Why? Because, according to the Maharal, subjecting oneself to the burden and authority of Torah, conceived and created as a Divine process, is a form of liberation, one that transcends all other systems, such as nature and government.

This is why our Torah linguists pronounce the word *charus* (engraved) – from the verse "The tablets are the writing of God, engraved [*charus*]" – as *cheirus* (emancipated), since the greatest freedom is to be able to be involved in an uplifting noble activity, namely the study of Torah.

꒰

"I have to tell you, Mrs. Buttinski," advises her doctor after a checkup, "that you have a fissure in your uterus, and if you ever have a baby it would be a miracle."

She immediately rushes home to tell Mr. Buttinski: "You vouldn't belief it. I vent to the doctah and he told me – 'You haf a fish in your uterus and if you haf a baby it vill be a mackerel.'"

꒰

Swine's Snout

Rabbi Yehoshua ben Levi said: Anyone who does not study Torah is called "rebuked," as the verse says, "As a golden ring in a swine's snout."

— *Mishna 6:2*

When this Mishna warns about "swine," it refers to the beast within, tamed not by mitzvos alone but by Torah study, a transformative event that frees the soul.

This startling observation is directed at religious Jews living a less than religious lifestyle.

Why is the non-learner called "rebuked"?

Better, say our Sages, a public scolding than love unrevealed (but the rabbis of the Talmud were pessimistic: they doubted whether anybody in their generation could accept rebuke, a course of action that the *Kli Yakar* said was "of no avail to the stiff-necked," using the same term that God did to describe the nation of Jews).

Does ben Levi tell us who has to study? No, but the answer, according to the Rambam, is *everybody*, "whether he is rich or poor, healthy or sick, young or old!"

Why?

Because of the fable of the Fish and the Fox, in which the hostile animal fails to entice the fish onto dry land, after the fish declares that, akin to Israel surviving only in the sea of Torah, a fish lives only in the ocean.

So what's more important? Study or prayer?

The Talmud announces: study! Why? Because prayer is "materialistic" in *this* world by its very nature, whereas Torah study is the means and entrée to the more spiritual World to Come.

It is an act of both passion and prayer, the highest form of Godly worship; this is why Jewish law allocates a higher degree of *kedusha* (sanctity) to a *beis medrash* (house of study) than to a synagogue.

❧

The town idiot comes to his Rebbe: "Rebbe! Rebbe! Last night I had a dream that I became the Rebbe and leader of your three hundred Chassidim!"

"Come back," replies the Rebbe, "when my three hundred Chassidim have a dream that you're their Rebbe!"

❧

Let's Study Together!

> One who learns from his fellow a single chapter of
> Torah, a single law, a single verse, a single statement, or
> even a single letter, must treat him with honor.
>
> — *Mishna 6:3*

This Mishna staples the concept of *derech eretz* (respect) to those who teach Torah ("even one letter"!), because they are engaged in the noble act of "giving" wisdom, helping another Jew navigate the trials and travails of life.

Since even a single letter's (correct) translation is of inestimable value to the overall comprehension of Torah, honor must be given to the teacher of that single letter. Rashi even extends the concept of honor to those who spread knowledge only in "general" terms.

The Mishna seeks an example of this advice to interact and focuses on Achitofel, who is upset at seeing King David studying Torah alone: "What are you doing?" he asks, adding that "those scholars who sit by themselves studying Torah will become fools!"

David, humbled, replies, "Let's study together!" and confides in his song of *Tehillim*, "I became wiser from every teacher!"

꩜

Two scholars are learning together in Chelm.

"Why is the sea so salty?" asks Beryl.

"Don't ask such ridiculous questions," scolds Shmeryl.

"No, really, I really want to know!" insists Beryl.

"It's obvious, you moron!" says Shmeryl. "It's because hundreds and thousands of herring live in the sea!"

꩜

Run Like a Zealot!

> Rabbi ben Azzai[264] said: Run to perform a minor
> mitzva and flee from sin, for the reward of a mitzva
> is a mitzva and the "reward" of a sin is a sin.
>
> — *Mishna 4:2*

There is an underlying lesson in this Mishna: not to "rate" mitzvos and decide which ones are more important than others.

This is why, in general, the Torah does not link rewards to deeds, and considers a mitzva done as an opportunity to do another one, a "reward" in and of itself!

And, adds Rabbi Yonah, if you get into the habit of "running" passionately and joyfully to do a "minor" mitzva, you'll continue the habit for "higher yielding" (or more difficult) mitzvos!

What's a "light" (or "minor") mitzva?

According to the *Tiferes Yisroel*, it usually entails something that provides immediate gratification (e.g., a Shabbas meal), or it has some "logic" to it (e.g., honoring a parent), or the convenience of repetition (e.g., daily *davening*).

Ben Azzai uses his words carefully: after "running" to do a mitzva, he doesn't use the same verb with sin, from which one must "flee"; nor does he use the adjective "minor" to attach to sin, on the theory that there's no difference between *minor* or *major* evil.

The Torah considers zealousness a virtue, complacency a curse.

꒜

The new *rav* was a bit overzealous and impatient. During a speech in *shul* one Shabbas morning, he was annoyed at ol' Yankele who was asleep and snoring in the back row. So the rabbi takes his *chumash* in a fit of fervor, and throws it at him. His aim is good and it hits Yankele right in the head.

"Hey! What are you doing?" Yankele shouts.

"Yankele! If you don't want to hear the Word of God, I'll make you feel it!"

꒜

The Domino Effect

> Rabbi ben Azzai said: One mitzva leads to another
> mitzva,[265] and one sin leads to another sin.
>
> — *Mishna 4:2*

This Mishna describes the phenomenon of a spiritual chain reaction, where one act, good or evil, leads to a similar act.

Ben Azzai was aware of human nature: a sin committed once and twice alters its chemistry, turning the particular sin into a "permissible" act, the repetition (with no immediate punishment) having chipped away at its perceived severity (the great nineteenth-century *mussar* master Israel Salanter warned often against the slippery slope of once unthinkable behavior becoming a routine reality, even, perversely, a "mitzva"!).

Similarly a mitzva acts as a catalyst for another mitzva, which, in turn, is considered the "reward" for the previous mitzva, and so on; good habits beget goodness!

Judaism requires a *pattern* of behavior (called a *chazaka*), which comes into play if any good or bad act is repeated three or more times. This reveals the compassionate nature of Torah, the benefit of the doubt concept: it is assumed that the first sin was accidental, the second also inadvertent or perhaps involuntary – whereas the third time it becomes a premeditated knowing act.

The concern of sin is thus not so much the punishment – but the progeny, the ultimate result! One lie needs another to prop it up; one crime leads to another crime of cover-up; one sin gives birth to another.

"If you start by *walking* in the counsel of the wicked," notes *Tehillim*, "you will end up *standing* in the way of sinners until, finally, you'll *sit* in the seat of scoffers!"

❧

Penelope decides to convert to Judaism and eventually ends up going to the *mikva* to finalize the process.

"Please immerse yourself fully under the water," the *mikva* lady explains.

"Oh, no! I can't!" she cries.

"Why not?"

"I just went to the beauty parlor and had my hair done. Can I go in without dunking my head?"

"Sure...but you'll still have a *goyishe kop!*"

❧

In Abundance!

> Chanania ben Akashia said: God wanted to give Israel merit;
> therefore He gave them Torah and mitzvos in abundance.
>
> — *Mishna*[266]

This Mishna reveals the motivation behind the giving of Torah to the Jews – in order to bestow merit upon them.

This Divine bequest turned Jews into the *am segula*,[267] "Chosen People," and its theme, that the Jewish people are a "jewel from among the nations" (*asher bachar banu mikol ha'amim*, "Who has chosen us from among all the peoples"), ripples throughout the Torah and all rabbinic writings.[268]

Rashi links *segula* to royalty, as in *segulas melachim*, "treasures of kings,"[269] whilst Abraham Ibn Ezra, a Jew who exerted great influence on both Rambam and Ramban, interprets *segula* as a "desired and honored" *a priori* object that can never be duplicated.

And yet the Rambam instinctively didn't like the term.

This twelfth-century Spanish Sage thought "chosen" hinted at a religious chauvinism of inherited biological differences between Jews and *goyim*,[270] divisions which didn't exist.

Chanania's reference to mitzvos "in abundance," is not an indication of excess difficulty, but a reminder that the Torah was given as an act of kindness ("Its ways are ways of pleasantness and all its paths are peace"), and as a disciplined road map of opportunity towards building a meaningful and rewarding relationship with God.

Why study Torah?

Phineas ben Yair provides one answer: because it leads to "exactness, exactness to ardor, ardor to morality, morality to restraint, restraint to purity, purity to holiness, holiness to mildness, mildness to fear of sin, fear of sin to saintliness, saintliness to the holy spirit, and the holy spirit to life eternal!"

❧

The rabbi is visiting a teenage boy in the hospital who believes he is losing his sight. He is relieved to find the boy calm, with his mother sitting nearby, knitting. As he approaches the bed, the boy starts screaming, "I can't see! I can't see! I can't see!" The *rav*, taken aback, turns to the mother and asks, "How long has this been going on?"

"It started," she says, without looking up from her knitting, "the moment you stepped in front of the TV!"

❧

THE FORTY-EIGHT WAYS

"Where's the self-help section?" Moishie
asks the salesman in a bookstore.

"Can't tell ya," he replies.

"Why not?!"

"If I told ya, it would defeat the purpose!"

The Forty-Eight Ways

> Torah is greater than priesthood and kingship, for kingship is
> acquired with thirty qualities, priesthood is acquired with twenty-
> four, whereas the Torah is acquired in forty-eight ways.
>
> — *Mishna 6:6*

In its "Human Challenge" section, the Mishna goes into a lengthy inventory, commonly referred to as "the Forty-Eight Ways," an extension and reiteration of previous positions, of distinct moral and spiritual skills that one needs in order to "acquire" Torah.

Unlike royalty and priesthood, Torah study, one of the few positive mitzvos not limited to a specified time ("Meditate in it," God tells Joshua, "day and night"), is unrelated to family rights, *yichus* (lineage), position, power, ability or wealth.

The common thread: "All who want Torah, come and take!"

Rabbi Akiva, one of the greatest of all Mishna scholars, discovered the *alef-beis* at age forty; Rabbis Shemaya, Avtalyon and Akiva himself were descended from converts. And they all had one common character trait: humility, a prerequisite, according to the Maharal, for anyone interested in the pursuit of Torah ("You will not find Torah among *gasei haruach* [arrogant people]").[271]

In explaining why the items on this list are called *kinyanim* (acquisitions), Rav Aharon Kotler notes that Jewish law uses the same technical term for an "acquisition"; in this context, it refers to the means ("forty-eight ways") by which property (Torah) changes hands, allowing the new owner to reach a higher level of spiritual perfection.

❧

When young David was asked by his father to say the evening prayer, he realized the boy's head was not covered...so he asked his little brother Henry to rest a hand on his head until prayers were over. Henry grew impatient after a few minutes and removed his hand.

The father said, "This is important. Put your hand back on his head!" – to which Henry exclaimed, "What, am I my brother's *kippa*?"

❧

Way One

"When I pray, I talk to God. When I study Torah,
God talks to me!" — *the Rugochover Rebbe*

The first of the forty-eight "ways" is *limud: study, study, study*!

Even the secularist Ahad Ha'am admits, "Learning, learning, learning – that is the key to Jewish survival!"

How?

Chassidus gives us a clue: as a spiritual pursuit it can convert *tzarah* (trouble and affliction) to *tzohar* (radiant light).

But the pursuit of knowledge and insight does not come easy. It requires diligence, conscientiousness, attentiveness, energy; thus laziness and idleness do not go along with Torah study, and lethargy is God's greatest enemy.

Wasting time and sleeping in ("How long," asks Proverbs, "must you lie a'bed, O sluggard?") are considered anathema, a curse, bordering on idolatry.

To study Torah requires perseverance; perseverance requires urgency, resolve, determination and zeal; it must be actively sought, warns Shimon ben Lakish, "for it will not come by itself!"

The *Mishlei Agur* defines a "lazybones" as one who thinks "pulling a hair out of milk is a difficult chore!" whilst a Yiddish proverb cautions: If you rest, you rust!

All successful students of Torah have one common character trait: they instinctively understand that failure to seize the moment creates "wasted" time, a *bizbuz z'man*, obliterated, lost forever, never to return.

Abraham Ibn Ezra was pragmatic: "A sleeping cat will never catch the rat!"

⤙

The rabbi, annoyed that Mendele always sleeps through his Shabbas *drasha*, has a brainwave. He approaches Mendele's young son and makes a deal with him, giving him twenty-five cents a week to keep his father awake during the *drasha*. This works for about three weeks, but then it's back to the same ol' disruptive snoring.

"What happened?" the angry rabbi asks the boy, "I'm paying you twenty-five cents a week to keep your father awake!"

"Yes, rabbi, I know. But my father's now paying me fifty cents a week to let him sleep!"

⤙

Way Two

"Man has two ears and one tongue in order that he may listen more than speak!" — *Abraham Hasdai, thirteenth-century scholar from Barcelona*

The Mishna's second of forty-eight "ways" is *shmias ha'ozen*: listen attentively (literally, "listen with your ears").

"Want to learn?" asks Ibn Gabriol. "Then listen!"

The vibrancy of Torah comes from being a good listener and training one-self to retain memory (memory loss for a Torah scholar was considered an acute tragedy).

The art of accurate listening is a major prerequisite for mastering Torah. Why? Because proper Torah study is not a solitary activity but a team effort, one that requires communication, articulation, interaction (*chavrusa*).

This is why the Mishna often doles out its words of wisdom from *zugos* (pairs of scholars).[272]

In fact, even God listens!

"When two students listen patiently to one another in legal discussion," observes Shimon ben Lakish, a famous Palestinian *Amora*, "God listens to them, too!" And if they do not? "They cause the *Shechina* [God's Presence] to depart from Israel!"

The Mishna is also concerned with the reverse: the risk of being inattentive.

Lacking concentration is a sure slide down the slope of carelessness and distraction. And worse! It leads to incomplete knowledge resulting in errors in Jewish law, life and lore.

When choosing body parts as allegory, the Mishna thus emphasizes the ears because retention of knowledge requires hearing (according to Jewish law, if one accidentally blinds an employee, he must pay for the value of the eye, but if he causes a servant to go deaf, he must pay for the servant's entire value!).

Moshe Ibn Ezra defined ears as "the gateways to the mind," whilst Job was more gastronomic: "The ear tries words, the same way the palate tastes food!"

꿎

Shmuel comes to work with both ears all bandaged up. "Hey," the boss yells, "what happened to your ears?"

"Last night," Shmuel explains, "I was ironing my shirt when the phone rang, and I accidentally answered the iron."

"OK. That explains one ear, but what happened to your other ear?"

"Well, I had to call Hatzolah!"

꿎

Way Three

"Regard the speech, not the speaker!" – *Yosef Caspi, fourteenth-century Provençal exegete*

The next of the forty-eight qualities is *arichas s'fasayim* (literally "arrangement of the lips"): the need for careful articulation, an argument for the virtues of verbalization.

But beware: on the one hand it was a special mitzva, according to Schneur Zalman of Liadi, founder of Chabad, to study Torah through speech, the "tool of Creation" (wisdom, notes ben Sira, "comes only through the tongue"), yet speech has its harmful flipside.

Gossip is deadly! Negative speech was considered "worse than a sword!" Why? Because it "kills" the multitude, even at great distances; and so King Solomon warned all who would listen, "Life and death are in the hands of the tongue!"[273]

So can one study Torah silently? Of course, but ultimately it's unrewarding.

Speak up! demands the Rambam ("One who raises his voice while studying will assure the retention of his learning; one who studies quietly will soon forget!"), and, in a letter to his son Nachman, the Rambam elaborates: "Let your utterance be clear, tranquil – and to the point!"

The *Tiferes Yisroel* goes one step further: say it, and then repeat it, he advises, and then say it over again!

⇢

The venerable rabbi invited one of his elderly congregants for Shabbas lunch. The Shabbas guest was very impressed with the respect the quiet *rav* gave his wife, after nearly seventy years of marriage, calling her by such endearing terms as *Ziskeit*, *Shaynkeit*, Darling, my Honey, etc.

When the rebbetzin was in the kitchen, he leaned over to the *rav* and whispered, "*Baruch Hashem*, I'm getting a lot of *nachas* from the respect you show your wife, still relating to her in such loving terms after all this time."

"I have to," the rabbi responded, "I forgot her name about ten years ago!"

⇢

Ways Four and Five

> The Jew needs *mazel* more than *seichel*, but in
> order to get *mazel* he has to have *seichel*!

The next two "ways," *binas halev* and *sichlus halev* (two different forms of "understanding" of the heart) are an ode to intuitive understanding; in short, *seichel* (which might be translated as "common sense") is critical!

Our Sages believe Torah is better suited to the brain than to the heart.

The English expression to "take it to heart" is a Judaic echo, in that *to know* is not enough; to know with emotion is the ideal!

To discern is to have acumen, and a certain instinctive sense of street-smart shrewdness to help clarify and grasp the concepts of Torah.

The *Malbim* wrote that facts alone are insufficient; only *seichel*, a certain form of ingrained quickness and intelligence, provides the ability to take hold of Torah concepts.[274]

In Jewish mysticsm, *seichel* (intellect) must rule emotion (*middos*), and not vice versa (e.g., in Chabad philosophy, there are only three levels of intellect – *chachma*, *bina* and *da'as* – and seven levels of emotion!).

"*Le sens commun n'est pas si commun*," Voltaire roared, "Common sense ain't so common!"

Meanwhile the *Tiferes Yisroel*, a scholar who had an instinct for ideas and ideals, linked *seichel* to "seeing," as in grasping concepts beyond one's immediate realm of knowledge.

The rabbis of the Talmud were blunt: A man with no sense deserves no pity!

꩜

Seichel is not an acquired trait; some have it by nature, many lack it. A priest, a lawyer and an engineer are about to be guillotined. The priest puts his head on the block, the executioner pulls the rope, and nothing happens. The priest declares that he's been saved by Divine intervention – so he's let go.

The lawyer is put on the block, and again the rope doesn't release the blade; he claims he can't be executed twice for the same crime, so he is set free, too.

They grab the engineer and shove his head into the guillotine; he looks up at the release mechanism and says, "Wait a minute, I see your problem…"

꩜

Ways Six to Nine

> "Where there is fear, there is no rejoicing, and where there is no rejoicing there is no fear — except in worshipping God!" — *Ba'al Shem Tov*

The list continues: we're now up to *eima*, *yira*, *anava* and *simcha* (awe, fear, modesty and joy), a complex recipe, one that sheds light on the dual (from exhilaration to fear) nature of Torah study.[275]

The Jew's challenge is to study with joy (because the Divine Presence only co-exists amidst joy), yet simultaneously knowing that the Presence he seeks requires the same level of "awe and fear" (*eima* and *yira*) as experienced at Sinai.

King David used this theme in his lyrics: "I feared in my joy and I rejoiced in my fear!"

He was not alone.

"There is no contradiction," wrote Der Alter from Slobodka, "between joyfulness and fear of God. On the contrary, no real fear can be achieved other than by gladness and rejoicing!"

Rabba bar Huna compares a Jew with knowledge and no fear of God to "a treasurer who has received the keys of the inside vaults, without the keys to the outer doors. How will he enter?!"

This is Jewish philosophy at its core: fear and wisdom, wisdom and fear — each needs the other to survive, as the Midrash puts it, "like a carpenter needs his tools!"

※

Morty is accidentally hit by a car one morning and, as he lies on the road, a priest suddenly appears and begins preparing him for the worst, demanding firmly, "Now's the time! Denounce the Devil and his evil!"

Morty says nothing.

The priest, raising his voice, repeats the order — but Morty remains mute, causing the puzzled priest to ask, "Why do you refuse to denounce the Devil and his evil?"

"Cause," replies Morty, "until I know where I'm headin', I ain't gonna aggravate no one!"

※

Way Ten

"Not what a man does but how he does it, is profane or sacred!"
— *Hermann Steinthal, nineteenth-century German-Jewish philologist*

The next "way" is that of *tahara* (purity), in that seeds of Torah can only grow in untainted and uncontaminated places.

This purity is metaphysical (of thoughts) and physical (of body), as Moses learned when he was told to remove his shoes in the presence of a burning bush.

The Ba'al Shem Tov approached everything, not just Torah, with pure reverence, in the belief that whatever God created had a spark of sanctity to it; the Chassidic master was armed with a Talmudic adage: if a man sanctifies himself a little, he will be sanctified much!

And so, throughout the centuries, Jews have tried to infuse their routine with purity.

Rabbi Eliyahu Botchko, *rosh yeshiva* in Montreux, Switzerland, would always go to the *mikva* before giving a *d'var Torah*, convinced that pure words of Torah could only come from a purified state of mind and body.

Rav Meir arrived late at all *simcha*s, not because he opposed punctuality, but because he thought the notion of leaving early would be impure and insulting to the *ba'al simcha* (host) – so he always stayed until the end!

❧

One day, Reb Velvele visited a wealthy Chassid of his and commented on a silver candlestick. "Doesn't it encourage pride in you?" he asks.

"Oh, no, Rebbe, it's not pure silver; it's only plated with silver."

"Oh, I see. There's no pride here, just deception!"

❧

Ways Eleven to Thirteen

> "He who is silent when he has nothing to say is not taciturn — he merely shows that he is not a fool. The truly silent man is the one who remains quiet when he has something to say. I remain silent, and whenever I am tired of remaining silent, I have a quiet rest, and then go back to being silent!"
>
> *— Reb Zev of Strykov*

The Mishna continues its inventory of "Forty-Eight Ways" by frowning on isolation and segregation, causing the Talmud to declare: "Looking after scholars is greater than studying with them!"

Jews are thus encouraged to perform *shimush chachamim* (serving the Sages), and to engage in *dikduk hachaverim* and *pilpul hatalmidim*, "careful and sharp discussion with colleagues and students."

Rashi, commenting on the Talmudic conclusion that "a Torah scholar's leaf does not wither," compares the leaf, the insignificant part of the tree, to the suggestion that even the ordinary conversations of Torah scholars are significant.

By attending to the needs of *rebbeim*, as role models, one could see, in close proximity, how couriers of Torah walked and talked, lived and laughed – and the effect that Torah knowledge had on even mundane day-to-day matters.

And by focusing attention on the teacher-student interaction, the Mishna reveals a natural progression: first study from a teacher, then review the lesson with a fellow student, and finally, pass it on to other students.

The advantages of "sharp discussions" are obvious: the to-and-fro exchange sharpens the mind, clarifies the issues, and prods the memory bank to retain what is important.

This methodology convinced Rabbi Yehuda that he had learned much from his teachers, more from his colleagues – but the most from his students!

❧

The rebbe asks his class, "We've all heard of the phrase 'from Dan to Beersheba,' but does anybody know the distance between the two?"

Moishie, known for his lazy, laid-back approach to Torah study, puts up his hand, "Do you mean these are places?"

"Yes," replies the teacher.

"Wow, that's news to me," says Moishie, "I always thought they were husband and wife. Like Sodom and Gomorrah!"

❧

Way Fourteen

> "To err is human!"
> — *Rambam*

The next "way" is *yishuv* (literally, "dwelling"), defined as being "deliberate" in words.

Why? "When error creeps in," notes the Babylonian Sage Dimi of Nehardea, "it stays!"

Don't rush to reply, cautions the *Machzor Vitry*, and think twice before answering, an echo of an earlier warning from Judah ben Ilai: "The errors of Sages are regarded as willful sins if the mistake is due to lack of study!"

Some interpret this Mishna's use of *b'yishuv* as "in calmness," in that Torah is best transmitted in a calm, steady ("deliberate") atmosphere; and so Eliezer ben Hyrkanos asks God to bless him with "tranquility," and Isaiah bluntly advises others, "Keep calm, keep quiet!"

In general, Judaism elevates the sounds of silence ("Even a fool," writes King Solomon, "who remains silent shall be thought of as wise!"), but the silence the Torah advocates is *not* total silence *per se*, but the avoidance of superfluous verbiage, and he recommends quiet deliberation.

In fact, the *Tiferes Yisroel* censures those who pursue silence for its own sake, and he especially condemns the Torah student who fails to express himself to his teacher, a cone of silence that threatens his learning.[276]

～

One day, in the lobby of a quiet retirement home in Florida, an elderly widower leaned over to a widow and whispered, "Will you marry me?"

After a few minutes of consideration, she said, "Yes, yes, I will."

The next morning, his memory fading, he was troubled. Did she say "Yes" or "No"? For several days he searched his mind but simply had no recall. So finally, gathering his courage, he went to the phone and called her room: "I'm sorry to bother you. But when I asked if you would marry me, did you say 'Yes' or did you say 'No'?"

She replied excitedly, "I said, 'Yes, yes I will' – and I'm so glad you called because I couldn't remember who asked me!"

～

Way Fifteen

Rabbi Mendel, who later became the Tzadik of Kotzk, was famed even in his youth as an outstanding scholar. Yet already then he disapproved of those who judged a man's greatness by his learning, maintaining that character and virtue were more important.

On one occasion the young Mendel appeared before an elderly scholar who asked him how much of the entire Babylonian Talmud he had learned.

"About half," Rav Mendel replied.

The scholar was amazed. "You mean to say that, though so young, you have already learned half the Talmud?"

"Well," said the young Mendel, "you can test me on it, if you like. Also, you can choose for yourself whether to test me on the first half or the second."

In this directive, the "fourteenth way," *b'mikra* and *b'mishna* (with Scripture and Mishna), we are told that before tackling the Talmud, one must be familiar with both Scripture and Mishna, the latter being the basis of the Oral Law.

The Torah was given at Sinai in two sections, the "written" Law and the "oral" Law; the latter, which helps explain the "written" law, was memorized and passed down orally from generation to generation.

Eventually, especially after the destruction of the Second Temple, when the Jews were staring at a long future of exile, our Sages realized that this *dor l'dor* memorialization was a great burden and enormous responsibility, tinged with human fallibility.

This led to putting these laws down in writing (known as the Mishna and Talmud).

Thus, *Torah sheb'al Peh* is the underpinning of the Written Law, which, by its very nature, was unable to be "cast in stone" (or parchment!); without this Oral Law, the Written Law is rendered incomplete.[277]

⇾

> A Chassidic rebbe, explaining a verse, elaborates, "The Torah is like three times squared plus eight times minus nine!"
>
> "Huh?" one confused Chassid turns to his friend, "What does the Rebbe mean?"
>
> "Don't worry," his *chaver* replies, "it's just another one of his parabolas!"

⇾

Ways Sixteen to Twenty-One

A Chassid complained to Rebbe Menachem Mendel of
Kotzk that the world was so evil that it was hard for him to
live in it. The Rebbe replied: "You are not as good as you
imagine, nor is the world as bad as you imagine. Think of
yourself less, and you will understand the world more!"

The next several "ways" (*miyut s'chora, miyut derech eretz, miyut ta'anug, miyut
sheina, miyut sicha, miyut s'chok*) are a combined ode to restraint and the virtue
of moderation, defined as "limitations," specifically in the areas of "business,
intimacy, pleasure, sleep, conversation, laughter."

The rationale?

Since life's only *raison d'être* is Torah, then all other activities and energies,
whilst certainly permitted, should be controlled.

The Mishna doesn't forbid them outright (after all, one *must* work to support
a family, *must* sleep to preserve strength, etc.), but simply suggests that pursuing them aggressively is detrimental to your spiritual health. The Ba'al Shem Tov
preferred to translate these "limitations" as arising from such a love of God that
all other "pleasures" are automatically rendered insignificant, and thus "diminished."

Rashi cautioned those who threw themselves into full-time communal and
civic duties that this preoccupation, whilst commendable, was an impediment to
full Torah growth; meanwhile the *Chasam Sofer* divided his days into two-thirds
for spiritual growth and one-third for his physical needs.

Our Sages credit moderation with prolonging life; meanwhile the Rambam,
echoing a thought from Aristotle, reminded his followers to "balance equally
[mitzvos] between too much and too little!"

❧

"Please cut the fat off," Feigie tells her butcher after asking to buy a huge tender-
loin steak.

"You sure you want all the fat off?"

"Yes, it's much easier to take it off here," Feigie explains, "than after I've eaten
it!"

❧

Way Twenty-Two

"Macht zach nisht azoy klein, bist nisht azoy groys! (Don't pretend to be so humble, you're not that great yet!)"
— *the Gerer Rebbe*

Next on the list is *erech apayim* (literally, "long nostrils), "slowness to anger," a salute to patience and composure, self-control and poise.

To hold one's anger is a generic quality, something good for both the wise and the unlearned; but for those who wish to lead lives of Godliness, being a "hothead" is incompatible ("An impatient person cannot teach"), anger and pettiness are an obstacle, and having an even disposition is a must!

"When the kettle boils," reminds a Midrash, "it spills hot water down its *own* sides!"

Our Sages embraced calm and quiet as virtues, especially for Torah study ("Anyone who gets angry will forfeit his learning"), and were convinced that anger not only caused errors but memory loss as well ("If a wise man becomes angry, he will lose his wisdom!").

The *Machzor Vitry* and Rav Shmuel de Uzeda remind us that anger is a major character interference, a breeder of both irrational behavior and tormented thought, incompatible with humility and patience; several Midrashim point out the common flaw in Moses' behavior: every time the leader of the Jews lost his temper, he made a mistake!

Rabbi Alexandri pitied the man who had even the slightest "haughtiness of spirit," convinced that he would be "disturbed by the slightest wind!"

Hezekiah warned such men that their prayers were wasted; Rabba was even tougher: a haughty person deserves excommunication – and Rav Nachman bar Isaac agreed: "Everyone that is proud in heart is an abomination!"

❧

"Doctor, doctor," cries Moishie into the phone, "you gotta help me. I can't control my anger and I keep losing my temper with people."

"Now, now, just calm down and tell me about your problem."

"I just did, didn't I, you idiot!"

❧

Way Twenty-Three

"A good heart includes all other virtues!"
— *Yochanan ben Zakkai*

The next prerequisite to mastering Torah is to have *lev tov* (a good heart).

This, says the *Tiferes Yisroel*, requires a disposition of geniality and empathy for others; the Midrash links it to being patient and the ability to forgive readily;[278] Rav Samson Raphael Hirsch extends the definition: "One who enjoys a good heart will rejoice in the spiritual achievements of his companions."

'Tis a poor heart that never rejoices, goes the old saying, echoing the early Proverbs: "Guard your heart, for from it flow the springs of life!"

The Hebrew word *tov* (good), whose *gematria* is seventeen, is the thirty-third word in the Torah; the *gematria* of the thirty-two previous words is *lev* (heart).

Jewish mystics link this to the seventeen days from Lag ba'Omer (the thirty-third day of *sefira*) to Shavuos, and make the point: a Jew must have a *lev tov* (good heart) in order to receive the Torah (when asked by Rabban Yochanan to choose the most important characteristic, Rav Eleazar said, "A good heart!").[279]

In relationships, a "broken heart" is one of sadness; in medical terms a "good heart" is a strong one; in friendships, a "good heart" describes a good-natured person, whilst a "cold heart" is one lacking compassion, emphathy, concern.

In Torah terms, "one heart" defines unity (the Jews camped before Mount Sinai "as one person with one heart") and is the resting place of Torah ("And these words which I command you today are to be in your heart").[280]

⇴

The young husband bursts into the *rav*'s office, "Rabbi, Rabbi! My wife is poisoning me!"

"How can that be?!"

"I'm positive, Rabbi! She's poisoning me! What should I do?"

"Why don't I go speak to her," the good-hearted *rav*, always ready to please, says. "Let me see what I can find out."

A few days later the *rav* calls the husband: "Well, I spoke to your wife. In fact, I spoke to her for three hours. Do you want my advice?"

"Yes, yes!"

"Take the poison!"

⇴

Way Twenty-Four

In 1934, Rav Abraham Isaac Kook was invited to the groundbreaking ceremony of the Beis Yosef (Novardok) Yeshiva in B'nei Brak. The large crowd sat silently in their seats listening as Rav Kook spoke at length. Only the *Chazon Ish* remained standing throughout, paying very close attention to the rabbi's words. Some people approached the *Chazon Ish* and suggested that he sit down. He refused, saying, "The Torah is standing!"

The next of the "forty-eight ways" is *emunas chachamim*, to "trust in our Sages" – even if "they tell you your right is your left and your left is your right!"

Does this mean rabbis are infallible?

No (that's the other religion), but it does mean that we are to have total confidence in the authenticity of their decisions. Why? Because, as Divine Couriers, they are Divinely inspired (to infuse confidence in their pronouncements, God gracefully promises, *Elokim nitsav b'adas kel*: He will try to help them in their deliberations).

Yet they are still capable of human error (and of different interpretations: don't forget, there are no less than seventy "faces" to the Torah!).

The concept of human flawlessness doesn't exist in a Torah that goes out of its way to reveal *tzadikim* as ordinary, frail human beings, warts and all, men who can succumb to sin at any time; in fact, Jewish law even envisioned errors by its rabbinic hierarchy and demanded that they offer a special communal sacrifice (*par he'elem davar shel tzibur*) if they issued an erroneous decision.[281]

Emunas chachamim (trust in the Sages) is a fundamental principle of Judaism: the *Gedolei Yisroel*, the "great ones of Israel," whilst not infallible, nevertheless have the clearest insight into God's wishes and are thus the most qualified leaders for the Jewish people.[282]

꩜

"My dear friends," the rabbi apologizes as he begins his Shabbas *d'var Torah*, "if my *drasha* is not as thorough or as lengthy as usual I hope you will forgive me. Tragically, after I had prepared my speech, my neighbor's dog chewed up all my pages – and I didn't have time to rewrite them."

When the *rav* is finished a visitor approaches him: "Rabbi, that was excellent! Can I ask you for a favor?"

"Sure, anything!" replies the *rav*, beaming with pride.

"Does your neighbor's dog have puppies? I'd like to borrow one for my own rabbi!"

꩜

Way Twenty-Five

> "It was only through suffering that Israel obtained three priceless
> and coveted gifts: the Torah, the land of Israel, the world."
>
> — *Rabbi Akiva*

The next "way" is a difficult one: *kabalas hayisurin*, to be of a mindset that is "willing to accept suffering."

To bear suffering is difficult, to "accept" it nearly impossible. The sight of a righteous individual or a Jewish youngster in pain is incomprehensible, leading to a theological and emotional inner conflict for any Jew.

However, the Mishna asks us not to "understand" but simply to "accept" seemingly senseless tragedies and injustices ("It is not in our power to explain either the tranquility of the wicked or the suffering of the righteous!").

And so the Mishna throws a challenge at us: the bitter obligation to come to grips with an idea known as *tziduk hadin*, an effort to reconcile the apparent contradiction between a "good" deity and a "bad" history of hatred, one that suffocates our senses, numbs our minds, chokes our joys.

We are forced to "accept," even though we cannot understand, the blood-stained torrents of *tzores* that are chronicled under Temples, Crusades, Inquisitions, Crematoria, Genocide and Intifadas by unlucky witnesses who struggled to put words to inconceivable sights.

"When a human being suffers, the Divine Presence responds, 'My head is heavy, My arm is heavy,'" to which Isaiah softly adds, "In all their troubles, He is troubled."

The absence of adequate responses is why our Sages were rarely philosophers.

❧

"Rabbi," Duvie cries, "I have to make arrangements to bury my wife."

"Duvie, Duvie!" the *chevra kadisha rav* replies, putting his arm around him, "Don't you remember, I buried your darling wife two years ago!"

"Of course I remember. That was my first wife. I'm here about my second."

"Second?" replies the overzealous *rav*. "Duvie! I didn't even know you remarried! *Mazel tov!*"

❧

Ways Twenty-Six and Twenty-Seven

*"Who seeks more than he needs prevents himself from
enjoying what he has. For in giving up what you don't
need, you'll learn what you really do need!"*
— *Solomon Ibn Gabirol, eleventh-century Spanish poet-philosopher*

The Mishna follows with a psychological observance: one needs to *makir es
m'komo* (know one's place) and be *sameach b'chelko* (happy with one's lot) – in
other words, be content with who you are, wherever you are.

When the Talmud suggests that we "eat onions and sit in the shade," it is telling us to be content with little and live at ease!

The *Tiferes Yisroel* views "place" as metaphoric, suggesting that one needs to
know where he stands as far as learning and knowledge is concerned, and must
make an honest assessment of where he wants to be versus where he is, "bringing," in the Maharal's words, "completion to the incomplete."

This is the challenge, balancing what we need with what we want in order to
become *sameach b'chelko*, "satisfied with our portion."

Rav Samson Raphael Hirsch taught that just as we should be satisfied with our
portion of earthly goods, so too should we rejoice in the measure of intellectual
talent we have been granted.

In summary: it is the "doing" – not the "acquiring" – that ensures satisfaction,
or as the nineteenth-century critic G.J. Nathan put it: "Be satisfied with life always,
but never with what you are!"

❧

"Doctor," Betty says to the psychiatrist, "my dear husband thinks he's a chicken!"

"Well, I suggest you bring him in to see me. Perhaps I can help him."

"No, I can't do that!"

"Why not?"

"I need the eggs!"

❧

Way Twenty-Eight

Loose lips sink ships!

— *World War II British proverb*

The next "way" is a poetic word of wisdom: *ha'oseh s'yag li'd'varav* (the making of a fence for words).

What does this mean?

The "fence" is symbolic of "safeguarding" our speech,[283] a metaphoric Mishnaic caution to "watch our words" (as articulated by the wise King Solomon, "He who guards his mouth and his tongue guards his soul from trouble!").

The study of Torah (known as *Talmud Torah*) is considered a "speech" mitzva, *k'neged kulam* (equal to all other mitzvos combined); in contrast, *loshen hora* is a "speech" transgression.

Upon Creation, man became a *nefesh chaya*, a "living creature,"[284] or as Onkelos puts it, a *ruach m'malla*, a "being that speaks."

Torah linguists note the similarity between the nearly identically spelled Hebrew words *metzora* (leper – leprosy being the traditional Divine punishment associated with sins of speech), and *motzi ra* (slanderer, literally "one who brings forth evil").

Rav Samson Raphael Hirsch sees this Mishna as a caution to Torah scholars to be soft-spoken, and judicious in words.

Less is thus more!

The less a scholar speaks, the more his followers will strain to listen; the less a scholar speaks, the less the chance of mistakes, innocent misinterpretation, misguided *machlokes* (argument).

Our Sages, aware of the power of holy speech, include its prayer in the daily *tefilla* ("Behold, I prepare my mouth to thank and praise my Creator"), whilst Rabbi Shimon bar Yochai pondered, "Had I been present at Mount Sinai, I would have asked God that we be created with two mouths: one mouth to speak in Torah, and one mouth for all of our mundane needs!"

⭒

"Hey, man!" the street kid asks the Jewish pawn shop owner, "What's my grandfather's violin worth?"

"Old fiddles aren't worth that much, I'm afraid," he replies.

"Whoa! What makes it a fiddle and not a violin?"

"Well, if you're buying it from me, it's a true violin, but if I'm buying it from you, it's only a fiddle!"

⭒

Way Twenty-Nine

"There are two ways that a man can be taller than his neighbor: he can himself climb to a higher position, or he can drag his friend down to a lower position. Never follow the second path. Instead of digging a hole for your friend, build a hill for yourself!"

— Reb Naftali of Ropshitz

The next "way" to a Torah path is *eino machzik tova l'atzmo* (not to take credit for oneself).

Go ahead and "humble yourself," writes ben Sira, "[*but only*] in all greatness!"

Consistency is thus not an automatic asset in humility. If it is counterproductive for the Jewish people, it would be best put aside (temporarily) so as to get the job done.

Humility, in *Jewish* terms, must not be unaware of the world of reality, in view of the fact that man was created to strive for greatness and dignity.

And so the Rambam goes for the golden mean, and *not* the extreme, whilst the *Divrei Yisroel*'s grandfather kept a list of examples of "hidden" Torah humility, convinced that whenever an event of humbleness occurs, the Torah prefers to hint in modesty, rather than explicitly.

Rabbi Simcha Bunim always carried two slips of paper. The one in his right pocket read, "The entire world was created just for me," and that in the left was Abraham's modest motto, "I am but dust and ashes."

When faced with a decision, the Rebbe would reach into his right pocket if he thought it was a time to shed some humility and step forward, or into his left pocket if he thought it was time to back off (in modern-day slang, "You gotta know when to fold 'em and when to hold 'em!").

꒚

The local *chazan* liked to hear his own magnificent voice at all times, so he never stopped singing. One day a pogrom was perpetrated in his small Polish shtetl and the Jews fled to the woods – but the *chazan* just kept on singing, louder. Concerned about the safety of his *kehilla*, the rabbi dragged the singing *chazan* deeper and deeper into the woods, finally throwing him into a local stream to shut him up.

It didn't help.

The *chazan* climbed out without missing a note – which proves you can lead a *chazan* to water, but you can't make him hoarse!

꒚

Ways Thirty to Thirty-Four

> "Anyone who is pleasing to his fellows is pleasing to God. Anyone who is not pleasing to his fellows is not pleasing to God!"

The next several "ways" to genuine Torah study have to do with love, ranging from *ahuv* (being loved) to *oheiv es haMakom, es habriyos, es hatzedakos v'es hameisharim* (loving God, mankind, uprightness and justice) and even *oheiv es hatochachos* (loving rebuke).

To "be loved" in Mishna terms is to be respected and admired, both "likable" characteristics that require a principled consistency and decency towards all people.

But to "love mankind, righteousness, justice" seems obvious. Why even mention them?

When the Mishna talks about "loving mankind," it has in mind *all* of Creation, which is why traditional Jews have a daily appreciation of Mother Nature (involving no less than a hundred daily blessings!).

In loving "uprightness," the Mishna uses the term *meisharim*, similar to *yashar*, which means "straight," as in upright, pure, sincere (i.e., no behavioral pretensions: what you see is what you get!).[285]

But why "love rebuke"? Doesn't this seem at odds with many Torah demands? In the time of the Mishna the expression "rebuke" had a different meaning than today, when it is more aggressive and intolerant.[286]

In those days it meant showing others the way not by bullying but by persuasion, not by destructive force but by constructive example, not as an enemy but as a caring friend: "You shall not hate your brother in your heart" is a strong admonition that cloaks any "rebuke" in the wardrobe of love and peace; in fact, we are warned not to rebuke a scoffer "lest he hate you!"

This explains the Mishna's choice of *tochacha*, which means "prove" (*not* rebuke!), and whose Hebrew root is the causative of *ko'ach*, "strength," in that we should strengthen others in their belief by "proving" *our way* is right, not that *their way* is wrong!

One day Beryl, the local doctor, has each patient lean out of the window and stick out his or her tongue. At the end of the day the baffled nurse asks him, "Doctor, why did you make dozens of our patients do this?"

"Well," replies Beryl, "there's no medical reason. I just don't like the neighbors!"

Ways Thirty-Five and Thirty-Six

"Let not the wise man praise himself for his wisdom, nor the strong man for his strength, nor the rich man for his wealth."

— *Jeremiah*

This Mishna argues for humility and meekness. How to achieve this? By being *misracheik min hakavod* (keeping far from honor) and *lo meigis libo b'salmudo*, avoiding getting "too conceited in study."[287]

Even Yehuda Hanasi, the noblest prince of them all, required a lesson in humility. Once, according to the Talmud Bavli, as he was compiling the Mishna, the town of Sepphoris found itself in the midst of a severe food shortage. Yehuda, a wealthy Jew, opened one of his storehouses of food, but only for the "learned Jews." This angered many young Torah scholars of Sepphoris who refused to benefit from their Torah status whilst other Jews went hungry. Yehuda then immediately ordered that his food be made available to everyone.

Smugness and snobbery, vanity and boastfulness are qualities that are the antithesis of everything the Mishna stands for, and so abhorrent to God that He defiantly confesses, "The arrogant and I cannot dwell together in this world!"

The Mishna uses the term *kavod* for "honor," a term closely aligned to *kaved*, "heavy," in that it's a "weighty" (i.e., full of himself) and selfish man who seeks honor and glory. Jewish mystics took the Hebrew word *ma'alot*, which means "steps," and equated it with arrogance and hubris (*bema'alot*), based on a Divine command that all who ascend the altar do so by way of a more modest ramp.

And more: the Rambam himself, Mr. Middle-of-the-Road, uncharacteristically comes out aggressive and uncompromising, convinced that the impulse to drive away the haughtiness factor was so inherently weak in the ordinary Jew that only an extreme defensive stance would be effective.

The Yiddishists get the last word: Honor is measured by those who *give* it, not by those who *receive* it!

꒰

A dog runs into a butcher shop and grabs a roast off the counter. The butcher, a humble and soft-spoken Jew, recognizes the dog as belonging to his neighbor, a lawyer. So he calls his neighbor and gently inquires, "If your dog stole a roast from my butcher shop, would you perhaps be liable for the cost of the meat?"

"Of course," the lawyer replies, "how much was the roast?"

The butcher shyly mumbles, "$7.98."

A few days later he receives a check for $7.98 attached to a bill that reads: "Legal Consultation Service: $250."

꒰

Way Thirty-Seven

> A mirror fools none but the ugly!
> — *Yiddish proverb*

As a reminder that all, even Torah scholars and Sages, are fallible, the Mishna's next "way" is *eino sameach b'hora'a*, a reminder not to "delight in dictating decisions."

The process of halachic decision-making is not an easy one, and thus "delighting" in it is a sign of spiritual arrogance at a time when humility is in order; a more appropriate quality is the feeling of being unworthy for the task.

The Midrash and the *Machzor Vitry* are unusually blunt in their description of those leaders who are "too self-confident" in handing down legal decisions, calling them "wicked fools, arrogant of spirit!"

There is an interesting exchange in the Talmud that mingles humor with humility.

"When Rabban Yochanan died, the splendor of wisdom ceased. When Rabban Gamliel the Elder died, the honor of Torah ceased. When Rabbi Yishmael died, the splendor of the priesthood ceased. When Rabbi Yehuda died, humility ceased – but Rav Yosef added, 'Do not teach the line about humility because there is still me!'"[289]

By tacking on Rav Yosef's witty remark, the compilers of the Talmud reveal the paradox of humility: there is simply no definitive standard.

Humility is, in fact, elusive; it can range from total self-flaggelation by one who believes that he has no good qualities at all, to perhaps refusing public honors.

But the *Netziv*, using Rav Yosef as an example, embraces the latter definition and totally rejects the former one, arguing that humbleness and accepting personal accomplishments are not mutually exclusive; in fact, being too under-confident can even undermine one's rabbinic duties![290]

❦

Moishie bumps into his rabbi on the way home from *shul* one evening. "*Nu*, rabbi, how was your day?"

"Today, *baruch Hashem*, I made seven hearts happy."

"Wow, that's great! Seven hearts? How'd you do that?"

"I performed three marriages."

"Three weddings? Isn't that six hearts?"

"What do you think? I do this for free?!"

❦

Way Thirty-Eight

> *"Hinei ma tov uma na'im, sheves achim gam yachad* (How good and
> pleasant, when brethren dwell in unity together)!"[291]
>
> — *From a Psalm used in the Shabbas liturgy*

The Mishna's next "way," to be *nosei b'ol im chaveiro* (bear one's yoke [*ol*] with
one's fellow), is a call for unity, communal cohesion and sensitivity towards
others.

The moment the Talmud added "Those who share in the community's troubles
are worthy to see its consolation," it was understood: Jews who think they can
live without other Jews may be wrong – but those who think that others cannot
survive without them are even more mistaken.

Putting sugar in your mouth won't help if you are bitter in your heart, our
Yiddishists would often grumble.

A pious Jewish leader once tried to justify handing over a "bad" (i.e., irreli-
gious) Jew to gentiles on the rationale that he was only "pulling out the weeds
from the vineyard." This was too much for Rabbi Yehoshua ben Karcha, who sar-
castically reminded him that God, as "the owner of the vineyard, is quite capable
of pulling out the weeds Himself!"

Once, the Ba'al Shem Tov continued longer than usual in his *Shemoneh Esrei*.
Unable to wait, the *minyan* slowly dispersed, each Jew going off on his own way.

When he finished, the Chassidic master complained that his being left solitary,
deprived of group prayer, had diluted the effectiveness of his *tefilla* and had created discord in Heaven: "I could have attained many things had we stood together
in prayer; once you left me, I could not attain those goals alone!"

꒰

Izzy survived a shipwreck and landed on an island. One day, miraculously, he is
discovered by a cruise liner.

"*Baruch Hashem*," he says as he hugs the captain, "I'm so glad you're here! I've
been alone on this island for years!"

"Then how come you've got three huts?"

"Well, I live in one and the other one is for prayer."

"And the third hut?"

"Oh, that's the *shul* I don't go to!"

꒰

Ways Thirty-Nine to Forty-One

> "Rebuke pays no dividends!"
> — *Talmud*

The next words of wisdom include a call not to rush to judgment, to be *machriyo l'kaf zechus* (judge one's fellow favorably), and *ma'amido al ha'emes u'ma'amido al hashalom* (set him on a path to truth and peace).

Instead of using the usual Hebrew word to "judge" (*dan*), the Mishna uses *machria*, which means "to cause another to bend." This is a much more proactive term, implying that one should "actively" judge others in a positive manner (*dan l'kaf zechus*).

Giving another Jew "the benefit of the doubt" eliminates enmity and grudge-bearing (in Yiddish, *Er hot a faribel*[292] *of mir*), and was explicitly mandated by the Torah's "*b'tzedek tishpot amisecha* (judge your fellow righteously)!"

Not surprisingly, the advice to help others pursue "peace" is quickly linked to "truth": after all, the Mishna has already defined the three qualities on which the world endures (justice, truth and peace).

It sounds so simple but it's quite complicated: truth is often very difficult to accept, and sometimes it's more "peaceful" not to know. But the Torah does not believe that ignorance is bliss, nor does it encourage us to look the other way, letting others "live in peace" when we see an obvious falsehood or injustice being committed.

This means that one must know when to speak and when to be silent; when to act and when to do nothing, for Torah "truth" (described as "ways of pleasantness") is an alien concept if it results in disunity, friction, animosity, bitterness and hostility.

In other words: the truth must be delivered, *peacefully*!

❧

"Ma!" Ernie calls home, "I'm coming right over. I just got engaged to a wonderful woman."

"Great," his mother says, "*mazel tov, mazel tov!*"

An hour later, there's a knock on the door and the Yiddishe mama is shocked to see her young son standing next to a tall non-Jewish Native American-Indian woman.

"Ma, her name is Shooting Star, and I'm changing my name to Running Water!"

"Pleased to meet you," his mother says, extending her hand, "you can call me Sitting Shiva!"

❧

Ways Forty-Two to Forty-Four

> One day the Kotzker Rebbe was asked what was the secret of his great wisdom. Rebbe Mendel replied, "The ability to stay focused on the study of a single topic for days on end!"

The Mishna then goes on to lobby for maturity and diversity: be *misyasheiv libo b'salmudo* (composed in your studies) and *sho'eil u'meishiv, shome'a u'mosif* (ask and respond, listen and add).

Why? In order to add to one's own knowledge!

Torah study cannot be superficial or haphazard. To be fully understood it needs to be handled with clarity and care, nurtured not by careless impertinence but by focused intellectual jousting (in order to avoid confusion in Torah, the Talmud cautions students not to ask their teacher about a different topic than the one being taught).

It's not enough to simply ask, "Is this the 'way' of Mishna?" No, one has to be both attentive and responsive, a give-and-take process that only succeeds if carried out with coherence and lucidity.

Rashi prided himself on his consistent accuracy, whilst the *Tiferes Yisroel*, convinced that Torah was not just context but also presentation, was always careful that his *divrei Torah* be offered in a clear, logical and rational manner.

Ben Sira described ambiguity in conversation as being akin to music in mourning; Ibn Ezra said clarity's absence is similar to food without salt!

⇥

It's *erev Shabbas* and the little ol' Jewish grandmother is at the store buying fish for Shabbas.

"Can I have some grayling?" she inquires.

"I'm sorry," replies the man behind the counter, "unfortunately, the grayling no longer exists."

"Any thoughts of bringing it back?"

"I'm sorry, Ma'am, I don't think that possible."

"Why not?"

"Because it's extinct."

"Still?"

⇥

Way Forty-Five

> If Torah is here, wisdom is here!
> — *Yiddish proverb*

The next "way" is *halomeid al m'nas l'lameid, v'halomeid al m'nas la'asos* (learn in order to teach, and learn in order to practice).

Studying and not teaching Torah? Rabban Yochanan compared this Torah *Weltanschauung* to "a myrtle in the wildnerness [whose] fragrance is wasted," and Koheles questions the "use" of "hidden wisdom."

The Talmud even elevates the honor (*kavod*) of teaching Torah to the level of the commandment to honor one's parents; some go beyond, claiming that a father only brings a child "into this world," whereas the teacher of Torah catapults the child, through adulthood, "into the World to Come" (it's no coincidence that *kavod* is derived from the Hebrew word *kaved*, "heavy" or "burdensome").

Our Sages, having traced this lofty conclusion back to the first Jew, Abraham – who "made" (i.e., converted) others to accompany him in his monotheistic trek to God's Holy Land – equate the Torah teacher's deeds to having "created him [his student] anew!"

This explains why the Rambam showed such great respect and esteem for converts ("regarding proselytes, our obligation is a great, heart-bound love"); whilst Jewish mystics even saw the positive in Abraham's non-Jewish father and purveyor of idolatry, deriving his Hebrew name Terach from *ruach* (spirit), in that, despite his idol-worshipping, he is still the foundation from which the House of Jacob was conceived and raised!

꙳

Pincus was a very religious man, but after nearly sixty years of strict adherence to Jewish law, he was fed up. "Esther," he tells his wife, "I've had it! No more getting up early every morning, putting on my *tefillin* and reciting the same prayers. I'm converting to Catholicism."

"Are you crazy?" asks Esther, but Pincus is determined. He goes to a local church, discusses his intentions with the priest, begins taking instruction and is baptized into the Catholic faith.

The next morning, as always, he gets up early, and, without thinking, puts on his *tefillin* and automatically starts to recite his morning prayers.

"What are you doing?" asks Esther. "I thought the whole point of becoming Catholic was so you wouldn't have to do that anymore."

"*Oy!*" cried Pincus, smacking himself in the forehead. "*Goyishe kop!*"

꙳

Way Forty-Six

With wisdom only, you don't go to the market!
— *Yiddish proverb*

King David might have sung that he became "wiser from every teacher," but this Mishna urges us to be *hamachkim es rabo*, make our own rabbi "wiser"!

The *Tiferes Yisroel* takes it one step further: the more wisdom your teacher has, the more you'll respect him. The more you respect him, the more you'll ask. And the more you ask, the wiser he gets!

Or, as the Talmud puts it: "Much have I learned from my teachers, more from my colleagues, but most from my students!"

This is a common theme in Torah study, that the student, via incessant prodding and probing, challenges and thus sharpens his teacher's skills.

On this everyone agrees: "A bashful person cannot learn," which is why there's no such thing as a "stupid question" (as long as it's not blasphemous, and is asked in a sincere effort to know).

On Pesach the father, as the family's main educator, is entrusted with the conduct of a question-and-answer form of disputation, *derech she'eila u'teshuva*. Why? Because listening is passive and stagnant; far better to inquire, probe, analyze, and create energy and enthusiasm that is fresh and jolting, invigorating and rejuvenating.

"If the other does not know how to ask," teases the Haggada, "ask on his behalf!" Why? "Because the finest quality of man is asking questions, since his wit is judged better by his questions than by his answers."

In fact, in a startling Talmud passage, students are urged to be aggressively inquisitive, to annoy and aggravate their teachers to new levels of exasperation with questions: "The student who gets his teacher angry at him, and who accepts his teacher's rebuke, will ultimately achieve greatness in Torah!"

꣒

The *cheder* rebbe enjoys the feedback from his students, so one day he points to little Yossi and asks, "Can you tell the class what the opposite of *simcha* is?"

"Sadness," replies the boy.

"That's right! And the opposite of depression?"

"Elation."

"Excellent! How about the opposite of woe?"

"I believe," thinks Yossi out loud, "that would be...uh...giddy up?"

꣒

Ways Forty-Seven and Forty-Eight

> "One may not steal even from one so poor as to
> own nothing more than Torah thoughts!"

To preserve the tradition of tradition [*mesora*], this Mishna urges Torah teachers to be *m'chaven es sh'mu'aso* (ponder what he has learned) and *ha'omer davar b'shem omro* (say a thing [or word] in the name of he who said it) – that is, not only to "quote *precisely*" but also to give "credit to the author."

The acknowledgment of indebtedness, explains the *Tiferes Yisroel*, is a moral argument for accuracy in transmission, and a meticulous attempt to avoid theft by falsely taking credit for the ideas of others (Yochanan ben Nappaha called those who don't quote their sources "robbers").

"Those who never quote," warns Isaac D'Israeli, nineteenth-century English author, "in return are never quoted!"

"The lips of a deceased scholar tingle pleasantly in the grave when a traditional statement is quoted in his name," declares Shimon bar Yochai – and, adds Eleazar ben Shimon, "It's also a virtue *not* to quote anything unauthentic!"

In his *Iggeros Teiman*, the Rambam gave no credence to any "word torn from its context," while Rabba ben Yosef was so obsessed with authenticity that he claimed an accurate "timely quote" was akin to "bread in a famine!"

Are our Sages more upset at taking undue credit, or depriving another of the quote's true source? Both.

In the Mishna's repetitive format of *derech eretz*, when "Rabbi X quotes in the name of Rabbi Y," the immediate and accurate identification of the source is considered a form of intellectual honesty.

In other words, the attribution is as important as the content.

The Mishna goes on to credit accuracy of quotation to *ge'ula la'olam* (deliverance to the world), which the Ba'al Shem Tov taught was a play on *giluy he'elem* (revelation of the unseen), as in disclosing what is concealed within one's own self.[293]

It is no coincidence that this is the final of the forty-eight ways, and one of the few Mishnas that, if followed, "leads to redemption."

꒰

The *cheder* rebbe picks up the phone and a voice says, "Rebbe, my son has a bad cold and won't be able to come and learn in yeshiva today."

Rebbe: "Who is this?"

Voice on phone: "This is my father speaking!"

꒰

EPILOGUE

Epilogue

Rav Meir of Tiktin once attended a *mussar drasha* given by a traveling *maggid*. The *maggid* spoke very harshly about the people's sins and urged them to begin changing their ways.

When he finished speaking, Rav Meir approached the *maggid* with a complaint. "Why did you have to humiliate me in public by spelling out all of my sins?"

The *maggid* was taken aback. "*Chas v'shalom*, I was not at all directing my words to you!"

"What do you mean — how could anyone think otherwise? I am the only one in this room guilty of those sins you mentioned! Everyone else here is a *tzadik*!"

What's the purpose of good deeds? The Midrash tells us: "The mitzvos were given to humankind in order to refine people!"[294]
This is the aim of *Pirkei Avos*, to improve our *middos* and, by acting as examples, hopefully to help others improve theirs as well. The key to this is only seeing the good in others. Goodness is a word that derives from "God," and when one sees and experiences the good in others, it opens the door to spirituality, to our own quest to know God.

꒰

The kindergarten teacher walks around her young art class and stops at Leah's desk.
"What are you drawing, Leah?"
"I'm drawing God, teacher."
The teacher pauses, and says, "But no one knows what God looks like, Leah."
Not missing a beat, Leah replies, "They will in a minute!"

꒰

The Rambam saw the world as being equally balanced between good and evil, with each individual's act able to tip the scales in either direction. Thus, acknowledging the limits of human behavior, he suggests the path of moderation.

Far better, he urges, to give $1 each to a thousand needy people than to go to the extreme and give one person $1,000. It is this very repetitiveness that makes giving *tzedaka* a normal part of your day.

That is why, whenever the Torah talks of helping others, it is repetitive. For example, *aser te'aser* (give…tithes), *nosein titen* (give…to the poor), *paso'ach tiftach* (open your hand…to the poor), etc. The double verb serves a purpose: it reminds that giving consists of "double dipping," in that not only are you helping another but you're helping yourself and building up your own character.

One of the most famous palindromes (words that read the same forwards or backwards) in the Torah is the Hebrew word *venasnu*, "and you shall give" – meaning, if you give, you get!

Avoid extremes, the Spanish Sage says, walk the balanced middle road, don't overindulge and don't underindulge! Except in one area: arrogance. The antidote to anger, hostility, arrogance and violence is to go to the other extreme: humility (*anava*), the only quality that God attributes to Moses.

～

> When asked, "How did you come to be the leader of the generation?" the *chacham* replied: "Throughout the course of my life I assumed that anyone I met was superior to me. If he was smarter than I, then I assumed he also had more *yiras Shamayim* on account of his wisdom. And, if the person had been given less intelligence than I by *Hakadosh Boruch Hu*, then I assumed he would have an easier time on the Day of Judgment since his sins remain unknown to him while mine are intentional. Likewise, if someone is older than I, I assume that he has accumulated more merit since he has lived longer. I also reckon that those who are younger have accumulated fewer sins than I have. Those who are richer probably merit this because they have given more *tzedaka* than I have, and have likely done more kindnesses for the poor. Of those who are poorer than I, I can safely say that their spirit is more humble, so that makes them better than I. Because of this outlook, I have always tried to honor everyone!"

～

Nearing death, the Ba'al Shem Tov hinted to his disciples that they should start looking for a new rabbi of the city.

"But how will we know who is the one?" they replied.

"Ask him for a way to avoid haughtiness," answered the Ba'al Shem Tov. "If he suggests a specific technique, he's too haughty and not suitable to be your *rav!*"

Our sages have always sought to teach us how to improve our *middos*, how to be better people both in our service of God and in our relationships with others. *Pirkei Avos* is a distillation of the essence of their insight: on every page we find a treasury of practical advice for living. So learn, laugh and live…with the wisdom of our fathers.

Notes

1. The most obvious Torah source for laughter is in the name *Yitzchak*, which means "he laughed," the name God gives the son of Abraham after the first patriarch laughs at God's prediction that he, a one-hundred-year-old man, and his wife Sarah, a ninety-year-old woman, will have a child.

2. *Tehillim* (Psalms) 59; 37:13; *Mishlei* (Proverbs) 1:20; 2:2–5.

3. *Koheles* (Ecclesiastes) 3:4.

4. *Pesachim* 117a; *Ruach Chaim*.

5. How is this possible with only six chapters in *Pirkei Avos*? After the entire *Pirkei Avos* has been read before Shavuos, it is then recommenced on the Shabbas after Shavuos, and then read twice more until Rosh Hashana.

6. The six chapters are: *Seder Zera'im* (which covers the cultivation of the soil and its products); *Seder Mo'ed* (on the *yomim tovim*, Shabbas, and fast days); *Seder Nashim* (covers the laws of marriage); *Seder Nezikin* (deals with "damages" in both civil and criminal law); *Seder Kodashim* (on "sanctity," of the Temple services and sacrifices, and dedicated objects) and *Seder Taharoth* (on cleanliness and purifications).

7. Abudarham, student of Yaakov ben Asher, was a famous commentator on Jewish prayers, and the last Jew to see the *siddur* of Sa'adia Gaon.

8. The plural of Mishna (which can also indicate a single paragraph) is *Mishnayos*; several *Mishnayos* form a *perek* (chapter), several *perakim* make up a *masechet* (tractate), a number of *masechtos* create a *seder* (order), whilst Shas, an acronym for *Shisha Sedarim*, the "six orders," forms the Gemora (which consists of 4,380 *Mishnayos*).

9. About two-thirds of the Sages quoted in *Pirkei Avos* are not from the first century (70–130 CE) but from the second century (135–200 CE). The six generations of the Mishna Sages include; First Generation: that of Rabban Yochanan ben Zakkai (circa 40–80 CE); Second Generation: Rabban Gamliel of Yavneh, Rabbi Eliezer and Rabbi Yehoshua, the teachers of Rabbi Akiva; Third Generation: Rabbi Akiva and his colleagues; Fourth Generation: Rabbi Meir, Rabbi Yehuda and their colleagues; Fifth Generation: Rabbi Yehuda Hanasi; Sixth Generation: that between the Mishna and the Talmud (Rabbis Shimon ben Yehuda Hanasi and Yehoshua ben Levi, etc.).

10. The catastrophe spanned three generations, from the destruction of Jerusalem by the Romans in 70 CE to the Bar Kochba failure. The entire long era of the Prophets witnessed a momentous Judaic upheaval of political, military and social elements. It included Judges, King Saul, the dynasty of David, the construction of Solomon's Temple, the secession of the tribes in the north that created the Kingdom of Israel, the exile and disappearance of ten out of twelve tribes, the destruction of the First

Temple and the "absence" of the Divine Presence, exile to Babylon, the rise of a Persian Empire, the return from Babylon to Zion, the building of the Second Temple and the subsequent flourishing of Torah study. The patient Sages of *Pirkei Avos* lump this entire period of Jewish history into one long moral aphorism, ignoring the upheavals of rulers and revolutions, persecutions and promises, insistent that the ultimate ethics of God is independent of "earthly" activity.

11. Out of the two-hundred plus rabbis in the Mishna, only about forty are quoted by name (even Gamliel II of Yavneh, Rabbi Yehuda Hanasi's grandfather, and Shimon ben Gamliel, his own father, two outstanding Torah Sages, are not mentioned). The "generations" of Mishna scholars are identified by locations that turned into major rabbinic centers; thus we have the era of Yavneh, from the Hebrew "God causes to build," a coastal town in central Israel which, after the fall of Jerusalem, thanks to Vespasian's honoring a request from ben Zakkai, became the epicenter of Judaic leadership and scholarship until the rise of Shimon bar Yochai. This reign lasted two generations (from 70 to 135 CE) and was dominated by such founding figures as ben Zakkai, Eliezer ben Hyrkanos, Yehoshua ben Chanania, and later leaders (during the "generation of Betar," the military center of the Bar Kochba insurrection) such as Rabbis Akiva and Ishmael. This was followed by the "generation" from Usha, Upper Galilee, which arose after Bar Kochba's uprising resulted in the Roman destruction of Jerusalem and the devastation of Judea. Usha was the home of Rabbi Meir, and it is this "generation" (mainly students of Rabbi Akiva, which included Judah ben Ilai, Shimon bar Yochai, Yose ben Chalafta, Eleazar ben Shamua and the Patriarch Shimon ben Gamliel) that contributed the greatest content to the Mishna.

12. On a typical page of Talmud, the Mishna passages are introduced with an abbreviation for the Aramaic *Matnitin*, "Our Mishna" (as distinguished from other Mishnas, in Aramaic *baraisos*). The Palestinian Talmud (Talmud Yerushalmi) is the earlier of the two Talmuds and consists of discussions by Palestinian rabbis (c. 400 CE); about a century later, the leading Babylonian rabbis compiled their own, much more extensive, discussions on the Mishna, known as the Babylonian Talmud (Talmud Bavli). The latter became the more authoritative compilation simply because more Jews studied Talmud Bavli than Talmud Yerushalmi. Who brought the Mishna to Babylon? Abba Aricha aka Rab (d. 247), a *talmid* (student) of Rabbi Yehuda. His work was expanded by Rav Ashi (d. 427), Sura *rosh yeshiva*, and Rabbi Abina (Rabbina, d. 499), the last of the *Amora'im*. The next generation of Torah scholars, at the end of the fifth and in the first half of the sixth century, were called *Sabora'im*, "those who reflect, examine," in that they "reflected" on what had been previously written. Is today's Babylonian Talmud identical to the original? No. Serious mutilations were caused by Christian censorship, especially in the first edition printed in Basle in 1578–81. Over the years, the excised portions have been (partially) collected and published (anonymously) in small treatises.

13. In a Talmudic exchange between Rabbis Yehuda and Rabba (Baba Kamma 30), reference is made to "the words of *Avos*" – not *Pirkei Avos*. Both Bahja (eleventh century) and the Rambam (twelfth century) use the term *Avos* – not *Pirkei Avos*; however the *Machzor Vitry* (c. 1100) does refer to *Pirkei Avos*, whilst the Medrash Shmuel (1579) calls it *Maseches Avos*. The first time the expression *Pirkei Avos* appears in print is in 1516, in a Christian work, *De Arcanis Catholicae Veritatis* by Petrus Galatinus (in 1612, Galatinus brought out the Latin version of *Pirkei Avos*, called *Capitula Patrum*).

14. *Avos* also denotes "general principles."

15. Generally, it is the parents, not *rebbeim*, who are charged with *chinuch*, education of the children. In real life, however, it is the daughters of Israel who inculcate Torah

into the home, within the context of a *Mishlei* directive: "Hark to the discipline of your father, and don't abandon the *teachings of your mother.*"

16. Joshua, the successor to Moses, together with "the elders" of his generation, led the Jews in their conquest and the tribal division of the Land of Israel. When the elders passed on, the period of the prophets, the spiritual leaders until the time of the Mishna (about a thousand years later) began. Unlike in the previous era (Exodus, etc.), God no longer revealed Himself openly, except through prophecy and Divine inspiration. With the passing of the prophets, at the beginning of the Second Temple period, the era of the Great Assembly, a religio-judicial body of 120 scholars, began.

17. The "men" of the Great Assembly were not rabbis as we understand the term today; in fact the word *rabbi* appears nowhere in the Five Books of Moses. In the days of the Talmud, rabbis never relied on their scholarship as the source of their livelihood: "As I have taught you statutes and ordinances without charge, so should you teach others without charge" (*Nedarim* 37a; Deuteronomy 4:5). This changed in the Middle Ages when, out of necessity, the rabbis became stipendiary spiritual leaders. A quick study of the Talmud finds the Sages working as wood choppers, water carriers, cobblers, even gladiators.

18. C. 517 BCE.

19. C. 444 BCE.

20. There is one exception: Antigonus Ish Socho "accepts" Torah from Shimon Hatzadik.

21. Why mention prophets at all? Until the Great Assembly there were no "real" prophets (prophecy didn't exist then) so why not go straight from "elder" to the Assembly, and include prophet as elder? I don't know. And more! What happened to the kings? Why did the elders bypass David and Solomon? Because God had already warned that the appointment of a king was fraught with danger; the Heavens obviously preferred rule by piety to rule by royalty.

22. The title *Nasi* was given to the official political representative of the Jewish people. Its holder, who also presided over the Sanhedrin, Judaism's supreme judiciary and legislative body, came to the position (mainly) by heredity, a tradition that went back to the time of Hillel in the first century BCE. (The title also means "uplifted," in that the leader was on a much higher spiritual rung than the rest of the people.)

23. The ancient Galilean town of Sepphoris (in Hebrew, *Tzipori*) was sacked by the Romans after the death of King Herod, and its inhabitants sold into slavery. The remains of Sepphoris's ancient synagogue have a magnificent mosaic-tiled floor depicting Abraham about to sacrifice Isaac. Imperial Rome is long gone, but the Jews returned and captured Sepphoris in 1949; today, it's the site of Moshav Tzipori, a thriving farming community.

24. Where is Rabbi Yehuda buried? No one's sure. Tourists to Israel are shown a grave in a deep valley near the Tel Tzipori archeological park, but Talmudic historians place the grave elsewhere in the Galilee.

25. The first revolt occurred in 69–70 CE, followed by the Bar Kochba rebellion of 135 CE.

26. The rabbis from the time of Hillel up to the compilation of the Mishna are known as *Tanna'im* (Aramaic for "teachers") and the rabbis of the Gemora are known as *Amora'im* ("explainers," or "interpreters"). Which views are more authorative? Those of the *Tanna'im*. Why? Because they were in closer chronological proximity to Moses and Mount Sinai.

27. To the Lubavitcher Rebbe, *Pirkei Avos* dealt not with *din* (law) but with *lifnim*

mishuras hadin, that which is "beyond [yet within] the line of the law" (Chassidus calls this *mili dechassidusa*, "guidelines for pious conduct beyond the measure of the law").

28. The "repetition" style of the Mishna established the traditional method of Torah learning, orally from teacher to pupil.

29. The Mishna, which contains very little "new" material (i.e., it is contemporary to Rabbi Yehuda, who died around 217 CE) was itself subsequently disseminated by word of mouth and then memorized, and, during the Babylonian era of the Talmud and well into the Middle Ages, continued to be studied orally.

30. What's the language of the Mishna? Mainly Hebrew, but not Biblical Hebrew, with some short passages in Aramaic and Chaldean, and some isolated words in Greek and Latin (in contrast, the Gemora is saturated with some four thousand Greek, Latin, Arabic, Persian and Syriac words and phrases).

31. Genesis 12:1, 17:11.

32. Psalms 90:12.

33. *Ta'anis* 20b.

34. Leviticus 19:32.

35. Ben Yehuda, a fifth-generation *Tanna* who lived in Kfar Acco, was a student of Rabbi Shimon bar Yochai.

36. Age, they say, is just a matter of time! "I don't feel old," said Bob Hope, "in fact, I don't feel anything until noon. Then it's time for my nap!"

37. These "seven righteous" qualities, says Shimon ben Menasya, were all fulfilled in Rabbi Yehuda Hanasi and his sons; however the Mishna lists eight qualities. Why the discrepancy? I don't know. In trying to go from "eight" to "seven," the Vilna Gaon omits "wisdom" and the Palestinian Talmud omits "old age."

38. Elisha ben Avuya was a third-generation *Tanna* who, tragically, became a heretic; however, since *emes* (truth) can be quoted from any source, the Talmud continued to refer to him but under a different name (*Acher*, "the other one"!) and recorded his halachic opinions as "Others declare..." A loyal Rabbi Meir explained why ben Avuya continued as his (misguided) teacher: "I only ate from the inside of the fruit and discarded the peel!" (*Chagiga* 15b). When asked why he was so hostile to Torah, ben Avuya blamed his father for displaying jealousy instead of *simcha* at his *bris* ("my Torah was [thus] not sustained!").

39. Children, it is said, are like books with blank pages, and a young mind like a savings account: no deposit, no interest!

40. Ben Yehuda was a student of Rabbi Eleazar ben Shammua and lived in Kfar Bavli.

41. God's greatest blessing is children; but then they grow up!

42. Was it always so? No. Originally the preferred method of Jewish education was based on the command within the *Sh'ma* that parents teach their children ("You shall teach them thoroughly [the words of Torah]"). The early Jewish elementary schools were *not* established, like today, for the general Jewish public but for orphans and for children whose parents were unable to teach them (that is why it is a great mitzva to teach other people's children). By the first century BCE, non-parental teaching was so ingrained (because of the rise and popularity of Greek-Roman schools, and the growing complexity of Jewish knowledge), that Shimon ben Shetach had no choice but to rule that all Jewish children must attend school, "for otherwise the Torah would be forgotten." How important was Jewish schooling? Rabbi Hamnuna linked the destruction of Jerusalem itself to the neglect of its school system; and Shimon bar Yochai even ordered that certain towns in Israel be abandoned, simply because they didn't maintain salaried teachers. Rabbi Yonah, concerned that all the attention

was being given to youth, turns his thoughts to the "ol' folks" and reminds them that God doesn't reward knowledge but effort.

43. Rabbi Ishmael ben Elisha, lovable grandson of a high priest who was executed by the enemy, was himself held prisoner by the Romans after the destruction of Jerusalem. His release was negotiated by Yehoshua ben Chanania. Unlike that of Rabbi Akiva, his style of exegesis followed the plain meaning of the text. Ben Elisha liked order, and wrote the thirteen principles of logic behind the study of Torah, which are recited daily in Jewish prayer. When he passed away, all the daughters of Israel, whom he defended in pragmatic piety, mourned him (*Nedarim* 66a).

44. Ecclesiastes 3:19–20; II Samuel 14:14.

45. *Sheol* is not to be confused with the concept of "hell." Originally, hell was on earth, a frightening place called the Valley of Gehinnom where children were sacrificed by a pagan cult (II Kings 23:10; Jeremiah 7:31; *Rosh Hashana* 16b, 17a).

46. Numbers 16:30; Ezekiel 31:14, Psalms 88:4–7, 13, 115:17; Isaiah 38:10; Lamentations 3:55; Job 10:21, 22, 26:5, 38:17.

47. Genesis 17:14, 25:8, 25:17, 35:29, 49:33; Deuteronomy 42:50; Exodus 31:14.

48. Daniel 12:2; Nehemiah 9:5.

49. *Zohar* II, 99b.

50. The Tanach contains no clear statement of a "recycled souls" dogma, and the rabbis of the Mishna never deemed it essential. Reincarnation as a doctrine was "resurrected" (pun intended) around the eighth century, but Sa'adia Gaon called it "foolish," and several super-rationalist philosophers (Chesdai, Yosef Albo) thought it opposed the true spirit of Torah. Was their opinion the general consensus? Far from it! Other scholars, such as Isaac Abravanel and Manasseh ben Israel, not to mention the formidable insightful *Zohar* ("All souls must undergo transmigration!") were supporters.

51. Ezekiel 37:11–12.

52. I Kings 17:17–24; II Kings 4:17–37, 13:21.

53. *Sanhedrin* 91b, 10:1; *Kesubos* 111b.

54. I Samuel 28:9, 13–15.

55. *Pirkei Avos* 2:16.

56. *Ta'anis* 25a; *Kesubos* 77b; *Baba Basra* 75a; *Brachos* 17a, 57b; *Mishne Torah*, Repentance 8.

57. This Mishna, the start of *Sanhedrin* (90a, ch. 11), was chosen as the introduction to the weekly study of *Pirkei Avos*, while the Mishna at the end of *Makkos* (23b, ch. 3) closes the weekly learning. Why? By acknowledging the Jews' place in the World to Come, this Mishna was intended to generate in them hope for, and elevate confidence in, their own destiny as a good, virtuous and moral nation, throughout periods of bitter exile and persecution. This declaration was made at a turbulent time, when sectarian and early Jewish-Christian adherents were spreading the theory that the majority of mankind was doomed to perdition, unless "saved" by their new messiah. The ultimate safety net is why the Mishna ends in *Makkos* (sometimes it's erroneously marked as 6:12), with Rabbi Chanania ben Akashia defining the glory of the Jew in the grandeur of Torah and mitzvos. It's also added for pragmatic reasons, since we only say *kaddish* at the ceremony held at the completion of a tractate after learning some *aggada* (defined as the the non-halachic portions of Talmud), which this Mishna is.

58. Rabbi Yaakov ben Kurshai was the grandson of Elisha ben Avuya and teacher of Rabbi Yehuda Hanasi. How do we know his father's name? The same verse appears in *Koheles Rabba* (4:6) with his full name.

59. *Prozdor* is a Latin term for vestibule; Rashi calls it a *portico*, which in today's English refers to the porch outside the front door.

60. Life has only one entrance door; death has many exits!

61. The inclusion of a *tefilla* in a Mishna (this is the original source for the traditional prayer for redemption) is, according to the *Tiferes Yisroel*, an anomaly. The Vilna Gaon claims it's a printing error: the line of redemption was originally intended as the concluding prayer, but somehow it got "tacked on" to this Mishna by mistake. Or, according to the Meiri's theory, the original Mishna ended here and this *tefilla* is correctly placed, meaning that all future *Mishnayos* were "add-ons."

62. Rabbi Eleazar, "the strong arm and right eye" of Israel, a disciple of Rabban Yochanan and an expert on *aggada*, came from Modiin, near Lydda, home of the Hasmoneans. This Mishna was directed against the non-Jewish Christians and Gnostics of the time who led many Jews down a path of spiritual nihilism. Eleazar was killed by his nephew (Bar Kochba) after being falsely denounced as a traitor by a Samaritan.

63. Genesis 4:9.

64. Isaiah 61:8; Psalms 146:7.

65. *Megilla* 26a; *Baba Basra* 8b; Naftali Tzvi Yehuda Berlin, *Ha'amek She'eila* 142:9.

66. *Kol-Bo* 142; Chaim Soloveitchik, *She'eilos u'Teshuvos k'Makor Histori*, ch. 9.

67. *Chullin* 11a.

68. Raavia, *Shut Mahrach Or Zarua* 222.

69. Chasam Sofer, *Choshen Mishpat* 116.

70. Deuteronomy 17:14–15.

71. I Samuel 8:5.

72. I Samuel 8:13–17.

73. Rambam, *Hilchos Gezeilah v'Aveidah* 5:17–18.

74. R. Moshe Feinstein, *Iggeros Moshe, Choshen Mishpat* 2:29.

75. *Pirkei Avos* 3:2.

76. Exodus 1:8. The distrust in rule and reign is justified: Pharaoh wished to curtail the fertility and fecundity of the Jewish people "*pen yirbeh* (lest they multiply)" by ordering their enslavement, oppression, forced labor, and finally, a direct genocidal decree on all newborn Jewish boys (Exodus 1:10–15).

77. Rabbi Chanina, who equated peace with being "as valuable as all Creation," was a deputy (*s'gan*) high priest who lived during the Hasmonean era, survived the destruction of Jerusalem, and painfully bore witness to the deterioration of Judaism in the Holy Land. According to tradition, he died on the 25th of Sivan – but we don't know which year, nor if he died a martyr.

78. Shemaya, a descendant of the Assryian king Sennaherib – and either a convert or a child of converts (*Gittin* 57b) – was a student of Rabbis Yehuda ben Tabbai and Shimon ben Shetach and rose to the position of *Nasi* during King Herod's rule at the end of the Hasmonean era. His advice in this Mishna was given after Herod tried to impose a vow of loyalty to himself. Shemaya, together with his *chavrusa* Avtalyon, were highly respected leaders who studiously avoided the mistakes of their rabbinic predecessors by refusing to get dragged into the civil political war of the times. Hyrkanos and Aaristoblus, sons of Queen Shlomtzion, were plotting her downfall with the help of the Roman enemy. When Hyrkanos won he rewarded his patron with Roman rule, and a major paving stone towards the destruction of the Second Temple was laid.

79. "When he sits on the throne of his kingdom, he shall write for himself a copy of the law" (Deuteronomy 17:18).

80. Hillel, the grandfather of Rabban Gamliel, used to earn a *trepik* a day, half of which

he gave to the guard at the *beis medrash* and half he retained to support himself and his family. Babylonian-born of Davidic descent through Shefatiah ben Avital. Hillel was a gentle, peace-loving, patient, modest and charitable student of Shemayah and Avtalyon. He became *Nasi* early during Herod's rule, about a hundred years before the Second Temple was destroyed, and served for forty years (dying at the age of 120), educating an entire generation of teachers and scholars. Hillel and Shammai, an engineer, were the fifth and last "pair" who, as the leaders of two opposing "Houses" (i.e., *yeshivos*), were often in disagreement (the Talmud records over three hundred differences of opinion between them). Yet Hillel mostly prevails (*Shabbas* 30b; *Succa* 28a). Why? Shammai was fearless, outspoken, and too strict (he once chased a potential convert away with a builder's measuring stick!).

81. A word of advice: if you are in questionable company, make sure you're not alone!

82. When the Gerer Rebbe noticed that some of his chassidim were loath to help outsiders needing assistance, he said: "Why is the *chasida* (the stork) not a kosher animal? Because of its habit of bringing food to the nests of its friends (*Chullin* 63). But if it is sensitive to the needs of others, why is it not eaten? The answer is because it is only concerned about its immediate circle, and not outsiders!"

83. The two Yoses (ben Yoezer and ben Yochanan) were the first and most senior "pair" (*zugos*, today called *chavrusos*) of scholars in the transitional period, around the time of the Hasmonean revolt against the Greeks. Ben Yoezer was a leader in his home town of Tz'redah, a *Nasi* and a student of Shimon Hatzadik and Antigonus. Ben Yoezer was murdered during a massacre of Torah scholars by his nephew Alcimus, a renegade high priest appointed by the Syrians against Judah the Maccabee. Ben Yochanan was ben Yoezer's second-in-command and head of the *beis din*.

84. The *Chazon Ish* interprets this to apply only to frivolous ("idle") talk intended to incite improper behavior; this directive is not opposed to essential neighborly conversations, which are conducive to friendships.

85. Ben Yehuda, the last *Tanna* and the third to bear the name Gamliel, succeeded his famous father as *Nasi*.

86. "Plenty of people," notes Rochefoucauld, "wish to become devout, but no one wishes to be humble!"

87. The *Anshei Knesses Hagedola*, translated alternately as "Men of the Great Synagogue" or "Men of the Great Assembly" (the confusion between the two terms is derived from the first *Pirkei Avos* translation into English: at the time "synagogue" was a Greek word referring *not* to any house of worship but to a religious assembly). The expression "Great Synagogue" referred to those Jews who followed Ezra's lead in the revival of Torah. When forming the Assembly, Ezra chose leaders of the community, together with prophets (e.g., Chaggai, Zecharia) and scholars (e.g., Mordecai, of Purim fame).

88. Ben Charash, a third-fourth generation *Tanna* and student of Rabbis Eliezer ben Hyrkanos and Eleazar ben Azariah, was a role model of piety and an expert in medical-halachic issues, who fled the country because of the Bar Kochba defeat. He opened a yeshiva in *chutz la'aretz* (Rome), crying as he left that "Living in the land of Israel is equal to all of the mitzvos!"

89. Isaiah 1:10–17.

90. *Sanhedrin* 35a.

91. *Sefer Hamiddos*, Chapter *Tzedaka* 12.

92. *Shulchan Aruch Yore Deah* 249:7, 251:10.

93. *Kiddushin* 40a.

94. Akiva ben Joseph (c. 50–135 CE), a refined and gentle Jew, was one of the greatest

intellectual and influential Torah forces in the history of Israel. Akiva rose from being a poor, semi-literate shepherd to become one of Judaism's greatest scholars and one of the first to systematically compile the Torah's Oral Laws. Akiva was inherently humble, a third-generation *Tanna* and son of a convert. At the prompting of Rachel, his wife (daughter of Kalba Savua, a wealthy shepherd who disapproved of his daughter's choice for a spouse), he began to study Torah under the tutelage of Rabbis Eliezer ben Hyrkanos and Yehoshua ben Chanania. At the time, he was forty years old, but had no objection to learning *alef-beis* side-by-side with young Jewish children, including his own son. Stripped of Rachel's inheritance because of her father's rejection of her marriage, the young family struggled to make a living (*Kesubos* 62b, 63a), however, Akiva managed to become wealthy over the years and set a standard of giving charity. Rabbi Akiva, who witnessed the destruction of the Temple, went on to become erudite in Jewish mysticism, and developed the exegetical method of the Mishna, a style that links each traditional practice to a basis in Torah; along the way he managed to also become proficient in languages, science, medicine and agriculture. After twenty-four years of study, Akiva attracted an incredible number of students (twenty-four thousand). Active in the unsuccessful Bar Kochba rebellion against Rome, the rabbi, a natural optimist, influenced by the feel-good philosophy of Nachum's "*gam zu l'tova* (all God does is for the best)!" was brutally tortured to death in Caesarea on Yom Kippur by the Roman enemy, at the age of 120. His students were decimated in the war and Bar Kochba totally discredited.

95. Note however that there is a minimum (10 percent) and a maximum (20 percent) of charitable giving in Jewish law. Why an upper limit? To prevent overly generous Jews from becoming a burden on society themselves.

96. Ben Yehuda, a student of Rabbi Yehoshua ben Chanania, was a third-generation *Tanna* and a contemporary of Rabbi Akiva. He was such a "notorious" donor to charity that beggars would hide from him so as not to take his last coin!

97. Tithe is derived from the Hebrew *aser* (ten – *ma'aser* means the "tenth" part). The concept makes its first appearance when Abraham offers Malchizedek, the king-priest of Salem, a portion (10 percent) of the spoils from his war against Kedorlaomer.

98. In some parts of prewar Europe, where the local *beis din* had more power than customary today, the rabbis could force people to give to the town coffers!

99. Proverbs 27:6.

100. *Ta'anis* 7a.

101. *Ta'anis* 23a.

102. *Brachos* 6b.

103. *Brachos* 17a.

104. *Bereishis Rabba* 8:7; *Zohar Chadash* 121c.

105. Leviticus 19:18.

106. *Pesachim* 113b; *Rosh Hashana* 17a; *Ta'anis* 20b; Exodus 34:6.

107. "I once didn't talk to my wife for three weeks," Yankie tells his friend. "Why, were you angry?" "No, I just didn't want to interrupt her!"

108. Ecclesiastes 7:9; Proverbs 15:1, 29:19, 22.

109. *Pirkei Avos* 5:14.

110. Rambam, *Mishne Torah*, Laws of Character Development 1:4.

111. Numbers 20:10.

112. *Pirkei Avos* 5:11.

113. *Ta'anis* 4a.

114. *Orchos Tzadikim* 12.

115. What do we know about Nittai? Nothing, except that his name is short for "Neth-anyah."

116. Shmuel lived in the first century CE at Yavne. At his death (childless and poverty-stricken), he (correctly) predicted the martyrdom of *Tanna'im*, and was thus compared to his namesake, Samuel the Prophet; hence his nickname, Shmuel the "small" – in that he was a "smaller prophet" than Samuel (although some claim that this was a description of his outstanding humility) (*Sanhedrin* 11a). So high in spirituality was Shmuel that nobody bothered to confer on him the tile "Rabbi," because his piety made any honor superfluous.

117. "If Aaron met an evil man on the road he greeted him with the words '*shalom ale-ichem.*' If that man wanted to commit a sin on the next day, he would say, 'Woe is me. How could I look at Aaron? I should be ashamed before him, for he gave me the greeting of peace!'"

118. The Gastinener Rebbe was able to control and, at the same time, express his anger by always waiting a day before reacting. Similarly, Rabbi Mendel Libavitzer, before reacting to a provocation, made it a custom to review the matter in the *Shulchan Aruch*, after which he would say, "How can one be angry after delving into the holy books?"

119. Some of the earlier *Pirkei Avos* manuscripts omit "Meir" and have "Rebbe" instead (i.e., Rabbi Yehuda Hanasi).

120. After his wife died, Rabbi Akiva Eiger's children urged him to remarry. In a letter to them, he replied, "Do you consider me so insensitive and heartless as to rush to accept a marriage proposal while still in mourning? Am I to forget the love of the beloved wife of my youth, with whom God allowed me to raise upstanding, blessed children? The little bit of Torah in me is only due to her help – she carefully kept watch over my health and bore all the financial worries of our home, so that I would not be distracted from the service of God. Now that she is gone, I am bereft and emotionally like a broken vessel. Who will pasture our young sheep (children); with whom shall I share my worries and find some respite? Who will care for me? Which person knows better than I of her righteousness and modesty?" (*Iggeros Soferim*)

121. Zecharia 8:16.

122. Deuteronomy 17:18.

123. Deuteronomy 16:20.

124. Shimon, a first-century *Tanna*, was second only to Yehuda ben Tabbai. Shimon's sister was Queen Salome Alexandra, the widow whose influential husband King Yannai reigned 76 BCE–67 BCE. Yannai opposed the Sadducees and supported the Pharisaic party that dominated Israel. Was this king good for the Jews? Yes. He mandated that Jewish law be observed by the halachic standards of the traditional *kesuba* and initiated Jewish schools for the young. Ben Shetach's plea to "examine witnesses thoroughly" was based on a tragic personal experience: his own rabbinic court accepted the testimony of false witnesses against his son, who was executed on a groundless accusation (Rashi, *Sanhedrin* 44b).

125. Ben Yose's father (ben Chalafta) was his primary tutor, and the father-son team acted as halachic adjudicators in Tzipori. A judge of high integrity, ben Yose, who lived in the latter half of the second century, was known for his conciseness (an entire *Sefer Torah* could have been written from his memory!). He attracted some enmity from the common folks after aiding the Roman government in the arrest of thieves, amongst whom were Jews.

126. Rabbi Tzadok was a first-generation *Tanna*, revered as a holy and mystic man, who fasted for forty years on a single fig that he sucked from Shabbas to Shabbas in an

attempt to prevent the Temple from being destroyed, but to no avail. After Vespasian destroyed Jerusalem, Tzadok continued his Torah study from Yavne, after Yochanan ben Zakkai successfully interceded for his life with the Romans, claiming that if there had been one more Jew like Tzadok, "Jerusalem could never have been conquered" (*Midrash Rabba Eicha* 1:5). The name Tzadok (and Eliezer and/or Eleazar) was repeated in several successive generations, so it's difficult to know which particular Tzadok or Eliezer/Eleazar ben Tzadok is which.

127. Israel, with a population of around six million, has twenty-five thousand lawyers; in contrast, Japan, with a population of 125 million, has only eighteen thousand!

128. Rabbi Eleazar was a close colleague of Rabbi Yehuda Hanasi, and probably the father of (the better known) Rabbi Eliezer Hakappar. Hakappar might mean "the man from Cyprus," or refer to a trade.

129. There are two men named Eliezer ben Yaakov in the Mishna, and we don't know which one made this comment. One was a fourth-generation *Tanna*, a great humanitarian, and one of the last students of Rabbi Akiva; the other was a contemporary of Rabban Yochanan ben Zakkai, who compiled the Mishna treatise called *Middos*.

130. Yehuda ben Tabbai followed in the footsteps of Yehoshua ben Perachiah and fled to Alexandria, Egypt, after King Alexander Yannai, a supporter of the Sadducees, the ruling priestly-aristocratic hierarchy during the two centuries before the destruction of Jerusalem, started harassing the Sages. After executing a Sadduccean witness, ben Tabbai was rebuked by Sanhedrin *Nasi* Shimon ben Shetach – his sterling-charactered *chavrusa* ("pair") – and never rendered another opinion without checking it with ben Shetach first. When it was safe to return, ben Tabbai paired up again with ben Shatach, safe now that his sister Queen Shlomtzion had taken over the reign of Israel, and the pair of Sages set out to ensure a "No Jewish Child Left Behind" educational program in the Holy Land. According to the texts, the years when brother and sister ruled Israel were the most peaceful and bountiful for the Jewish nation (*Ta'anis* 23a).

131. This is why "Thou Shalt Not Erect an Auschwitz" is absent from the Commandments, for those who choose decency and morality are simply incapable of designing, building and operating horrendous crematoria.

132. *Makkos* 1:10.

133. "The worst thing about falsehood," Rabbi Yosef Yitzchak of Lubavitch would say, "is not that it is not true, but that it presents itself as truth."

134. *Mishne Torah, Hilchos Lulav* 8:15; Deuteronomy 28:47.

135. *Shabbas* 30a.

136. "Rebbe" (an endearing term) is Yehuda Hanasi, "the Prince" (c. 135–219 CE), descendant of Hillel in the seventh generation, student of Shimon Hasheni (his father) and of Rabbi Yaakov ben Kurshai. Yehuda was a wealthy, learned, humble, cultured patrician and respected patriarch of the Jewish community. Rebbe, who formed a close relationship with Antonius even before he became the mighty Roman emperor, achieved his aim "to ensure unity of religious observance" by, for the first time in Jewish history, collecting and reducing to writing the decisions and opinions of earlier Torah teachers, a work now known as the Mishna, the foundation of all Talmudic study (completed about 200 CE, the Talmud being completed some three hundred years later). According to Jewish tradition, Rebbe was born in Beis Shearim on the day Rabbi Akiva died, and it is he who is referenced in the verse "The sun set, the sun then shone!" (*Koheles* [Ecclesiastes] 1:5). A lover of Hebrew, Yehuda Hanasi objected to the extensive use of Aramaic in the Holy Land, and insisted on only speaking Hebrew, even to his non-Jewish staff (*Baba Kamma* 82b, 83).

137. Shimon ben Gamliel, the humble father of Yehuda Hanasi, was the *Nasi* (in hiding) during the Bar Kochba period. He is extensively quoted in the Mishna (more than a hundred times!) and died before the siege of Jerusalem. Had he lived, theorizes the *Tiferes Yisroel*, he, and not Yochanan ben Zakkai, would have taken the lead in reorganizing Jewish life after the turbulent Roman years. "Gamliel" is Greek for the Hebrew of "God is my reward/recompense," indicating the loss of children in the family. It was a common name. The Torah refers to Gamliel ben Pedahzur, chief of the tribe of Manasseh (Numbers 1:10; 2:20; 7:54, 59; 10:23); in Christian mythology, the first-century Gamliel the Elder was declared a saint (Saint Gamaliel); there is Gamliel II of Yavneh; Gamliel IV, grandson of Shimon from the latter half of the third century (of whom very little is known); Gamliel V, son and successor of Hillel II; and Gamliel VI, grandson of Gamliel V, the last of the patriarchs. (And what was the middle name of US President Warren G. Harding? Gamliel!)

138. This saying, which ends the first chapter of *Mishnayos*, is unique. Why? It's the first Mishna that comes with an explanatory text.

139. Shimon Hatzadik (the Righteous), one of the last survivors of the *Anshei Knesses Hagedola*, served as high priest for forty years in the early Second Temple period after Ezra. He led the Jewish delegation to greet the conquering Alexander the Great at the gates of Jerusalem (every Jewish child born in Jerusalem that year was named "Alexander"). Shimon, inspiring and kind, and the only Sage in the Talmud referred to as "the Tzadik," was the transitional teacher between the period of the Great Assembly – the first generation to be led by select individuals knowledgeable in Torah – and that of the "pairs [of students/scholars]," an indication that in these follow-up generations there was a severe shortage of learned Jews capable of "transmitting" Torah. What was his full name? We're not sure. It's either Shimon ben Onias I (the high priest from 310 BCE to 291 BCE), or, since his contemporary was Yehoshua ben Sira, more likely his grandson (high priest from 219 BCE to 199 BCE).

140. Why Bilam? Why was he chosen as the "false teacher opposite" of Abraham? I don't know; but he appears frequently in the Midrash as a typical tempter and deceiver of Jews.

141. Rabbi Dosa ben Horkinos, a name of Greek origin, was very wealthy, lived a long life (to 120), and followed the teachings of Hillel. His younger brother Yonathan followed those of Shammai. His words seem directed to those in his social and economic circle.

142. "I would never belong to a group," declared Groucho Marx, "that would accept someone like me as a member!"

143. When he was an infant Rabbi Yehoshua ben Chanania's mother would bring his cradle to the *beis medrash* so that the first sounds he heard were men studying Torah. Together with his close friend Rabbi Eliezer, ben Chanania, a blacksmith by trade, helped Rabban Yochanan ben Zakkai escape from Jerusalem. A Levite singer in the Temple, he was a gentle, witty, calm and unextravagant scholar at Yavne who authored the universalist dogma, "The righteous *of all nations* have a share in the World to Come!" He was also well versed in astronomy (he correctly predicted Halley's comet), which helped him calculate the time of Jewish festivals.

144. *Nidda* 16b; *Beitza* 16a.

145. *Megilla* 6b.

146. *Sanhedrin* 99b.

147. Deuteronomy 6:5; *Brachos* 61b.

148. Leviticus 26:3–13; Deuteronomy 11:13–16, 25:15; Proverbs 22:4.

149. Deuteronomy 15:10, 16:11; Isaiah 1:17–19; Proverbs 19:17; *Eruvin* 86a.

150. *Bava Basra* 9b; *Chagiga* 5a; Rambam, *Hilchos Matanos Aniyim* 10:7–14.

151. *Ta'anis* 9a.

152. *Nidda* 70b.

153. Rambam, *Hilchos De'os* 3:1.

154. Proverbs 21:17.

155. Rabbi Addah bar Ahavah once saw a woman wearing a karbalta, an ostentatious red garment, and tore it off her. Turned out she wasn't Jewish. The rabbi was fined.

156. *Chullin* 84a, b; Proverbs 27:26.

157. *Makos* 24a; Micah 6:8.

158. *Pirkei Avos* 4:1.

159. Polygamy survived Hillel for many centuries, but there's not a single instance of a polygamist rabbi; in the year 1000 CE, Rabbi Gershom ben Yehuda ("the Light of the Exile") banned polygamous marriages for a thousand years; however, even when that time was up, Jews still maintained monogamous unions.

160. Caesarea-based Yose ben Kisma, a pacifist and survivor of the Bar Kochba revolt, was a third-generation *Tanna* and colleague of Rabbi Chanania ben Teradyon, one of the ten martyrs executed by the Romans. What do we know of him? Hardly anything. Why? Because he is rarely quoted (in fact, this is the only first-person experience quoted in the Mishna, with perhaps the exception of 1:9).

161. A Yiddish proverb: You can tell what God thinks of money by looking at some of the people he gives it to!

162. The shopkeeper complained to the Premislaner Rebbe that someone had opened a similar store next door and was threatening his livelihood. The Rebbe said: "Watch a horse drink water from a pool. He stamps his hoof in the water. The reason is that when he bends down to drink he sees his shadow. He imagines that another horse is also drinking next to him and he tries to frighten him away. In reality there is plenty of water for plenty of horses. You too are afraid of an imaginary enemy. God's abundance flows like a river. No man can touch another's livelihood!"

163. Rabbi Yehuda would go to the yeshiva bearing a pitcher on his shoulders, saying, "Great is labor, for it honors the person who does it!" Although Abba Joseph was a rabbi, he was also a builder's laborer. One day, when he was working, he was confronted by a man who wanted to drag the rabbi into a long theological conversation. The rabbi refused. "I am a day laborer," he said, "and I must not leave my work, so say what you want quickly and then leave" (*Midrash Rabba*).

164. If you think a dollar has no value, try borrowing it from a bank!

165. There is an important exception, known as the Yissachar-Zevulun partnership. Zevulun and Yissachar are role models who, in a unique form of spiritual partnership, agree to "share their work": the former performs hard labor to generate the funds necessary to support the latter's time which is committed exclusively to toiling in Torah. (The Rambam, for example, worked as a doctor and sent money to support his brother, engaged exclusively in Torah study.)

166. What's the difference between a tailor and a doctor? A generation!

167. *Kesubos* 5:5; *Pesachim* 113a.

168. Eleazar ben Azariah, a third-generation *Tanna*, had *yichus* (he was a descendant of Ezra), wealth, popularity, piety and such a vast knowledge of Torah that he became a *Nasi* (temporarily succeeding the deposed Rabban Gamliel II after he had thrice shown disrespect to Yehoshua ben Chanania) of the Yavne Sanhedrin at the young age of eighteen! He was so sensitive about his age that he prayed for gray hair (*Brachos* 28a). Ben Azariah's vote was the decisive one in the debate as to whether to

include *Koheles* and *Shir Hashirim* into the Tanach. His colleagues said he was "a pleasant container, and a merchant's store of knowledge" (*Gittin* 16a).

169. A Yiddish proverb: If poverty were of any value, the rich would buy it!

170. *Sotah* 4b–5a.

171. *Mishne Torah, Hilchos De'os* 1:4.

172. *Vayikra Rabba* 9:3.

173. *Eiruvin* 55a.

174. *Pesachim* 66b.

175. Numbers 12:3; *Yevamos* 49b; Exodus 16:8; Rav Chaim Volozhin, *Ruach Chaim* 1:1.

176. Malbim, Proverbs 22:4.

177. "If I only had a little humility," said Ted Turner, "I'd be perfect!"

178. *Midrash Targum Sheni*, Esther 1:3.

179. Genesis 1:3.

180. *Koheles* (Ecclesiastes) 5:2.

181. This quote appears in different versions attributed variously to Mark Twain, George Eliot, and others. No one knows who really said it first, but it has a *yiddishe ta'am* (a Yiddish "taste," or flavor).

182. *Pirkei Avos* 5:9.

183. *Eiruvin* 54b.

184. *Pesachim* 3b.

185. Proverbs 18:21; 21:23.

186. "Half the world is composed of people who have something to say and can't," observed Robert Frost, "and the other half who have nothing to say and keep on saying it!"

187. God even advises Hosea what to name his children, after the prophet had already changed his own name (which means "God delivers") to Joshua (which means "God is noble").

188. Parents who give their children odd names are inflicting cruelty on their kids: When she turned sixteen, the daughter of singer Bob Geldof publicly accused her father of causing her ridicule by naming her "Peaches Honeyblossom Geldof"! (The extra names Michelle Charlotte Angel Vanessa were added to her Wikipedia entry by a mischievous blogger and widely reported as part of her name, but Peaches Honeyblossom is unusual enough all by itself…)

189. Rabbi Shimon bar Yochai (c. 100–160 CE) was a self-confident and highly independent disciple of Rabbi Akiva, with whom he studied for thirteen years. His conclusions are quoted over three hundred times in the Mishna. One of the most preeminent Sages of the time, and a role model for future Jewish mystics (kabbalists credit him with authoring the *Sifrei* and the *Zohar*, the "Bible" of kabbalism), bar Yochai was a hater of Rome and a lover of Jews ("Every Israelite is to be regarded as of royal descent!"). He survived Bar Kochba's revolt and spent many years in hiding with his son (Elazar) in a cave in the upper Galilee after the Roman authorities had sentenced him to death. He died at age eighty and is buried together with his son on Mount Meron, the preferred place of pilgrimage every year on Lag ba'Omer, the anniversary of his death.

190. The Torah records only a few cases of Nazirites, such as Samson and Absalom.

191. The Rambam, in his *Sefer Hamadda, Hilchos Teshuva*, was able to reduce the legal road to *teshuva* down to four steps: regret, abandonment of sin, resolve for the future, confession. The first three are man-to-man related whereas the last, and most important, is man-to-God related.

192. We know very little about Rabbi Shimon ben Nethanel except that he was a "sin-

fearing" priest, a second-generation *Tanna*, son-in-law to Rabban Gamliel Hazaken, and Yochanan ben Zakkai's fourth student.

193. The rabbis of the fifteenth century, faced with the rise of the printing press, ruled that printed *seforim* are subject to the same level of *kedusha* as handwritten works.

194. Avtalyon, descendant of proselytes, became a beloved and influential Sage and *av beis din*. He gave this warning to his colleagues after witnessing the persecutions by King Alexander Yannai and the fratricidal conduct of his successors. Many Jewish teachers fled to Alexandria, then the intellectual capital of the world (despite its being "a place of evil [heretic] waters"), where they stopped speaking Hebrew and related to mitzvos as mere "symbols" of Judaism. Avtalyon and Shemaya (another proselyte descendant), the first to be known as *darshanim*, became "celebrities" after rescuing Hillel from freezing to death when they found him on the roof of their *beis medrash* on Shabbas listening to their words of Torah (*Yoma* 35b).

195. Shimon, the wise and practical son of Rabban Gamliel I, was killed during the destruction of the Second Temple. He was concerned at the excessive talkativeness in rabbinic literature and speech, and stressed that the aim of Torah was practical (to *do*), not theoretical (to *think*), a position confirmed by the famous Lydda rabbinate in 13 CE: "Study is most important, because it leads to deed!"

196. Rabbi Yose ben Chalafta, a fourth-generation *Tanna* from Usha who started a *beis din* in Tiberias, was an author (*Seder Olam*, a treatise on Jewish history) and one of the most distinguished of Rabbi Akiva's five students (*Yevamos* 82b). His famous *vort* was that since Creation God has kept Himself busy by being a *shadchan* (matchmaker), as difficult a task as "splitting the Red Sea" (*Bereishis Rabba* 68:4). Ben Chalafta, a tanner by trade who received his *smicha* from Rabbi Yehuda ben Bava after Akiva's death (ben Bava was also murdered by the Romans), had married his sister-in-law after his childless brother died, as prescribed by Jewish law (*yibum*), and left five sons (Ishmael, Elazar, Chalafta, Avtilas, Menachem) who were referred to as "five cedar trees." Why? Because they grew tall in Torah! (*Shabbas* 118b) Rabbi Yose was prolific: there are over eight hundred rulings in his name sprinkled throughout the Mishna and Tosefta (*Moed Katan* 25b).

197. "I am glad I am guilty of some sins," confided nineteenth-century Galician Rabbi Meir Hurwitz in his *Sefer Imrei Noam*, "otherwise I might be guilty of the greatest sin of all – conceit!"

198. After Shammai died, ben Mehalalel, contemporary of Hillel, was the first to describe God as "King of the king of kings" (repeated by Rabban Yochanan ben Zakkai on his deathbed). His stature was so great amongst his colleagues that he didn't need any rabbinic titles. As the epitome of humility, he turned down an offer to become *av beis din* because he refused to compromise on some of his halachic positions ("Let men not say that, for the sake of office, I changed my views!").

199. We do not know where or when he was born, nor to whom, but we know that Rabbi Meir, a descendant of the Roman emperor Nero (*Gittin* 56a), and husband of Beruria, daughter of Rabbi Chanina ben Tradyon, was, after Rabbi Akiva, the most important and original figure amongst the fourth-century *Tanna'im* (even God announced that Meir had no equal in his time. Yehuda Hanasi, when asked how he had achieved his own success, traced it to seeing Rabbi Meir's back: "Had I viewed him from the front, I would have achieved much more!"). We're not even sure what his name is because *Meir*, meaning "one who enlightens," was how others, in awe of his erudition, called him. Rabbi Meir received *smicha* from Rabbis Akiva and Yehuda ben Bava and was such a brilliant orator (dividing each talk into three segments – one part halachic, one part parable, one part homiletic – that he is quoted

on nearly every page of the Mishna. Whenever the Mishna quotes an anonymous source ("others say"), it almost inevitably refers to Rabbi Meir! Eventually, because of taking sides in a *machlokes* (difference of opinion) between Rabbis Nosson and Shimon ben Gamliel, he left Eretz Yisroel and settled in Asia Minor. When he died, he requested that his coffin be placed along the Mediterranean shores facing the Holy Land, so he could stay connected through the motions of the waves (*Kila'im* 9:3).

200. Rabbi Levitas, a third-generation *Tanna* in Yavne, contemporary of Rabbi Akiva, and a student of Yehoshua ben Chanania, is a bit of a mystery; this, on humility, is his only quote in the entire Mishna (although he reappears in *Pirkei d'Rabbi Eliezer*). Even his name is different: it is Greek, formed from a Hebrew original!

201. The Talmud recalls that even kings can self-destruct when stricken with arrogance and egotism. After God offers Yerovam a spot in *Gan Eden*, he asks, "Who will be first?" When told, "Ben Yishai will be first," Yerovam, hungry for honor, turns down a portion in *Olam Haba* with an arrogant response: "If so, I don't want to go!"

202. Rabbi Elazar ben Shammua, a fourth-generation popular and cheerful *Tanna* (the "happiest of scholars"), colleague of Rabbi Meir and mentor to Rabbi Yehuda Hanasi, was one of the five "new students [from] the south" whom Rabbi Akiva selected to preserve the Torah after his own twenty-four thousand students had been killed in a horrendous epidemic. What caused this tragedy? Some scholars point to the lack of respect the students showed towards each other. This helps explain ben Shammua's high degree of sensitivity to "honoring" *your own* "students, colleagues, teachers." When asked to explain his longevity (105 years), he replied that he had always shown respect for others. Ben Shammua, whom the Mishna quotes often, taught Torah during a dark period for the Jews. Among his students were Yehuda Hanasi and Rav Yosef of Babylonia (*Eruvin* 53a; *Menachos* 18a).

203. Early Jewish history shows how fatal these underlying character flaws are. Korach, Gechazi and Yerovam ben Nebat were killed because of unbridled envy (Korach of Moses and Aaron), unbridled lust (Gechazi's desire for a reward from Naamon) and unbridled desire for honor (Yerovam denied Jews their pilgrimage to Jerusalem because he thought it was an insult to his dignity).

204. Samuel I 1:12–13, 15.

205. *Ta'anis* 2a; Deuteronomy 11:13; Rambam, *Mishne Torah, Hilchos Tefilla* 1:1.

206. *Akeidas Yitzchak* 58, 3:17a.

207. In Hebrew *tzedaka* means "righteousness," which should not be confused with *zedek* (which means "justice") or *chesed* (which means "loving-kindness"), nor "charity" (an act for which there is no Hebrew word), derived from a root which means "love," in that true charity is a loving, respectful approach, and not just an action. *Chesed* is a mitzva, but it is not *ipso facto* tzedaka or charity. Nor is "compassion" technically righteousness. It is a popular fallacy that a mitzva occurs each time you give someone money. It does not. For the mitzva of *tzedaka* to take place, there are several very specific halachic imperatives, ranging from the resources of the giver and the needs of the recipient to certain moral priorities (e.g., placing the needs of female orphans ahead of those of males). Thus it is entirely possible to do an act of *chesed*, *motivated* by compassion, and yet *not* have performed the mitzva of *tzedaka*.

208. Very little is known about Rabbi (and maybe priest) Shimon ben Nethanel except that he married the daughter of Rabban Gamliel I and was a close friend of Rabbis Eliezer and Yehoshua. How do we know which "Shimon" the Mishna is referring to? When "R. Shimon" appears, with no further elucidation, it is Shimon bar Yochai, whereas the other "Shimon" is Shimon (ben Nethanel), with no mention ever of his father's name.

209. The English word "miracle" is derived from the Latin *mirari*, which means "to wonder," or "to marvel at" or "be amazed by."

210. D. 46 BCE.

211. In Babylonia, the term *Mar* was added to create the *Ge'onim* title of *Mar Rabbi*; the Jews who lived under Ottoman rule preferred the title *Chacham*.

212. In order of importance, *Rabbi* was greater than *Rab (Rav)*; *Rabban* was greater than *Rabbi*; the simple name was greater than *Rabban* (the title given to the presidents of the Sanhedrin). Unfortunately, in the twenty-first century, the title doesn't have the same aura anymore, vying for attention in a plethora of confusing honorifics: there's *Rav, HaRav, Moreinu HaRav, Reb, Moreinu, Moreinu v'Rabbeinu HaRav, Moreinu v'Rabbeinu, Rosh Yeshiva, Rosh HaYeshiva, Mashgiach, Mora d'Asra, HaGaon, Rebbe, HaTzadik, HaKadosh, Admor*, ad infinitum.

213. This Mishna bridges the generations of Torah scholars, from Yose ben Yoezer and Yose ben Yochanan to ben Perachia and Nittai of Arbel. Ben Perachia fled to Egypt about two hundred years before the destruction of the Second Temple in order to escape King Yannai's reign of terror after Yochanan, the high priest, defected to the Sadducees. He returned to Israel under the protection of the king's wife (Queen Salome Alexandra), the sister of a student of his (Shimon ben Shetach).

214. Typical of Rav Leib Lazarow's aphorisms: "Watch out for people whom nobody likes – but be more careful of him whom everybody likes!" and, "I measure your wealth by your friends and your greatness by your enemies!"

215. Rabban Shimon ben Gamliel was the grandson of Hillel and the first first-century *Nasi* in the post-*zugos* ("pairs") era that immediately preceded the destruction of the Second Temple. He tragically witnessed the disintegration of the Jewish community in the Holy Land, and its defeat at the Roman sword. During his time as high priest, the office became such a "prize" that it was sold to the highest bidder. Ben Gamliel, a juggler, was known for his love of the Temple (*Succa* 53a), and together with Rabbi Ishmael ben Elisha, was the first of the ten martyrs butchered by the enemy. In order not to confuse him with his grandson (Rabban Gamliel of Yavne), Gamliel (who instituted the "equalizer" of plain burial shrouds for all) was known as Rabban Gamliel Hazaken, "the Elder" (and was the first to be honored with the superior title of *Rabban*, "our Master"). Gamliel is one of the few Mishna rabbis who appears often in the New Testament, where even Paul recalls "learning at his feet." His granddaughter (Imam-Shalom) became the rebbetzin of the outstanding Sage Rabbi Eliezer ben Hyrkanos.

216. "I hate the rabbinate," fumed the frustrated German Rav Yaakov Emden, eighteenth-century Talmudist and author (*Edus B'Yaakov*), echoing the Mishna's Shemaiah, "Love work; hate the rabbinate!"

217. What does "cleaving to their dust" mean? This is not to be taken literally, although in the olden days of no furniture, students would actually sit "at the feet" of scholars, or perform "menial" (i.e., dusty) tasks for their teachers. Today it means to stay in close proximity to rabbinical role models.

218. This passionate warning comes from personal experience. After refusing to accept a decision by the majority of his colleagues, Rabbi Eliezer was excommunicated and died a lonely and bitter man.

219. Eliezer ben Hyrkanos, married to Rabban Gamliel's sister (Imma-Shalom), had an encyclopedic knowledge (which is why they called him "the cistern," in that he retained his learning just like a cemented cistern retains its water). After he arrived in Jerusalem at twenty-two to learn Torah from Rabban Yochanan, his father disinherited him, only to change his mind later when his son, now a *rosh yeshiva* in Lod,

became known as *Eliezer Hagadol*, "Eliezer the Great Scholar"! His attitude was so determined that he refused to accept majority decisions on halachic matters, and was often "cold-shouldered" by his colleagues. Nevertheless, the Mishna quotes him over three hundred times, and the Talmud recalls how he died (age 100) in the midst of answering a *she'eila* (*Sanhedrin* 68a).

220. Rabban Yochanan ben Zakkai was one of the most remarkable of all Jews, one in a (fortunate) generation, a man who doesn't get enough credit for single-handedly changing the course of Jewish history. A Jew who elevated the mitzva of charity and who loved all men, making sure to be the first to say "hello!" to others (*Brachos* 17a). A modern-day merger between Jeremiah (who mourned the destruction of Jerusalem) and Zerubavel (who went about laying the foundation of a new edifice for Torah), ben Zakkai was living proof of a famous Benjamin Disraeli saying ("There is no education like adversity!"), and found himself in that rare position in Jewish history of having to make decisions, some of which he was unsure of until he went to his death. Trusting Roman General Vespasian was like hugging Osama bin Laden or Arafat; it required a certain suspension of disbelief of reality (or as that great American novelist Saul Bellow put it: "A great deal of intelligence can be invested in ignorance when the need for illusion is great!"). Ben Zakkai, a committed pacifist, survived the fall of Jerusalem in 70 CE by faking "burial" and escaping the besieged city with the help of his nephew (Abba Sikra) and two students (Eliezer and Yehoshua), making his way to the Roman camp (*Gittin* 56a, b). An elderly man by then (he died at the age of 120), he was instrumental in reorganizing the religious life of the surviving Jewish remnant, and helped move the Great Assembly, the Jews' chief spiritual and learning center, to Yavne. He modestly succeeded Shimon ben Gamliel, which seems odd, because he was not a direct descendant of Hillel; the natural successor should have been his son Gamliel II, who finally accepted the leadership only after ben Zakkai died. However, this interruption in the chain simply shows how valuable ben Zakkai was to the continuity of Judaism. Incredibly, we know more about this Mishna Sage from Josephus than from rabbinic sources. The Talmud recalls the negotiations between ben Zakkai and an (unnamed) king (identified by Josephus as Titus), appointed by Vespasian, who had already left for Egypt. The term of "transmission" is used here for the last time, which makes Rabban Yochanan the last to receive Torah in the traditional means, which is especially significant since he "received it" from the two masters Hillel and Shammai (he was the youngest of Hillel's eighty students). From that moment on, the "transmission from Moses" was under very different conditions, but, to his credit, it was ben Zakkai who founded a new world order of Judaism compatible in the context of Sinaitic continuity. On his deathbed his last words were, "May you fear God as much as you fear man!"

221. This challenge was not lost on America's preeminent twentieth-century Talmudist teacher, Rabbi Joseph B. Soloveitchik (the Rav, who served as *rosh yeshiva* of Yeshiva University for more than forty years). At a lecture in honor of the fourth yahrzeit of his wife, Rebbetzin Tonya Soloveitchik, he warned: "We, the harbingers of Torah Judaism to the non-Torah Jewish community, are under strict scrutiny from a moral point of view. Precisely because we place the study of Torah at the center of our existence, the topic of humility is very relevant, as the explosion of knowledge in the modern world *can and does result in human arrogance.*"

222. *Sota* 1:7.

223. Exodus 20:12; Deuteronomy 22:7, 25:15.

224. Deuteronomy 11:16–17.

225. Rashi, Exodus 12:22.

226. Antigonus of Socho, a high priest in the first generation after the Great Assembly, succeeded his teacher Shimon Hatzadik as *rosh yeshiva/Nasi* during the days of the Second Temple. A contemporary of Alexander the Great, he is the first noted Jew with a Greek name! Why does the Mishna have Antigonus "receive" Torah instead of having it "conveyed" from Shimon? Because Shimon's generation, especially the upper-class Jews, suffered from a deterioration in the quality of teaching. Thus it was more a case of "getting" than "giving"! Tragically, two of his students (Tzadok and Baytos) misunderstood his teachings about Divine reward and punishment and abandoned traditional Torah Judaism to become leaders of the *Tzadokim* (Sadducees) and the *Baytosim* (Boethusians), both sects rooted deeply in Hellenism.

227. This is the final Mishna; from here on the sayings are "add-ons," appended to *Pirkei Avos*.

228. The concept of a "Heavenly Book" comes from Exodus 32:32, *Malachi* 3:16 and Daniel. Jewish mysticism declares that every night, while the body sleeps, the soul ascends to Heaven and records the day's activities, sinful or otherwise.

229. Is Noah included in this ten? No. He is the tenth in the *previous* generations.

230. The other two are Purim and Chanukah.

231. This is the only quote in the Mishna from Rabbi Yannai, father of Rabbi Dostai and Rabbi Elazar. Why such a tone of despair? Because the Sage lived through the Roman persecution.

232. Deuteronomy 6:7; Haggada.

233. Deuteronomy 28:10.

234. Isaiah 11:6–9; Amos 4:15; Joel 2:21–6.

235. *Brachos* 55a.

236. *Brachos* 40a.

237. Proverbs 9:9.

238. Proverbs 10:8.

239. Reish Lakish, *Pesachim* 66b.

240. Proverbs 3:7; Psalms 111:10.

241. Proverbs 3:13, 3:35, 9:8.

242. *Bava Basra* 12a.

243. Matza (for Passover) must be baked within eighteen minutes of the time the flour and water come into contact with each other, as the definition of *chametz* is one of the five grains (wheat, spelt, oats, barley and rye) that has been in contact with water for more than eighteen minutes, allowing the leavening process to begin.

244. *Avos* 5:7.

245. Deuteronomy 26:10.

246. Rabbi Tarfon, a priest from his mother and father's side, was one of the most prominent Sages in Yavne (because of his encyclopedic knowledge his opinion was always the first sought), and a wealthy, generous Jew from Lod with a stern temperament. A contemporary of Rabban Yochanan and a teacher to Rabbi Akiva, Rabbi Tarfon was very strict about honoring one's parents (one Shabbas, his mother's sandals split; rather than have her walk barefoot, Rabbi Tarfon kept stretching his hands under her feet so she could walk on them). He was twenty years old when the Temple was destroyed, and he established a yeshiva in Lydda where he continued to teach promising students for the next fifty years who would become the famous scholars of the next generation (including Rabbi Yehuda), earning him the title "Rabbi Tarfon is the father of all Israel" (*Yevamos* 4:12).

247. Shimon ben Zoma, a third-generation *Tanna* and student of Rabbi Yehoshua, died too young to receive the title of "Rabbi" (after "delving too deeply" into mysticism),

yet was considered the epitome of *chachma* (wisdom). According to the Talmud, anybody who sees ben Zoma in his or her dreams will "acquire wisdom" (*Brachos* 57b). Absorbed in his Torah, Shimon ben Zoma never married.

248. Elazar ben Chisma, a brilliant student of Rabbis Gamliel, Yehoshua and Akiva, was a third-generation *Tanna* with a unique knowledge of geometry, astronomy and physics, which he considered "supplemental" to his Torah studies. Was "Chisma" his real name? No, it was given to him after he perfected his ability to *daven* in front of the *omed*, i.e., lead the *tefillos* (*chisma* means "stronger;" *nechsam* means "was strengthened").

249. Most of the Mishna is written in Hebrew, so why did Hillel, who was born in Babylon, pen this one in the less "formal" Aramaic? The context of this Mishna is of a conjectural rather than a doctrinal nature (e.g., there is no halacha that *not* studying Torah will lead to death!); thus Hillel presents it in the language of the masses, in order that it be easily understood by its intended "street" audience.

250. "Crown" in Hebrew is similar to the Latin *toga,* which would make Hillel's saying read, "Anyone who takes to the *toga* [i.e., the culture of Rome, as many upper-class Jews did in his day], passes away [meaning, leaves his people and his faith]."

251. Rabbi Chanina ben Dosa was an inspiring mystic and poverty-stricken wonder-worker who saved the lives of the sons of Rabban Gamliel and Yochanan ben Zakkai. Pious and righteous, ben Dosa was a first-generation *Tanna* and student of Rabban Yochanan.

252. Is the reverse also true? Are Jews punished for thinking of sinning if they don't actually go ahead with their plan? No.

253. Rabbi Chanina ben Tradyon, a role model for collecting and distributing *tzedaka,* was a third-generation *Tanna,* father to Beruria (wife of Rabbi Meir), and a *rosh yeshiva* in Sichni, the lower Galilee. He was one of the ten Sages executed by the Romans, dying a horrible death by being wrapped in a Torah scroll and burnt alive. His last words were, "The parchment is being burnt, but the letters are soaring upwards!" (*Avoda Zara* 18a). His wife and son were also murdered and another daughter given to Roman soldiers as a "play toy." She was rescued by her brother-in-law (Rabbi Meir) who was then forced to flee for his life to Babylon.

254. A certain contemporary of Hillel was known as ben Bag Bag. This was not his real name, but an acronym of *ben ger, ben giyores,* "son of male and female proselytes." Why did he keep his name secret? As a descendant of converts (as was ben Hai Hai [*Chagiga* 9b]), another pseudonym, he was concerned that the Romans would harass his relatives (the *hei* was added in honor of the letter *hei* added to Abraham and Sarah's names at the time of Abraham's circumcision). The two Sages lived at the time of Hillel, about a hundred years before the destruction of the Temple.

255. Rabbi Yishmael, who is rarely quoted in the Mishna (but frequently in the Tosefta and in the *baraisos*), was a fourth-generation *Tanna* at Yavne who studied with his distinguished father (Rabbi Yochanan ben Beroka) and at Rabban Shimon ben Gamliel's yeshiva in Usha, in the Galilee.

256. Rabbi Yehuda bar Ilai was a fourth-generation *Tanna* from Lod, a student of Rabbi Tarfon, and one of the five students of Rabbi Akiva. An author (*Toras Cohanim,* a Midrash on Leviticus) and sought-after public speaker, Rabbi Yehuda lived in Usha and spread Torah through the Galilee. He was pacifist, pious and poor (sharing one coat with his wife), and a widely quoted halachist (the Mishna, Midrash and Tosefta quote him hundreds of times), described by the Talmud as an *ish chassid* (*Baba Kamma* 103b), who outlived most of his rabbinic peers.

257. If, in English society, ignorance of the law is not an acceptable defense, then ignorance

within Torah study (a positive obligation to "do") is a crime peculiar to Jewish law (this led to the rabbinic maxim that narrowed the "sin of error" down to those who "lack study"!).

258. The Talmud recalls how Rabbi Eleazar ben Arach, on a trip to Progissa and Diomisis, became so distracted by the local wines and waters that he ignored his Torah studies. The result? Instead of reading the Torah verse "*hachodesh hazeh lachem* (this month shall be for you)," he read instead, "*hacheresh haya libom* (their hearts have become dumb)." His stunned colleagues prayed for him, and his knowledge was restored.

259. Homiletically, the word *apikoros* comes from *pakar*, to "break loose" – i.e., unrestrained, without direction – whilst a common associated Jewish term, *hefker*, means "free," or "abandoned." Those early *apikorsim* (an epithet that is still considered an insult) who deserted Judaism for another religion were called *minim*, a term no longer in use. The Midrash describes them as *am ha'aratzim* (simpletons, ignoramuses), a term which came into the Judaic vocabulary in order to differentiate between the masses of ignorant Jews and the few learned ones who had simply stopped believing.

260. What do we know about Rabbi Nehorai? Nothing, despite the fact that he, a *chaver* of Rabbi Yehuda and one of Rabbi Akiva's students in the Valley of Rimon, is mentioned in the Midrash-Talmud over two hundred times. We don't even know his real name, which could be Nechemia. "Nehorai" is a knickname, given to several rabbis, that simply means "enlightened." In this case, his esteemed colleagues referred to Rabbi Nehorai, a mystic who made a meager living as a potter, as "a light to the students" in the context of studies in halacha (*Shabbas* 147a).

261. Ben Chachinai, a fourth-generation *Tanna* and one of the ten martyrs killed by the Romans, was a contemporary of Rabbi Shimon and a disciple of Rabbi Akiva who was so engrossed with his Torah study that his wife had to send him a message, after twelve years, to return home and help marry off their daughter.

262. Yehoshua ben Levi, a wealthy, humble and prominent student of Rabbis Yehuda and ben Kappara, who excelled in aggada and homiletics, lived in Lod and Tiberias and was one of the outstanding pious Sages who bridged the gap between the end of the *Tanna'im* (Mishna) and the beginning of the *Amora'im* (Talmud), together with Rabbi Chiya, Rav and Rabbi Yannai. As a respected and active communal leader, he represented the Jews in their dealings with the Roman authorities in Rome and Caesarea. Ben Levi fasted two days for Tisha b'Av to make sure he covered both the 9th and 10th of Av, initiated the saying of the nightly *Sh'ma*, and is one of the few in Jewish history to have entered *Gan Eden* while still living, the result of his last wish (*Kesubos* 77b).

263. Ben Hakanah, an affable and likable Sage who avoided *machlokes* at all costs, was a contemporary of Rabban Yochanan, a teacher of Rabbi Yishmael, and a writer of mystical works (*Sefer Habihar*) and morning prayers (*Ana b'Choach*). When asked why he was privileged to live a long life, he replied: "I was liberal with my money, I never went to sleep before eliciting forgiveness from friends, and I never derived honor at the expense of another!"

264. Shimon ben Azzai, without the title "rabbi" because he had no *smicha*, lived in Tiberias and was a sensitive, brilliant student of Rabbi Yehoshua, a popular Torah lecturer who was murdered at a young age together with Rabbi Akiva. He delved into mysticism in a disastrous way (*Chagiga* 14b), and was one of the few Sages who never married (he thought that his Torah study would be adversely affected by marriage and a family). One legend has it that he was engaged to Rabbi Akiva's daughter but

it was never consummated and thus annulled, or that they simply divorced (*Brachos* 17b; *Yevamos* 63b; Tosefta *Brachos* 7:7).

265. Good deeds, they say, can never save you, but without them you can't be saved!

266. Technically, this is not part of *Pirkei Avos* but is the final Mishna of Tractate *Makkos*, which deals with civil law; it is a custom to recite this Mishna at the end of any Torah study held in *shul*. Why? In order that the "Rabbi's Kaddish" can be said (it is only said after the study of scriptural verses or Mishna).

267. *Segula* is similar to the Latin *seligere*, whose root meaning is "choice"; in Aramaic it means "that which is preferred." The King James Bible's Jacobean translation translates it as the "peculiar people," but in those days "peculiar" stemmed from the Latin *peculiaris*, which means "special."

268. Deuteronomy 26:18; Exodus 19:5,6; Leviticus 20:26.

269. *Koheles* (Ecclesiastes) 2:8.

270. In classical Hebrew the term *goyim* originally meant "nation" or "people" and applied to Jews *and* gentiles. "The nations of the earth" were *goyei ha'aretz* (Genesis 18:18), Israel was called a "*goy echad ba'aretz* (a unique nation on the earth)"; later, the term came to denote "them" (as in, not "us"), as per "*hagoyim asher s'vivotechem* (the nations that surround you)" (Leviticus 25:44).

271. Maharal, *Nesivos Olam, Nesiv Hatorah* 2; *Eiruvin* 55a.

272. The Talmud shows a mystical concern regarding demons that are connected to an activity involving "pairing" (*zugos*), such as drinking two cups of the same wine, or eating the same food twice (*Pesachim* 109, 110). Should contemporary Jews be worried about this? Yes, says the *Tur* (*Orach Chayim* 170); no, says the *Beis Yosef*, the *Chida* (Rabbi Chaim Yosef David Azulai), and the *Ben Ish Chai* (Rabbi Yosef Chaim of Baghdad), who thought that those negative "spiritual influences" were no longer applicable. In Baghdad, Jews would *davka* send two similar baskets of gifts to show they no longer feared these metaphysical forces; however, Ashkenazi Jews make it a point of not paying a *shiva* call twice, either going only once or adding a third time.

273. Proverbs 18:21.

274. The term *seichel* makes its first appearance in the Torah in Genesis: "The woman saw that the tree was good for food, appealing to the eyes, and an attractive means for gaining understanding [*l'haskil*]" (Genesis 3:6). *Haskil*, a verb form of *seichel*, represents a higher level than knowledge, and thus Jews pray for it in their daily *Shemoneh Esrei* (the fourth blessing).

275. The Torah usually uses the Hebrew word *es*, which appears at the beginning of the verse "The Lord your God you shall fear" (Deuteronomy 10:20) as a connective (this syntactic element has no equivalent in English). The term (*es,* or in modern Hebrew *et*) means "with," which couples man's fears with God's, leading the Mishna's Antigonus to break fear into two categories: the plain, everyday visceral fear, and, more importantly, the fear of punishment for displeasing God. Rav Shimon of Amson asserted that he was able to derive a new law from every appearance of the word *es* in the Torah. This was a remarkable claim. Why? Because *es*, like the word *a* in English, is one of the most common words in the Torah. However, he changed his mind when he got to this verse ("The Lord your God you shall fear") and was unable to derive anything new from it. He then rescinded all his previous *divrei Torah* on *es*, declaring, "Just as I received reward for the expounding, so too will I receive reward for the refraining!"

276. *Pesachim* 99a; *Eiruvin* 54a.

277. An example? The Torah says, "You shall slaughter (the animal) as I commanded you";

however, the laws of *shechita* are nowhere to be found in the Written Torah. Another example? The Torah says, "Seven days shall you dwell in a *succa*"; yet, the definition of a *succa* or how to build one is also not found in the Written Torah.

278. During the British Mandate in Palestine, a Royal Commission asked Rav Abraham Isaac Kook why the Jews make such a fuss over the Western Wall. "After all," drawled an English officer, "it's just a bunch of rocks!" Rav Kook replied, "Just as there are hearts made of stone, there are also stones made of heart!"

279. "To harden the heart" (as in the case of Pharaoh) is a figure of speech that suggests one is drained of such feelings as anguish or compassion for another; an image conjured up of the most human of organs turned to rock. When the Torah blamed Pharaoh for his increasingly *kaved lev* nature, it identified "a heart heavy with stubbornness;" one that was self-generated and thus, according to the sixteenth-century kabbalist Eleazar ben Moses Azikri, predisposed to gratuitous hatred.

280. Deuteronomy 6:6.

281. There is no such thing as "infallibility" in the Torah; in fact, not only can rabbis make mistakes, there is an entire Talmud tractate (*Horiut*) that assumes they can – and will! Even the Sanhedrin was known to err occasionally in halachic matters.

282. The Rambam includes in his definition of heretics the "one who contradicts his teachers [*mach'chish maggideha*], and, in 1973, Rav Moshe Feinstein declared, in a speech: "A central aspect of the Jewish commitment is the authority vested in the Torah leadership of each generation. Our obligation is to follow those of our age. One who does not accept the Torah leaders of his generation cannot claim to believe in *Torah sheb'al Peh*…. One who says that he does not need the Sages anymore is an *apikoros* (heretic)."

283. Judaism is replete with warnings against excessive and nonsensical speech; even the truth, if degraded into gossip (*loshen hora*), is seen as treacherous. The Midrash defines *tzara'as* as a skin disease punishment for gossip and slander; the Jew suffering from this is called a *metzora* because he was *motzi shem ra* (spread derogatory reports – *Vayikra Rabba* 16:1). Of the forty-three sins enumerated on Yom Kippur in the *Al Cheit* confession, eleven are tied to speech. The tongue was considered so potentially dangerous that the rabbis of the Talmud said it needed to be hidden from view, behind two protective walls (the mouth and teeth) to prevent its abuse. The *Chofetz Chaim* lists a staggering number of mitzvos (thirty-one) that are violated during the "art" of telling or listening to *loshen hora*.

284. Genesis 2:7.

285. The Torah's role model is Aaron, an *ish tam*, a "plain, natural, uncomplicated man," the quintessential "straight" man of peace.

286. This approach was already under attack in the days of the Talmud: "I doubt whether in this age there is a single person who accepts rebuke!" (*Arachin*).

287. The Gerer Rebbe once asked a young boy, "Have you learned any Torah?" "Just a little," the boy replied, to which the Rebbe nodded, "That is all any of us have ever learned!"

288. *Avos* 4:4, 21.

289. Rav Yosef and Rabba were both candidates to become *rosh yeshiva* in Pumbedita. Rav Yosef was selected but relinquished the position to Rabba, who served for more than two decades. During this time, Rav Yosef repeatedly refused, in humorous ways, any special honors, in order not to detract from Rabba's authority (*Sota* 49a, b; *Horiyos* 14a). Rav Yosef was not the only one to request an emendation: similarly, Rebbe Nachman told the *Tanna* not to include "fear of sin" as a trait that ceased whilst he was still alive.

290. Rabbi Naftali Zevi Yehuda Berlin, *Ha'amek Davar,* Numbers 12:3.

291. Psalms 133.

292. The Yiddish noun *faribel* describes those who take pleasure in bearing a grudge, and comes from the German *verübeln,* to "take offense" (*übel* being akin to the English "evil," as in to think evil of someone).

293. Chassidus connects the Hebrew word for world, *olam,* with *he'elem* (oblivion), in that the world is a concealed mystery.

294. *Bereishis Rabba* 44:1.

JOE BOBKER COLLECTION

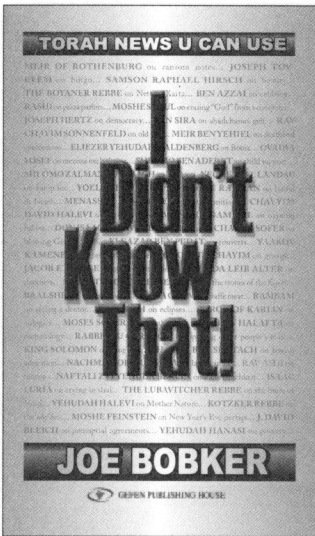

TORAH NEWS U CAN USE

I Didn't Know That!

JOE BOBKER
GEFEN PUBLISHING HOUSE

Hardcover • 400 pp
ISBN 978-965-229-398-5
$14.95 • 70 NIS

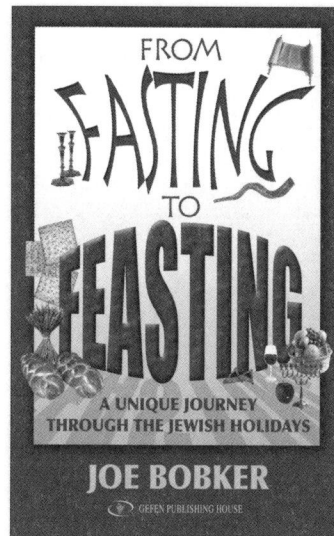

FROM FASTING TO FEASTING

A UNIQUE JOURNEY
THROUGH THE JEWISH HOLIDAYS

JOE BOBKER
GEFEN PUBLISHING HOUSE

Hardcover • 280 pp
ISBN 978-965-229-378-7
$18.95 • 80 NIS

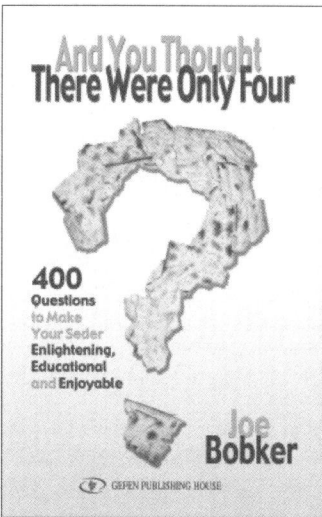

And You Thought
There Were Only Four

400
Questions
to Make
Your Seder
Enlightening,
Educational
and Enjoyable

Joe Bobker
GEFEN PUBLISHING HOUSE

Paperback • 338 pp
ISBN 965-229-366-0
$14.95 • 70 NIS

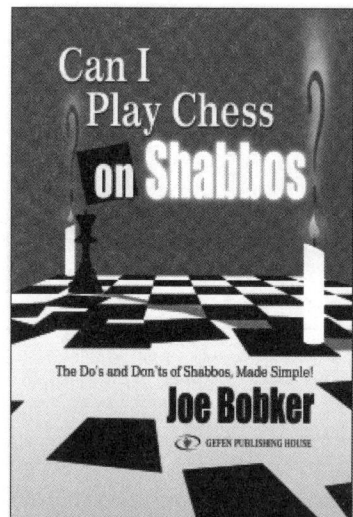

Can I
Play Chess
on Shabbos

The Do's and Don'ts of Shabbos, Made Simple!
Joe Bobker
GEFEN PUBLISHING HOUSE

Hardcover
ISBN 978-965-229-422-7
$18.95 • 80 NIS